The Ethnic History of Chicago

Melvin G. Holli, Editor

Advisory Board

Josef Barton
Kathleen Niels Conzen
Lawrence J. McCaffrey
William McCready

The Irish in Chicago

The Irish in Chicago

Lawrence J. McCaffrey
Ellen Skerrett
Michael F. Funchion
Charles Fanning

University of Illinois Press
Urbana and Chicago

MAY 2001

This book is printed on acid-free paper.

Library of Congress Cataloging-in-Publication Data

The Irish in Chicago.

  (The Ethnic history of Chicago)
  Bibliography: p.
  Includes index.
  1. Irish Americans—Illinois—Chicago—History.
2. Chicago (Ill.)—Ethnic relations. 3. Chicago
(Ill.)—History. I. McCaffrey, Lawrence John, 1925–
III. Series.
F548.9.I6I75   1987   977.3'110049162   86-24977
ISBN 0-252-01397-2 (alk. paper)

to
Thomas N. Brown
who informed us all

Contents

Preface

In its early days the Irish were the most numerous of Chicago's foreign born. Once the largest ethnic component in the city, now they are low on the list. Recently they began losing the political power that distinguished them and gave Chicago such an Irish tone. Most of the metropolitan-area Irish are now suburbanites with a middle-class lifestyle that makes it difficult to differentiate them from Anglo-Americans. Not only do they practice their Catholicism in a more casual way than their parents, but the distinguishing characteristics of their religion have changed as well. Gone is most of the authoritarianism, clericalism, devotionalism, rigidity, and certainty that defined Irish Catholicism all over the English-speaking world. As a result of changes in the Catholic Church since Vatican II much of the contemporary liturgy and spirit of American Catholicism resembles evangelical Protestantism.

Although their separate identity has apparently vanished, the Irish have had a dramatic impact on Chicago and other American cities. As pioneers of its urban ethnic ghettos, they were the United States' first cultural and religious aliens and first large-city group social problem. These roles and their religious, political, educational, cultural, and labor leadership of American Catholicism have made the Irish the most significant ethnic group in many American cities, including Chicago.

This volume discusses some dimensions of Irish Chicago. I place the Chicago Irish within the Irish-American context. Ellen Skerrett analyzes their Catholicism: how it both retarded and advanced their social, economic, and cultural progress and shaped the character of Chicago Catholicism. Michael Funchion describes the beginnings, growth, nature, strengths, and weaknesses of Chicago Irish politics and its ties with

Irish-American nationalism. In his portrait of Chicago Irish writers, Charles Fanning examines the pioneering contributions of Finley Peter Dunne and James T. Farrell. In addition to describing Irish communities, fixed and in transition, they established an Irish-American literary tradition and created models for America's urban ethnic literature. In the Conclusion, I discuss how success and changes in American Catholicism challenged Irish ethnicity.

While preparing these essays I wrote and published "Building an American Power Base: The Irish, the Cities and the Church," *Loyola Magazine* 13 (Summer 1984); "Irish-America," from the *Wilson Quarterly* 9 (Spring 1985) by the Woodrow Wilson International Center for Scholars; "Irish-American Politics: Power with or without Purpose?" *Irish Studies,* vol. 4, *The Irish in America,* ed. P. J. Drudy (New York: Cambridge University Press, 1985); and "Irish Catholics: America's First Urban Ethnics," in *The Ethnic Enigma: The Salience of Ethnicity for European Origin Groups,* ed. Peter Kivisto (forthcoming). I want to thank these journals for permission to repeat some of my interpretations of Irish-America. I also express appreciation for typing funds from Research Services at Loyola University of Chicago, directed by Professor Thomas J. Bennett.

Lawrence J. McCaffrey

The Irish-American Dimension

Lawrence J. McCaffrey

Contemporary Chicago testifies to the success of Irish-America. Because of their twentieth-century adaptation to the life-style, values, and aspirations of the dominant culture, few people, including many of their own, view the Irish as a portion of the American ethnic mosaic. However, nineteenth-century Irish immigrants, the "Classic Ethnics," pioneered the American urban ghetto, challenging Anglo-Protestant cultural homogeneity.[1] Their poverty culture generated a massive social problem which, combined with their Catholicism, goaded Anglo-American nativism. Their enemies branded them alien and a threat to American values, culture, and institutions.

Their psychological and physical passage from rural Ireland to urban America; their effort to surmount the burdens of their history, their poverty, their ignorance, and the hostility of the host society; and their successful quest for power and respectability, all of these made the Irish the paradigm of the American ethnic experience. Their turbulent pilgrimage through American history previewed the adventures of other non-Anglo Protestants.

Ireland has a long tradition of emigration. After English conquest deprived them of influence, property, and prospects, seventeenth- and eighteenth-century members of leading Irish Catholic families sought opportunities on the Continent. During the eighteenth century, British mercantile restrictions and Church of Ireland Ascendancy drove hundreds of thousands of ambitious, skilled Ulster Presbyterians to North America to help develop a new nation. Few members of the impoverished and oppressed Catholic peasantry had the funds, confidence, courage, or skills to escape from their misery to the New World. Many, however, went to Britain as seasonal harvest workers or as part of the unskilled labor force for the industrial and transportation revolutions.[2]

By the close of the eighteenth century the potato had become the main item in the Irish peasant diet. For the very poor, about one-third of the population, it was the sole source of sustenance. The potato crop failures of the 1820s meant famines that made rural Catholics so pessimistic about the future that those who could afford to go decided on America. By the mid-1830s they were a majority of their countrymen entering the United States.

Ireland's Great Famine (1845–49), which killed between one and one and a half million people, propelled about one million mostly poverty-stricken survivors to America—some arrived literally naked. The Famine institutionalized emigration as a safety valve to relieve pressure on a limited agrarian economy. Many Irish parents had to endure the anguish of raising most of their children for export. Since 1820 about five million Irish have come to the United States, the overwhelming majority young, single, and Catholic. Today over forty million Americans claim some Irish ancestry.

Like other European Catholic immigrants who would follow them, most of the Irish avoided farming in the United States. An inefficient landlord system in Ireland had crippled their ability. As subsistence spade, hoe, and scythe farmers, they lacked the techniques and confidence to till America's vast fields. Small farms in Ireland meant conversations with neighbors across ditches, hedges, or stone walls. Evening visits between cottages were frequent. Letters from the few Irish in rural America described space and loneliness. Some Catholic bishops in Ireland and the United States tried to steer the Irish from "wicked" cities to the spiritual tranquility of the country, but Catholicism's corporate and communal emphases encouraged urbanization. Protestantism's individualistic values seemed more appropriate to American rural living. Thus, with few exceptions, the Irish settled in cities as proletarian pioneers of the ghetto.[3]

Without skills Irish men had few employment opportunities. They cleaned stables, drove horses as draymen or cabbies, loaded and unloaded ships and riverboats or served in their crews, dug building foundations or carried bricks and mortar in hods, melted and molded iron. Hotels hired them as bellhops, janitors, and barmen. The Irish mined coal in Pennsylvania, gold in California, copper in Montana. Black slaves were a considerable capital investment so an unlimited supply of Irish immigrants drained swamps in Louisiana, risking and often suffering death from malaria.

As in the United Kingdom, adventure, glory, uniforms, bed and board, money to spend, and comradeship attracted the Irish in America to the armed forces, where they fought well in the Mexican and Civil wars. After the latter the Irish were numerous in the army policing the western frontier. Those in the predominantly Irish Seventh Cavalry were among the 250 or so who died with its general, George Armstrong Custer, at the Battle of the Little Big Horn in 1876.

Promises of adventure as well as security also attracted Irish males to professional police and fire departments in record numbers during the second half of the nineteenth century. Thus on the frontier as well as in the cities, the Irish were early enforcers of the law, a duty which pitted them against their own people during America's violent labor disputes and urban riots.

Many Irish laborers found final resting places in graves alongside American canals and railroads. "Paddies" digging canals and cutting trails through forests and mountains before laying track brought the Irish west to help establish an urban frontier. In 1836 navvies from the Erie Canal came to Chicago to dig the Illinois and Michigan Canal as a link between Lake Michigan and the Illinois and Mississippi rivers. Seven years later natives of Ireland were 10 percent of the city's 7,580 people. They hovered close to the Chicago River, settling on the north side at Kilgubbin (named after a town in County Cork where most originated); just below the south branch at Hardscrabble, renamed Bridgeport in 1848, at the canal terminus; and on the west side near Adams and Desplaines. Famine refugees greatly increased Chicago's Irish numbers. By 1850, the 29,963 Irish-born were 20 percent of the population, making them and the Germans the city's largest ethnic contingents.[4]

The Irish were a unique European emigration in that women were about equal in numbers to men and that a vast majority of both were single. Irish women made a better adjustment to the United States than did men and were more successful economically than Irish men or other women. After leaving Ireland, where they were lightly regarded, Irish women in America aggressively pursued economic independence. As a result of the Famine, late marriages and permanent celibacy became characteristics of family life back home. Unpleasant aspects of many Irish marriages—absent husbands, battered wives, early widowhood— did not make marriage in the United States seem much more attractive than it did in Ireland. Once wed, however, and if not deserted or widowed, Irish women were less likely to be in the work force than those of other nationalities. Instead, they concentrated on managing large families, leading a slow but tenacious Irish drive toward middle-class respectability.

Anglo-Americans scorned domestic service as degrading. Ethnics who arrived in the United States as families did not want their young women in the homes of strangers. But Irish women flocked to jobs that paid reasonably well and provided food, housing, uniforms, and a taste of civilized living. Widowed or abandoned Irish wives with children to care for or single women living with their families drifted toward mills and factories. When American textile and shoe manufacturing shifted from hand to factory production, many Irish women operated the machines.[5]

Irish misconduct obscured the contribution of "Paddy" and "Biddy" labor to the American industrial revolution. A poverty culture carried from the Old Country and nourished in American urban ghettos, an ethnic predisposition to flee the demons of unhappiness in drink, and the psychological problems involved in the transition from a rural to an urban environment made the Irish America's first group social problem. Their ugly, dirty, and dreary neighborhoods spawned crime, violence, and mental and physical disorders.

Still, Irish antisocial behavior irritated their enemies less than their religion. Rooted in the English historical tradition, anti-Catholicism was the intrinsic ingredient in American nativism. Early American Catholicism represented such a small number that antipopery was more paranoia than reality. Irish-initiated waves of Catholic immigration with their urban settlements seemed to substantiate nativism by contradicting the nation's image of itself as rural and Protestant. Many Americans considered the swarming mass of Irish immigrants as alien invaders, agents of popery and European despotism, an unassimilable menace to Anglo-Protestant culture and institutions.

With their super siege mentality, Ulster Presbyterians hated Irish Catholics even more than English or Anglo-Irish Protestants did. To avoid association with their hereditary enemy, in the United States they claimed Scotch-Irish nationality. Their alliance with Anglo-American Protestants tightened the connection between Irish and Catholic identities even more than in Ireland.

Bitter memories of British colonialism and the Protestant Ascendancy in Ireland and confrontations with nativism in the United States persuaded Irish-America to build its own Catholic institutional structure of schools, hospitals, asylums, and orphanages. Since American public schools featured anti-Catholicism and taught morality through the King James Bible, education became a dominant Catholic concern. In 1884, at the Third Plenary Council in Baltimore, the predominantly Irish-American Catholic hierarchy commanded that each parish should have a school and that Catholic parents should enroll their children.

Irish troubles did not translate into empathy for other victims of poverty or oppression. Adopting American racial prejudices, reacting to the anti–Irish Catholicism of many abolitionists, and competing for urban turf and jobs, the Irish were hostile to free blacks, particularly those employed as strikebreakers. They considered it hypocrisy for middle-class Anglo-Protestants to weep for the black plantation slave of the South while ignoring the plight of the industrial "white wage slave of the North."[6]

The July 1863 New York anti-draft riot was the most infamous display of anti-black Irish prejudice. During five days of carnage, Irish mobs, enraged by drink, burned a black orphanage and killed eleven blacks plus an Indian mistaken for a black. Riot police and soldiers summoned from the battlefield killed twelve hundred rioters and wounded many in combating the disorder. Most of the police and many of the soldiers were as Irish as the rioters. Irish-born Archbishop John Hughes exerted moral authority in persuading members of the mob to return to their homes.[7]

Post–Civil War Irish-America expanded its net of prejudice to include groups other than black urban Americans. In California during the 1870s and 1880s, Denis Kearney, Workingman's party leader, agitated against the Chinese. At the same time Patrick Ford's Irish nationalist and American populist *Irish World* (New York) described Jews as exploiters of the working class.

Hostility to blacks and complaints against the unfairness of conscription did not prevent the Irish from fighting courageously for the Union. Although the Irish in the South fought just as well for the Confederacy, the performance of Irish troops in blue did much to diminish nativism. America's industrial revolution, which swung into high gear after the Civil War, also softened xenophobia. Demands for immigrant labor helped inspire the melting-pot vision of the United States.

Improved emigration as well as a lull in nativism relieved pressure on Irish-America. The continued flow of people to the United States reduced the strain on the agrarian economy of Ireland, increasing the proportion of landholders and the size of their farms. Additional factors also contributed to the rise of rural Ireland's standard of living: declining population, steadily rising agricultural prices matched with stable rents and good harvests, a significant decline in evictions between 1850 and 1878, dollar gifts from Irish-America, and the 1881 legislation of secure tenures at fair rents with compensations for improvements to the farm. Peasants supplemented the potatoes in their diet with bread, butter, vegetables, meat, and, to some extent, fish. They wore better clothing, and they lived in roomier, healthier, and more comfortable cottages.

British government attempts after 1890 to solve the "Irish Question" short of Home Rule, which included land purchase loans, also lifted the rural standard of living.

Education as well as material comfort improved the quality of Irish life. In 1831, two years after conceding Catholic civil rights, the British government established a national school system to civilize (Anglicize) the Irish. Following the Famine the impact of mass education was visible in the large numbers able to read and write. By the 1890s about 95 percent of the Irish entering the United States were literate.

Literacy was an important tool for upward mobility for the urban American Irish. So was an evolving Catholicism which disciplined their character. Pre-Famine Catholicism became more devotional and disciplined, particularly in prosperous parts of Ireland, but still featured many poorly educated priests and a laity largely indifferent to its doctrines and practices.

The Famine and a surge in Irish nationalism assisted a dramatic devotional emphasis in Ireland's Catholicism. Famine deaths and emigration eliminated the most ignorant, superstitious, and lax Irish Catholics, clearing the way for reform. And the Famine made the people realize that excessive population was a factor in the great calamity. Therefore, they decided to adjust marriage patterns to the grim realities of a primitive agrarian economy. Catholicism provided religious motivation and sanction for the sexual abstinence involved in delayed marriages or celibacy.

Because many Irish leaders charged Britain with genocide in regard to Famine-related depopulation, the "holocaust" of the 1840s fueled Irish nationalism; so did the national schools. While the schools did have Anglicizing features, they also abetted nationalism by expanding its propaganda-reading audience. Nationalism also cultivated the historical associations between Irish and Catholic identities. Consequently, the Irish became more dutiful in practicing their religion as they became more dedicated to national liberation.

As apostolic delegate and archbishop of Armagh (1850–52) then cardinal archbishop of Dublin (1852–78) Paul Cullen, ultramontane Catholic, channeled a more aggressive Catholicism and links between faith and fatherland into a "Devotional Revolution" which molded the Irish into exceptionally loyal and enthusiastic Catholics.[8]

Better educated, more sophisticated and disciplined Irish emigrants arrived in the United States with more expectation than those who came before. They and non-English-speaking newcomers to urban America, who pushed from below, speeded Irish mobility. Early in the twentieth century Irish-Americans were more likely to be in the skilled than in the unskilled labor force and a number had penetrated the borders of the middle class. Progress, however, was not uniform. Gender and geography were factors in mobility.

Irish-American women continued to postpone or avoid marriage and to be more successful than Irish-American males or other members of their own sex. Second-generation Irish-American women were the largest ethnic group in the teaching profession and were prominent in nursing and skilled office work. In addition, they had visibility in medicine, business, and labor union leadership. Irish-American women were much more unselfish than men in sending money to relatives in Ireland, financing Irish emigration, and contributing to the Catholic Church.[9]

Nuns were vital to the success of Irish-American women. While male leaders of American Catholicism ignored women's problems, nuns, many from Ireland, sheltered the poor and afflicted and educated the young, emphasizing economic self-reliance rather than marriage. Since teaching nuns concentrated on the needs of their own sex, Irish-American women were far better educated than the men, enhancing their role as civilizers of Irish-America.[10]

Both Irish men and women on the "urban frontier" achieved more than those in the East, with New England and the Midwest providing sharp contrasts. In New England the Irish settled in a highly structured society. Yankees regarded them as inferior and dangerous. Their scorn and Irish technological and cultural deficiencies constructed disabling mental and physical ghettos. When the Irish managed to win political power, it was not always accompanied by economic advance or social respectability.[11]

Unlike New England, the Midwest was a relatively open society with a dynamic economy. Since its factories, mills, stockyards, and railroads needed workers, nativism was more muted than in the East. Production and profit took priority over prejudice. Opportunity encouraged the Irish to overcome pessimism and moved them into the skilled working and lower middle classes.

In 1870 "urban frontier" Chicago had an Irish-born population of almost 40,000. At the beginning of the twentieth century it was the fourth-largest Irish urban center in the United States, trailing New York, Philadelphia, and Brooklyn. Some 237,479 first- and second-generation Irish-Americans lived in the city. Census data does not show a large third generation. Most of the Irish lived on the south and west sides with a small community on the north. Unlike those in the eastern United States, Chicago's Irish mixed with other nationalities, mostly Germans, and did not inhabit exclusive ghettos. In 1884 they were a majority in only 11 out of 303 census districts.

While their city offered myriad employment opportunities, the Chicago Irish did not do as well as those in "urban frontier" San Francisco, St. Paul, Louisville, Milwaukee, Detroit, Pittsburgh, or St. Louis.[12] Although not ghettoized, perhaps they were too numerous in the city for individuals to summon the initiative and courage to surmount their limited ethnic self-image and restricted vocational horizon. Irish social disorder and graft-ridden politics did provoke a more pronounced nativism than in other cities of the Midwest and West. In 1868 the *Chicago Evening Post* complained that the Irish filled prisons, reform schools, hospitals, and charitable institutions and commented "Scratch a convict or a pauper and the chances are that you tickle the skin of an Irish Catholic at the same time—an Irish Catholic made a criminal or a pauper by the priest and politicians who have deceived him and kept him in ignorance, in a word, a savage, as he was born."

While both their own complexes and nativism might have prevented the Chicago Irish from matching the accomplishments of their countrymen on other parts of the urban frontier, by the end of the nineteenth century their mobility was obvious. A large number had become work-crew foremen or engineers, firemen, switchmen, levermen, clerks, and telegraphers for the railroads. There were still quite a few Irish foundation diggers and hod carriers on building sites but they were outnumbered by Irish bricklayers, carpenters, plasterers, plumbers, and, after the turn of the century, electricians. As in other cities, the Irish took a prominent place among the leadership of the skilled labor unions.

Public service, respectability, and pension security attracted the Irish to the civil service and police and fire departments. They operated streetcars and the elevated railway that moved people around the city. Curiosity, adventurous spirits, fascination with a good story, and writing talent qualified the Irish for journalism. Connections between law and politics produced an abundance of Irish lawyers. And quite a few became physicians, earning reputations as dedicated general practitioners and skilled specialists, particularly surgeons such as John B. Murphy and Loyal Davis. Considering the Irish appreciation for drink, it is not surprising that many were in the saloon business. They purchased other kinds of small shops as well.

Two religious orders originating in Ireland, the Sisters of the Blessed Virgin Mary and the Sisters of Mercy, were active in Chicago. Irish-American women also were the majority in other congregations. In their schools, nuns prepared young women for careers in nursing and teaching. While the Chicago Irish remained loyal to Catholic education, they made a substantial teaching contribution to public education. In the early 1920s George Cardinal Mundelein estimated that about 70 percent of Chicago's public school teachers were women educated by nuns in Catholic secondary schools. The vast majority of them would have been Irish.[13]

Following the 1871 fire, Irish workers helped rebuild Chicago. At the same time, the skilled working and middle classes led an Irish migration away from the central city. New neighborhoods with prosperous-looking homes, churches, and schools testified to Irish social mobility. So did the marble mausoleums in Calvary cemetery, on the shores of Lake Michigan between Rogers Park in Chicago and the affluent northern suburb of Evanston.

In much of New England, Irish political power did not result in significant economic or social advancement. This was not the case in other places, including Chicago. While the Irish landed in America lacking in technological skills, they did come with political experience. Daniel O'Connell, the founding father of modern Irish nationalism, educated them in the principles of liberal democracy and the techniques of agitation. His successful effort to achieve Catholic civil rights in the 1820s and his failed campaign to reestablish a sovereign Irish Parliament in the 1840s exhibited model political organizations.

Although they were acknowledged as the best politicians in the country, the Irish political style and their power offended many Americans. Nativists charged that they endangered Anglo-Protestant foundations. Reformers, often with nativist leanings, complained that the easygoing Irish political conscience corrupted urban governments. As late as the 1960s, Daniel Patrick Moynihan, Irish-American scholar and politician, argued that while the Irish excelled at getting power they failed at using it constructively.[14] Some authors of Irish-American political novels such as Thomas J. Fleming, Edward R. F. Sheehan, and James Carroll have supported the Moynihan thesis.[15]

Chicago exhibited some of the most negative aspects of Irish politics. During the last two decades of the nineteenth century and the first two of the twentieth, especially when Carter Harrison I and II were mayors, gambling and prostitution flourished. Policemen and politicians prospered from vice payoffs. Irish politicians also fattened wallets by selling city franchises to businessmen, a practice known as "boodling." Johnny Powers, "Bathhouse John" Coughlin, and "Hinky Dink" Kenna were prominent "boodlers."

Alderman of the Nineteenth Ward from 1888 to 1927, Johnny Powers provided bail for jailed constituents and fixed their court cases; paid the rent of hard-pressed tenants; placed thousands on the public payroll; attended weddings and funerals, bringing presents to the former, often paying the expenses of the latter; provided railroad passes for poor people needing to visit relatives; purchased tickets for benefits and church bazaars; and one Christmas personally distributed six tons of turkeys and four tons of ducks and geese.[16] Powers, like Irish political counterparts in other cities, also served Italians, Poles, and Jews. To their multiethnic constituents they were modern-day Robin Hoods, taking from the rich and giving to the poor. Powers survived numerous reform efforts, even those of Jane Addams, to unseat him, bragging that his saloons produced more voters than did reformers or clergymen.[17]

Later in this volume Charles Fanning will discuss Finley Peter Dunne as a social historian and the creator of the first rounded, realistic ethnic community in American literature. When writing newspaper editorials Dunne condemned "Boodlers" but his fictional proprietor of a Bridgeport saloon in the 1890s, Martin Dooley, did not view Irish-American politics in black and white terms. He observed that young lads from his community who used politics to make their way in the rough and tumble of urban America learned from Anglo-Protestant political and business examples. Dooley decided that the American urban environment corrupted the Irish more than they did it.[18]

Moynihan's thesis distorts the nature of early American reformism as much as it does the character of Irish-American politics. Reformers tended to be more concerned with moral improvement than social justice. Catholic belief in the concept of original sin influenced the Irish to be cynical about the Enlightenment's optimism concerning the essential goodness and perfectability of man. Irish Catholics also scorned the fashionable laissez faire Social Darwininism of the late nineteenth and early twentieth centuries. Irish-American politicians mitigated constituent poverty by dispensing food, clothing, coal, and patronage jobs. Inadvertently, they advanced the United States toward twentieth-century social justice liberalism.

Some prominent leaders of Irish nationalism in the United States such as John Devoy, editor of the *Gaelic-American* in New York, despised compromising Irish-American politicians for turning their people's attention from Ireland's freedom to Democratic party interests. However, in most cities, and Chicago was a good example, there were close associations between Irish politics and Irish nationalism.

One scholar has observed that "in the alembic of America the parochial peasant was transformed into a passionate nationalist."[19] Irish-America was a catalyst for the nineteenth-century Irish freedom movement, providing funds and passion for its constitutional and physical manifestations. In the 1840s the American Irish organized Repeal clubs to support Daniel O'Connell's agitation to liberate Ireland through constitutional methods. They gave the name Fenian to revolutionary Irish nationalism in the 1860s. During the 1870s and 1880s the American-based Clan na Gael sustained the Irish Republican Brotherhood in Ireland. In the late 1870s the Clan also initiated the New Departure. It mobilized the Irish peasantry against landlordism, thus energizing the Irish Parliamentary party. From the time of Charles Stewart Parnell, Irish party chairman (1880–90), until 1916, American dollars financed the Home Rule cause in Ireland and at Westminster. After the Easter Week Rebellion, Irish-Americans aided revolutionary nationalism, pressuring American foreign policy to acknowledge Ireland's claim to sovereignty.

More than sentimental attachment to Ireland, Irish-American nationalism expressed hate, a loathing for Britain as the source of Irish misery and exile, and a search for respectability in the United States. Acceptance-seekers were convinced that Ireland's colonial status reflected badly on them. They believed that an independent Ireland would give Irish-Americans a dignified homeland, persuading other Americans to respect them as equals. Because of Anglo-America's close emotional and cultural ties with Britain, Irish-American pressure on American foreign policy has not been particularly successful. But it and the association of a free mother country with status in the United States established a strategy for other ethnic groups.

Chicago had Repeal and Fenian manifestations. For a time, in the 1880s, Clan na Gael activities centered in Chicago. Archbishop Patrick Feehan championed the Clan and was a friend of Alexander Sullivan, the dominant member of the Triangle, its executive committee. John Devoy temporarily moved to Chicago to contest the leadership with Sullivan. And Henri LeCaron, a British spy, also located in the city and successfully infiltrated the Clan.[20]

Like other Irish-Americans, those in Chicago celebrated March 4 as Robert Emmet's birthday. (The British had executed Emmet in 1803 after a failed revolution, but his defiant "Speech from the Dock" continued to inspire the Irish at home and abroad.) On August 15, the Feast of the Assumption or Lady's Day, the advent of the harvest season and the anniversary of two sixteenth-century victories over the English, the Chicago Irish gathered at picnics and listened to patriotic rhetoric. On November 23, they honored the memories of W. P. Allen, Michael Larkin, and Michael O'Brien, the Manchester Martyrs, executed in 1867 for killing a constable in a successful rescue of Fenian Head Centre, Irish-American Thomas J. Kelly, from a police van.

Politics gave the Irish the wealth and opportunities denied them in business. Nationalism provided Irish immigrants and their children with an identity, a hope for American respectability, a hate for the hereditary enemy, and a heritage. Despite a strong commitment to nationalism, however, the Irish in Ireland and America invested their strongest enthusiasm as well as their best talent in the Catholic Church. With the early exception of Belgian James Van de Velde (1845–49), from the first appointee in 1844, William J. Quarter, until the death of James Quigley in 1915, every bishop or archbishop of Chicago came from Ireland or Irish-America. From the inception of the office of chancellor in 1859 and for over a hundred years after, every one of its holders was of Irish heritage. In the twentieth century, Catholic immigration, mostly Polish, made Chicago the largest American archdiocese, but the Irish remained in leadership positions.[21]

Priests and politicians shared the leadership of Irish-America. In many ways the abilities and professional personalities of the two were not dissimilar. Irish bishops and priests who nurtured the Catholic Church in the United States into the largest, most powerful, and wealthiest religious body in the country did so with more political genius than spiritual fervor. Priests and politicians incorporated other ethnics into the institutions and causes they directed, enlarging the presence and influence of Irish-America while expanding the strength of the Catholic Church and the Democratic party.

Many American Catholic critics have insisted that Irish leadership has restricted the intellectualism and sophistication of American Catholicism and given it an authoritarian, peasant, pietistic, puritan quality. While certainly more urbane, continental Catholicism was not more intellectual or liberal than the Irish version. Before the 1950s Catholicism exhibited a universal Counter-Reformation defensiveness. John Henry Newman, a nineteenth-century convert from Anglicanism, possessed one of the few minds that made Catholic thought somewhat creative. Post-Famine Irish Catholicism exhibited strict adherence to Rome in matters of faith and morals. Unlike continental Catholics, the Irish were Anglicized as well as Romanized. Not only did they take Church teachings and rules seriously, but Victorian notions of respectability encouraged them to heed Catholic views on sex more docilely and earnestly than French or Italian Catholics did. As previously mentioned, Famine memories also fostered prudery along with sexual abstinence and delayed marriage.

Nationalism, too, colored Irish Catholicism. Not only did it encourage Catholic pietism as a sign of Irishness, it also demanded that the Church be concerned with the secular needs of the people. Since Daniel O'Connell injected the liberal principles of British Whiggery and Radicalism into the lifeline of Irish nationalism, he politically civilized its ally, Catholicism.

Remembered conflicts in Ireland with Anglo-Saxon and Anglo-Irish

Protestants and Scotch-Irish Presbyterians, experienced confrontations with American nativism, and historical connections between religion and ethnicity made Irish-Americans cautious in dealing with Anglo-America. Still, they were more in tune with political culture in the United States than were Catholics from the Continent, where bishops were of the aristocracy and an authoritarian Church bolstered the established regimes.

In contrast, Irish bishops, originating in the strong farmer and shopkeeper classes, were close to the laity. They submitted to Rome's religious and moral authority, but ignored many of its reactionary social, economic, and political guidelines. Irish prelates and priests participated in agitations that eventually transferred the soil from landlord to tenant farmer. They endorsed and served as lieutenants in nonviolent efforts to replace British rule with an Irish liberal-democratic state. While less politically involved than in Ireland, many Irish priests in America carried on the tradition of leadership in secular as well as spiritual matters and concern for the general welfare of Catholic communicants.

Inclusion in the Irish spiritual empire did not make American Catholicism a duplicate of the Irish model. Secularism, pluralism, egalitarianism, and liberalism in the United States made Irish-Americans more emphatic in resisting clericalism than the Irish in Ireland. This has been particularly true on the "urban frontier," where Irish Catholics have been more confident and open and less ghettoized than in Boston or New York.

Irish Catholicism evolved as cultural identity more than theology. The Irish have detoured around the psychologically troubling paradox of loyalty to western civilization's most authoritarian religious system, Roman Catholicism, and its politically most liberal, Anglo-Protestant constitutionalism. Unable intellectually to reconcile them, they have worshipped their God without much speculation, investing their intelligence in literature and politics.

Perhaps, as its critics suggest, Irish Catholicism's shallow intellectualism is a weakness. But in the United States, a place without much interest in theology or philosophy, it has been a strength. Continental Catholicism's rejection of the liberal tradition and its isolation from a changing world cut against the American grain. Irish Catholicism's emphasis on pastoral care rather than theology and acceptance of liberal democracy fit the New World. The Catholic Church in the United States would have been more alien if its leaders had been Germans, French, Italians, or Poles.[22] In conjunction with Irish-American politics, Irish-American Catholicism brought Catholic America into conformity with the nation's political consensus.

In addition to politics and the priesthood, athletics and entertainment were other Irish opportunity routes. For middle-class Anglo- and other Protestants with business and professional prospects, sports essentially was recreation. For ghetto-toughened Irish and poor rural Protestants it was a chance for fame and possible fortune. Triple jumper James B. Connolly in 1896 became the first American Olympic gold medal winner. The Irish continued to be prominent track and field athletes. From before the days of John L. Sullivan in the 1880s until Joe Louis knocked out James J. Braddock in Chicago on June 22, 1937, the Irish were the dominant ethnic element in professional boxing. As players and managers they helped baseball emerge as the national pastime. One of the great managers, Charles Comiskey, founded the Chicago White Sox. The University of Notre Dame became the most successful college football power when "fighting Irish" accurately described its personnel. Many of the excellent Irish football players in other colleges and universities, mostly Catholic but not necessarily so, came out of Chicago.

Irish interest in sports as adventure, opportunity, excitement, and competition inspired writing as well as athletic excellence. Experts acknowledge Walter "Red" Smith as the greatest sports writer in the history of American journalism. New York's Jimmy Cannon and Chicago-based John Carmichael, Warren Brown, Bill Gleason, and Jack Griffen have also added to the quality of sports journalism.

Athletics have distracted American minorities from misery and mischief, but they also have tended to confirm negative stereotypes. Like anti-Irish nativists of an earlier time, racists today argue that the physical prowess of blacks is not matched by intelligence. And emphasis on sports has distorted priorities in minority communities. Even today many Catholic schools remain preoccupied with games to the detriment of more important academic matters.

Show business as well as sports opened the doors of fame and fortune to the Irish. Captain Francis O'Neill, Chicago's police chief from 1901 to 1905, collected and helped preserve traditional Irish music on both sides of the Atlantic. But for the vast majority of Irish-Americans their music was Thomas Moore's drawing-room *Irish Melodies,* the ballads of the *Nation,* the catchy songs of Percy French, and the stage Irish words and tunes of the English and American music halls. And they quickly adjusted to and became skilled in the popular entertainments of their adopted land, becoming prominent on stages all over the country. Perhaps amusing others is a way of escaping a heritage of troubles. History's victims wear survival masks. Pretending is therapy and a school for performers.

As a singer, dancer, playwright, and actor, George M. Cohan accurately represented the Irish-American personality. He wrote America's

World War I songs—"It's a Grand Old Flag," "Yankee Doodle Dandy," "Over There." They thrilled the country again in World War II. The blatant, openhearted patriotism of these songs revealed the Irish-American love of the United States. They also suggested anxieties about really belonging.

Irish actors Jimmy Cagney, Pat O'Brien, Frank McHugh, Spencer Tracy, and Bing Crosby presented the Irish as quintessential urban ethnics, America's politicians, priests, policemen, and hoodlums. Movie director John Ford advertised his Americanism in western classics, with many Irish characters, and his Irishness in such films as *The Informer, The Quiet Man,* and *The Last Hurrah.* Gene Kelly, in many outstanding movies, and James Cagney, particularly when he portrayed Cohan in *Yankee Doodle Dandy,* contributed an Irish clog-dancing tradition to the choreography of the American musical comedy. Jackie Gleason and Art Carney still entertain large television audiences with an Irish-American comedy tradition of boisterous one-liners, pratfalls, and double takes.[23]

While Americans laughed at the antics of the stage Irishman and cheered Irish sports heroes, athletic and theatrical prominence did not lead to social acceptance. In fact Irish athletic and entertainment success might have contributed to a post-1880 resurgence in nativism touched off by economic hard times. Experiencing recessions and depressions, many Americans demanded that their country's resources be reserved for the native born. And they blamed alien ideas transported in the minds of immigrants for radicalizing workers and fostering class conflict. While some Irish were active as Industrial Workers of the World (Wobblies) and later as Communists, most were involved with trade unionism. But even the principle of collective bargaining offended advocates of private enterprise and unlimited property rights.

In addition to aggressive capitalism, late nineteenth-century nativism featured racism. It was directed against the Irish as well as against linguistically or physically more obviously non-Anglos such as Slavs, Latins, and Jews. British and American Anglo-Saxonism described Celts as colorful and entertaining, but essentially irresponsible, emotional, superstitious, and servile with childlike or feminine dispositions needing the guidance of responsible, rational, efficient, industrious, liberty-loving, masculine, Anglo masters. Subscribed to by scholars and popularized by novelists, poets, journalists, and politicians, racism gave nativism an ideological dimension attractive to upper- and middle-class metropolitans. However, in small town and rural America, and for many Protestant clergymen and academics, Catholicism continued to be the most dangerous enemy of the nation's culture and institutions. From this vantage point, the Irish, as political, religious, educational, and labor leaders of an expanding American Catholicism, remained the chief enemy.[24]

Although it inconvenienced them, nativism did not halt Irish-Americans' march toward respectability. Between World Wars I and II about one-fourth of their secondary school graduates went on to higher education. Most were women pursuing teaching and nursing careers. Some men also became educators, while others practiced law or medicine. Since so many of the Irish were in vocations and occupations less seriously affected by the Great Depression—railroad and urban transport, education, law, medicine, crime and fire prevention, journalism, urban government, and civil service—they survived better than most. Following World War II the GI Bill provided a springboard for their longest leap forward. After earning their bachelor's degrees many Irish-Americans enrolled in graduate and professional schools, increasing their representation in law and medicine, becoming significant in academic life and in business.

Social mobility, a sharp decline in Irish immigration, the Irish Free State and its evolution into the Irish Republic, and the Gaelic or Irish-Ireland thrust of twentieth-century Irish nationalism tended to wean Irish-America from Ireland. Americanization and social mobility made Irish-Americans more respectable. Common suffering during the Depression and common cause in World War II were cohesive forces diminishing nativism. While increased contact with Catholics in the work force and military services did much to allay fears about their loyalty, the American movie industry also played a role. In the 1930s and 1940s, popular stars Spencer Tracy, Bing Crosby, and Pat O'Brien portrayed priests as social workers in Roman collars rather than celebrants of sacred mysteries. As a result, Catholicism seemed less alien.

Not all Irish-Americans became prosperous and self-confident. The drunks, sexual neurotics, and political reactionaries featured in the novels of Jimmy Breslin, Joe Flaherty, Tom MacHale, Pete Hamill, and John Gregory Dunne had and have real-life counterparts. Failures and insecurities also fostered paranoid politics. In the 1930s Father Charles Coughlin, the Detroit radio priest, recruited a number of Irish-Americans into his Social Justice movement. Despite his early support of Franklin D. Roosevelt, Coughlin's recipe for American revitalization soon degenerated into anti-Semitism and fascism. While Senator Joseph McCarthy's 1950s anti-Communist crusade drew support from many Irish Catholics, the evidence is clear that Irish-America evolved into a solid middle-class community, second only to Jewish-America in its concern for social justice, civil liberties, and international peace.[25]

Politics more concerned with purpose and less with power indicated a successful, more relaxed Irish-America.[26] Progressive administrations of former Chicago Mayor Edward F. Dunne as governor of Illinois (1912–16), and Tammany product Alfred E. Smith as governor of New York (1919–21, 1923–29), signaled the shift in Irish politics. Smith's defeat in the 1928 presidential race revived Catholic fears that they indeed were "strangers in the land," but Roosevelt did much to restore their psychological security. He awarded Catholics, mostly Irish, with about one-fourth of federal appointments. Irish-American government officials, senators, congressmen, Supreme Court justices, and civil servants were important agents in the New Deal liberalization and regeneration of the American social and economic systems.[27]

Increasing Irish visibility in and influence on national politics balanced their decline in urban government. Edwin O'Connor's best-selling 1956 novel, *The Last Hurrah,* argued that the New Deal as Santa Claus trivialized Irish political machines. However, the previous year Chicagoans elected Richard J. Daley mayor. His twenty years in office contradicted O'Connor's thesis. As mayor and chairman of the Cook County Democratic Central Committee, Daley controlled patronage and exercised more power than any of his city hall predecessors. And by persuading the federal government to route funds for social programs through the local Democratic organization, he enhanced its power and his own. There were many things wrong with Daley—he was authoritarian, insensitive to the problems of nonwhites, intolerant of intraparty opposition, and oblivious to the mutual concerns and interests of city and suburbs. Still, his genius ended chaos in Cook County Democratic politics and made Chicago the best administered, most dynamic and progressive large American city. Daley's accomplishments suggest that declining Irish political power in the cities has more to do with flight to the suburbs than with Washington, D.C.[28]

Toting university degrees and wearing middle-class respectability, hordes of post–World War II Irish-Americans abandoned urban neighborhoods. This migration intensified in the 1950s and 60s when impoverished blacks flooded into northern cities, squeezing white ethnic residential areas. As in so many other metropolitan places, the Irish are more numerous in Chicago suburbs than they are in the city. They have moved to such places as Oak Lawn, Evergreen Park, and Burbank to the southwest; Oak Park, River Forest, and Lombard to the west; and Evanston and Wilmette to the north.

Irish-America's journey from urban ghettos of economic and cultural poverty to suburban prosperity and respectability and the transformation of its politics from obsession with power to purpose climaxed in the 1960 election of John F. Kennedy as thirty-fifth president of the United States. If his bid for the White House had failed, the psychological effect on Catholic America could have been devastating. That is why so many clerical and political leaders of Irish-America were not originally enthusiastic about his candidacy. A number of priests frowned on Kennedy for another reason. Eager to obtain public funds for Catholic education, they believed that in his effort to defuse nativism Kennedy would scrupulously insist on the separation of church and state. His opponent, Richard M. Nixon, indicated more flexibility on the school issue. Mayor Daley, however, insisted that it was time for an Irish-American president to establish first-class citizenship for Catholics in the United States. He sold this conviction to other Irish political leaders across the nation.

A number of self-consciously Catholic intellectuals would have preferred someone like themselves, say Senator Eugene McCarthy, as the first Catholic chief executive of the United States. However, the combination of Harvard pedigree with shrewd Irish political judgment made Kennedy more suitable. While he may have been more style than substance, his charm, mental quickness, self-deprecating wit, energy, and physical attractiveness camouflaged meager legislative accomplishments, improved the image of the Irish and other Catholics, and made most Americans feel good about themselves, a self-esteem they never have quite recaptured.[29]

For those who can remember, America never seemed bleaker than in those bright but cold late November days of 1963 when the nation mourned the passing of so much promise. Since he liberated them from their doubts about belonging, no group grieved the loss of Kennedy more than Catholics, particularly the Irish. But they did so with the confident conviction that never again could others question the contribution of their talent and patriotism to the greatness of America.

NOTES

1. Moses Rischin refers to the Irish as the "Classic Ethnics" in his Introduction to *The San Francisco Irish,* ed. James Walsh (San Francisco: Irish Literary and Historical Society, 1979).

2. For recent surveys of Irish history in the period covered by this essay see Lawrence J. McCaffrey, *Ireland from Colony to Nation State* (Englewood Cliffs, N.J.: Prentice-Hall, Inc., 1979) and Karl Bottigheimer, *Ireland and the Irish* (New York: Columbia University Press, 1982).

3. For useful surveys of the Irish-American experience see Carl Wittke, *The Irish in America* (New York: Russell and Russell Publishers, 1970); William V. Shannon, *The American Irish* (New York: Collier Books, 1974); Andrew M. Greeley, *The Irish Americans: The Rise to Money and Power* (New York: Harper and Row Publishers, 1981); and Lawrence J. McCaffrey, *The Irish*

Diaspora in America (Washington: Catholic University of America Press, 1984), and "Irish-America," *Wilson Quarterly* 9 (Spring 1975), 78–93.

4. Comments on Irish Chicago history are based upon Charles Fanning, Ellen Skerrett, and John Corrigan, *Nineteenth Century Chicago Irish* (Chicago: Center for Urban Policy, Loyola University of Chicago, 1980); and Michael F. Funchion, "Irish Chicago: Church, Homeland, Politics, and Class—The Shaping of an Ethnic Group," and Paul Michael Green, "Irish Chicago: The Multiethnic Road to Machine Success" in *Ethnic Chicago,* ed. Peter d'A. Jones and Melvin G. Holli (Grand Rapids, Mich.: William B. Eerdmans Publishing Co., 1981).

5. Hasia Diner, *Erin's Daughters in America: Irish Immigrant Women in the Nineteenth Century* (Baltimore: John Hopkins University Press, 1983), effectively argues that Irish women adapted better to and were more successful in America than Irish men and achieved more than other women. However, her contention that gender segregation among the Irish in Ireland and America was a factor in the low and late marriage rate will not stand careful scrutiny. Other ethnics from Europe had as much if not more separation between the sexes as did the Irish.

6. Shannon, *American Irish,* p. 55.

7. Joel Tyler Headley, *The Great Riots of New York: 1712–1873,* with Introduction by Thomas Rose and James Rodgers (Indianapolis: Bobbs-Merrill, 1970). Richard Shaw, *Dagger John: The Unquiet Life and Times of Archbishop John Hughes of New York* (New York: Paulist Press, 1977), pp. 362–69.

8. Emmet Larkin, "The Devotional Revolution in Ireland," *The Historical Dimensions of Irish Catholicism* (Washington: Catholic University of America Press, 1984); Eugene Hynes, "The Great Hunger and Irish Catholicism," *Societas* 8 (Spring 1978), 137–56; and McCaffrey, *Ireland from Colony to Nation State,* p. 89.

9. According to Patrick Blessing, "The Irish," *Harvard Encyclopedia of American Ethnic Groups* (Cambridge, Mass.: Belknap Press, 1980), p. 532, "In 1900 daughters of Irish born parents composed 10 percent of all female teachers of foreign parentage in the United States, exceeding the combined total of female teachers with English and German parents." Diner, *Erin's Daughters in America,* pp. 70–105, discusses the mobility and professionalization of Irish-American women, and also their role in the labor movement.

10. Diner, *Erin's Daughters in America,* pp. 120–38. See also Eileen M. Brewer, "Beyond Utility: The Role of the Nun in the Education of American Catholic Girls, 1860–1920" (Ph.D. dissertation, University of Chicago, 1984).

11. JoEllen McNergney Vinyard, *The Irish on the Urban Frontier: Detroit, 1850–1880* (New York: Arno Press, 1976), and Stephan Thernstrom, *Poverty and Progress* (Cambridge, Mass.: Harvard University Press, 1964) and *The Other Bostonians: Poverty and Progress in the American Metropolis, 1860–1970* (Cambridge, Mass.: Harvard University Press, 1973), contrast Irish mobility in midwestern and eastern settings.

12. Vinyard, *Irish on the Urban Frontier,* p. 420.

13. Mundelein's statement was in the *New World,* June 25, 1920.

14. Daniel P. Moynihan, "The Irish," *Beyond the Melting Pot,* ed. Nathan Glazer and Daniel P. Moynihan (Cambridge: M.I.T. Press, 1963).

15. Thomas J. Fleming, *All Good Men* (New York: Doubleday and Co., 1961), *King of the Hill* (New York: New American Library, 1965), *Rulers of the City* (Garden City, N.Y.: Doubleday and Co., Inc., 1977); Edward R. F. Sheehan, *The Governor* (New York: World Publishing Co., 1970); James Carroll, *Mortal Friends* (Boston: Little, Brown and Co., 1978).

16. Jane Addams, "Why the Ward Boss Rules," *Outlook* 58 (1898), 879–82.

17. Allen F. Davis, "Jane Addams and the Ward Boss," *Journal of the Illinois State Historical Society* 53 (1960), 247–65.

18. Charles Fanning, *Finley Peter Dunne and Mr. Dooley: The Chicago Years* (Lexington: University Press of Kentucky, 1978), pp. 105–38.

19. Thomas N. Brown, "Nationalism and the Irish Peasant," *Review of Politics* 15 (Oct. 1953), 445. This essay is also indebted to Brown's "Origins and Character of Irish-American Nationalism," *Review of Politics* 18 (July 1956) 327–58 and *Irish-American Nationalism* (Philadelphia: J. B. Lippincott, 1966).

20. Michael F. Funchion, *Chicago's Irish Nationalists, 1881–1890* (New York: Arno Press, 1976).

21. Charles Shanabruch, *Chicago's Catholics: The Evolution of an American Identity* (Notre Dame, Ind.: University of Notre Dame Press, 1981); James W. Sanders, *Education of an Urban Minority: Catholics in Chicago, 1833–1965* (New York: Oxford University Press, 1977).

22. This is the thesis of Philip Gleason's "Thanks to the Irish," *America*, May 14, 1966.

23. Joseph M. Curran's "The Irish in American Film," paper presented to the Midwest Conference of the American Committee for Irish Studies, Oct. 16, 1982, influenced my comments.

24. John Higham, *Strangers in the Land: Patterns of American Nativism, 1860–1925* (New York: Atheneum Publishers, 1965); L. P. Curtis, Jr., *Anglo-Saxons and Celts: A Study in Anti-Irish Prejudice in Victorian England* (Bridgeport, Conn.: Conference on British Studies, 1968) and *Apes and Angels: The Irishman in Victorian Caricature* (Newton Abbot, England: David and Charles, 1971); John J. Appel and Selma Appel, *The Distorted Image* (New York: Anti-Defamation League of B'Nai Brith)—a slide collection containing examples of anti-Irish cartoons in American newspapers and periodicals; Stephan Garrett Bolger, *The Irish Character in American Fiction, 1830–1860* (New York: Arno Press, 1976).

25. In *The Irish Americans: The Rise to Money and Power,* Andrew M. Greeley summarizes poll evidence present in his other books indicating Irish-American liberal attitudes. The conduct of such Irish-American politicians as Senators Edward Kennedy, Daniel Patrick Moynihan, Thomas Eagleton, Joseph Biden, and Patrick Leahy, and Congressmen Thomas P. O'Neill, Thomas S. Foley, Edward Markey, and Congresswoman Patricia Schroeder confirm the liberal thrust of Irish-America. Over thirty years ago even prominent Catholic-baiter Paul Blanshard had to concede, "On the whole, Irish Catholicism in the United States tends to be left of center, and the voting record of its congressmen in Washington is generally progressive on every issue concerning which contrary orders have not come from Rome" (*The Irish and Catholic Power*

[Boston: Beacon Press, 1953], p. 289). And now Rome does not make much difference.

26. The transformation in Irish-American politics is the theme of Thomas N. Brown, "The Political Irish: Politicians and Rebels," *America and Ireland, 1776–1976,* ed. David Noel Doyle and Owen Dudley Edwards (Westport, Conn.: Greenwood Press, 1980), pp. 133–49.

27. George Q. Flynn, *American Catholics and the Roosevelt Presidency* (Lexington: University Press of Kentucky, 1968); and Shannon, *American Irish,* pp. 327–48.

28. Daley has attracted a considerable bibliography, including William F. Gleason, *Daley of Chicago* (New York: Simon and Shuster, 1970); Eugene Kennedy, *Himself: The Life and Times of Mayor Richard J. Daley* (New York: Viking Press, 1978); Edward M. Levine, *The Irish and Irish Politicians* (Notre Dame, Ind.: University of Notre Dame Press, 1966); Len O'Connor, *Clout* (Chicago: Henry Regnery Co., 1975); Milton L. Rakove, *Don't Make No Waves— Don't Back No Losers* (Bloomington: Indiana University Press, 1975) and *We Don't Want Nobody Nobody Sent* (Bloomington: Indiana University Press, 1979); Mike Royko, *Boss* (New York: New American Library, Signet Books, 1971).

29. In *The Kennedy Imprisonment* (Boston: Little, Brown, 1982), Gary Wills presents a negative Catholic intellectual critique of Kennedy. Shannon, *American Irish,* pp. 392–413, gives a favorable evaluation. Hermet S. Parmet, *Jack: The Struggles of John F. Kennedy* (New York: Dial Press, 1980) and *The Presidency of John F. Kennedy* (New York: Dial Press, 1983) present the most definitive portrait of Kennedy yet published.

The Catholic Dimension

Ellen Skerrett

The Irish community in nineteenth-century Chicago was shaped by three major forces: Catholicism, politics, and nationalism. Although the Chicago Irish were deeply involved in politics and the cause of Irish freedom, Catholicism remained their primary loyalty. It was the one common bond among the mass of Irish immigrants, continuing to claim their allegiance in the New World. Whereas politics and nationalism tended to divide the Chicago Irish into warring factions, Catholicism remained a unifying force well into the twentieth century. Not only did it hold the central institutional position in the lives of Chicago's Irish Catholics but, even more important, it mirrored their changing concerns as they ceased to be an immigrant minority and entered the ranks of the middle class.

The Irish who came to Chicago were essentially rural people, and like other Catholic immigrants they brought with them a concept of a parish-centered church.[1] While parish building was an important activity for nearly all Catholic immigrant groups, it was especially meaningful for them. Unlike Germans and Poles who settled in Chicago, the Irish did not form ethnic enclaves. Although Irish neighborhoods did exist, particularly near industrial sections of the city, the majority of the Chicago Irish were not ghettoized, and their parish building resulted in Irish communities throughout the city.

As the Chicago experience makes clear, the Irish used their parishes to create cohesive communities, especially in middle-class residential neighborhoods where Catholics were a minority. Far from limiting mobility or participation in the larger society, their parishes accelerated the integration of immigrants and their children into American life. The

Irish parish in Chicago was a powerful force in transforming peasants into devout, disciplined urban dwellers. In the early years, it eased the burden of dislocation for immigrants and provided working-class Irish with models of middle-class behavior. As they improved their economic status and moved to residential neighborhoods, the parish once again provided structure, this time for an emerging Catholic middle class. As the middle-class Irish parishes became bastions of respectability, they also contributed the lion's share of financial support for Catholic second-ary schools, and from the 1930s on they supplied much of the leadership for Catholic social action movements.

At its best, the parish filled important religious and social needs and became the heart of Irish-American community life. At its worst, the Irish parish turned inward and bred a fortress mentality. For generations of Chicago Irish men and women the parish reduced the awesome experience of urban life to a manageable scale. Not only did it play a large role in the development of Chicago neighborhoods, but the parish experience profoundly affected Irish attitudes about city life. Indeed, after more than a century as urban dwellers, the Chicago Irish remain a largely parochial people. To evaluate the legacy of the Chicago Irish parish experience it is necessary to view it in historical perspective.

Although the Irish controlled the hierarchy of the Church in Chicago during its formative years, the poverty of the Catholic community hampered institutional development. Chicago Catholic beginnings were inauspicious and gave little indication that Catholicism would emerge as the largest denomination in the city by the 1890s. When William J. Quarter, Chicago's first bishop, arrived in 1844 he found a single Catho-lic church, St. Mary's. So poor were the city's few hundred Catholics that they had been unable to complete the church's interior, much less liquidate an indebtedness of $3,000.

In many ways, Quarter was the ideal candidate to establish the new diocese of Chicago on a firm footing. Born in Kings County (Offaly), Ireland, in 1806, he emigrated at the age of sixteen in order to prepare for a career as an American priest. After ordination in 1829, he was assigned to New York City, which was in the process of becoming "the capital of American Catholicism."[2] During Quarter's tenure as a parish priest and pastor, New York's Catholic community experienced phenomenal growth as Irish and German immigrants flooded into the city. An estimated 90,000 Catholics lived in New York in 1840 and Irish-born priests like Quarter were faced with the challenge of building churches and establishing schools, orphanages, and hospitals. The new bishop came to Chicago, then, with firsthand knowledge of urban life and an appreciation of the multiethnic character of the fledgling American Catholic Church.

The pressing need for more Catholic churches in Chicago was compounded by the problem of language. Prior to Quarter's appointment, St. Mary's on Madison Street had operated as a multilingual parish with separate services for French, Irish, and German Catholics. Chicago's first bishop was a pragmatist and in forming new parishes he arrived at a solution that satisfied each of the city's ethnic groups.

Quarter's years in the East had made him acutely aware of the diversity of the Catholic population and he was especially sensitive to the desire of German Catholics for priests who could minister to them in their native tongue. In 1833, German Catholics in New York established the national parish of St. Nicholas, just a few blocks from St. Mary's Church on Grand Street, where Quarter began his pastorate. This was a new kind of parish based on language rather than territory, and it became "the trademark of German American Catholicism."[3] Quarter endorsed the relatively new concept of the national parish in 1846 when he designated St. Joseph's and St. Peter's as churches for Chicago's growing German Catholic population. At the same time he established the territorial parish of St. Patrick's for his own countrymen who had settled west of the Chicago River.[4]

Quarter's decision to form parishes based on language had important consequences for the structure of the Catholic Church in Chicago. First and foremost, the system of national parishes effectively separated ethnic groups from each other. Although the national parish was intended as a temporary solution to meet the needs of immigrants, it came to play a crucial role in the formation and preservation of ethnic communities. As the drive for ethnic solidarity intensified, so did the demand for national parishes, with the result that separate parishes became the norm for succeeding waves of German, Bohemian, Polish, Lithuanian, Slavic, and Italian Catholics.

German and Polish Catholics in particular created national parishes on the grand scale. In addition to building magnificent churches, both groups established schools, hospitals, orphanages, and cemeteries. For the majority of Catholic immigrants, religion and nationality were inextricably linked with the mother tongue. Understandably, national parishes as they developed in Chicago sought to preserve old-world customs and language as a way of strengthening faith and ethnic identity. Yet their success created a vacuum insofar as English-speaking parishes were concerned.

As the largest group of English-speaking Catholics in Chicago, the Irish had the most to gain from the proliferation of national parishes. Not only did the creation of national parishes isolate the Irish from other Catholic immigrants but it guaranteed Irish domination of the English-language territorial parishes. Although in theory territorial parishes were open to any English-speaking Catholic who lived within a circumscribed area, in practice virtually all English-speaking parishes established in nineteenth-century Chicago were de facto Irish. By default, the Irish gained control of English-speaking parishes throughout Chicago, and in a very real sense they dominated the Catholic Church from below as well as from above.

Like the national parishes of the Germans and Poles, the Irish territorial parishes fulfilled important religious and social needs. However the preservation of an ancestral language was not a concern of the Irish and it played no part in the formation of their parishes. Because the language question had already been decided for them before they emigrated, it did not become an issue in the New World as it did for every other Catholic ethnic group. While familiarity with English put the Irish at least a full generation ahead of other European immigrants, it also made them the most visible ethnic group. For Chicago's Irish this was a mixed blessing.

Until the Civil War, the Irish were the city's largest—and poorest—ethnic group. From a few hundred canal workers in the 1830s, the city's Irish population grew to more than six thousand by 1850 and within the next decade it tripled.[5] When construction was halted on the Illinois and Michigan Canal in 1842, Irish laborers sought employment and housing in the city and its adjoining communities, especially Bridgeport, which was the terminus of the canal. Their numbers were swelled by refugees of the Great Famine who arrived in Chicago during the late 1840s. Not only did this flood tide of newcomers overwhelm the city's small Irish community but it strained the charitable resources of the emerging metropolis.[6]

At mid-century, the presence of Irish and German immigrants was deeply felt in Chicago, where fewer than half of the city's 29,275 residents were native-born Americans. Transplanted New England Yankees decried the increasing number of foreigners in their midst and they supported legislation aimed at restricting the right to vote, drink, and hold public office. Despite the fact that the Irish spoke English, which made them in one sense the least "foreign" of Chicago's immigrants, they bore the brunt of nativist attacks for reasons that had more to do with religion and politics than with their poverty or their regular appearance on the criminal court docket.

Unlike the Germans, who were divided along religious and political lines, the Irish were identified with the Douglas wing of the Democratic party and the Catholic Church.[7] While it is not clear what proportion of Irish immigrants were churchgoers, nativist attacks in the 1850s hammered away at the link between the Irish and the Catholic Church. Staunchly Republican, the Chicago *Tribune* took the lead in denouncing the increasing influence of the Irish in local politics and its editorials warned that the Catholic Church sought political and religious supremacy in America. In 1855, it supported the mayoral campaign of Levi D. Boone, who ran as a Know Nothing candidate on a temperance ticket. In advocating temperance legislation known as the Maine Law Alliance, the *Tribune* charged that "The great majority of the members of the Roman Catholic Church in this country are Irishmen. The fact is peculiarly true in this city. . . . Who does not know that the most depraved, debased, worthless and irredeemable drunkards and sots which curse the community, are Irish Catholics? Who does not know that five-eighths of the cases brought up every day before the Mayor for drunkenness and consequent crime, are Irish Catholics?"[8]

Groups such as the Hibernian Benevolent Society were fully aware of nativist sentiment and their St. Patrick's Day celebration in 1855 reflected the tensions which existed between Irish, Catholic, and American identities. It followed the convention of the day with speeches and musical selections. However the choice of "sentiments" and "airs" indicated a defensiveness on the part of the Irish. Except for the customary tributes to St. Patrick and Ireland, the celebration was heavily patriotic, with speeches ranging from "The Memory of Washington" to "The President of the United States" and "The Army and Navy." But for all the singing of the "Star Spangled Banner" and "Yankee Doodle," the *Tribune* recoiled at the sentiment expressed by Rev. Bernard O'Hara of Holy Name Church that America ultimately "would be Catholic throughout its borders." The newspaper suggested that if the Catholic Church flourished in America, then the "fruits of Romanism here shall be seen in as full and abundant a harvest of beggary, degradation and want as is seen in the Catholic portions of Ireland."[9]

Throughout the 1850s and 1860s, the *Tribune* portrayed Chicago's Irish Catholics as priest-ridden and the newspaper cited the immigrant's loyalty to the Church as evidence that the Irish could never become fully American. Contrary to the *Tribune*'s opinion, at the time the Chicago Irish were not obsequious slaves of the Catholic Church or her clergy. A large segment of them were locked in disputes with bishops Anthony O'Regan and James Duggan over their arbitrary dismissal of diocesan clergy. These controversies, which pitted congregation and priests against their bishops, raised questions about the limits of episcopal authority and they also revealed the increasing importance of the parish as a vehicle for Irish respectability.

The first crisis to galvanize Irish Catholic sentiment occurred in 1855 when Bishop O'Regan dismissed Rev. Jeremiah Kinsella and three priest-professors who served Holy Name Church and St. Mary of the Lake University. In one fell swoop the bishop fired the men who had been handpicked by Quarter to organize the first institution of higher learning in the city.

Bishop Quarter had been acutely aware of the need for an American-trained clergy and he had established St. Mary of the Lake University to include a seminary department. Finances for such a venture were a constant problem, and in his will Quarter left all his personal property to the university rather than to his successor, Bishop James O. Van de Velde. This bequest had enabled Father Kinsella to pursue an independent course. Not only was he able to keep the university running, but he hired Edward Burling, one of the city's foremost architects, to design a church for Irish Catholics who had been attending Mass in the school chapel. Kinsella's plans for Holy Name Church were ambitious. At a time when the city's Irish population worshipped in frame churches, if at all, estimates for the new Gothic structure ran as high as $100,000. To members of Holy Name parish, however, the new church was more than just a place to attend Mass. It was a powerful symbol of Irish Catholic respectability in a city where few Irish families had achieved middle-class status. As one observer recalled, "The foundations were laid as never foundations were laid in Chicago before or since. The buttresses were massive enough to have sustained an edifice the size of St. Peter's and millions of bricks were stowed away in the massive tower."[10]

That Father Kinsella borrowed heavily to build the new church had not bothered Holy Name parishioners but it had alarmed Bishop Van de Velde, who regarded such initiative as "Irish insubordination."[11] These conflicts remained unresolved when Van de Velde resigned his post in 1853.

Bishop Anthony O'Regan, like his predecessor, was reluctant to head the Chicago diocese, but once in Chicago he acted quickly to assert his authority. In January 1855, he dismissed Father Kinsella and three other well-known priests, Rev. John Breen, Rev. Lawrence Hoey, and Rev. Thomas Clowry. This action stunned Holy Name parishioners, who held a meeting to protest the bishop's decision. In a formal statement a committee of parishioners acknowledged respect and reverence for the authority of the Church and their bishop, but they disputed his reasons for removing their priests. The committee, composed of leaders of the Irish community, expressed "utmost confidence in the energy and zeal of our priests to complete our new church" and they pledged continuing financial support if O'Regan reconsidered his decision. But the bishop remained firm and the four priests had little recourse but to leave Chicago.[12] While Irish Catholics were unable to alter O'Regan's decision about their clergy, they succeeded in completing Holy Name. On Nov. 5, 1855, the Court of Common Pleas ruled that the cornerstone blessing constituted approval of the church and awarded contractor Charles O'Connor $6,263.96 in his suit against the bishop.[13]

The fact that the Chicago Irish paid serious attention to the issue of clerical rights indicates that they were already well on their way to thinking of themselves as American Catholics. O'Regan's arbitrary dismissal of the local clergy was an embarrassment to the city's Irish community because it gave credence to nativist charges that the Catholic Church was an institution incompatible with the American spirit of democracy. In the Protestant tradition, local congregations played an important role in forming churches and selecting ministers. Many Protestants regarded as un-American the near absolute freedom enjoyed by Catholic bishops in appointing and dismissing priests. Nor did this state of affairs go unnoticed by officials of the Congregation de Propaganda Fide, which had jurisdiction over the Catholic Church in the United States until 1908. Following an extensive tour of this country in 1853, Archbishop Gaetano Bedini filed a long report on the relationship of bishops and priests. He noted in particular that it was "difficult for a priest to work hard in his mission, to build churches and schools at great sacrifice, to obtain the good will of the parishioners and then suddenly to be transferred by the unexpected inclination of the Bishop."[14]

As the targets of nativist propaganda, the Irish were especially sensitive to claims that they could not be loyal Americans because their first allegiance was to the Church. Irish-born priests such as Quarter and Kinsella had been optimistic that the Catholic Church would thrive in Chicago and they believed that American-trained clergymen would accelerate the process. Quarter was confident that Catholic institutions such as St. Mary of the Lake University could play an important role in the life of the city and the Church, and by the 1860s the school had fulfilled this promise.

Considering the virulent anti-Catholic and xenophobic sentiments which became commonplace in the 1850s, Quarter's plans for the Church in Chicago may have appeared overly optimistic. However as far as the Irish were concerned, nativist attacks had the effect of strengthening the bond between their Irish and Catholic identities. Indeed, the Holy Name controversy underscored the prominent role accorded priests in the Chicago Irish community and it revealed the increasing importance of church-building as a sign of Catholic power.

For many Irish immigrants, the process of forming parishes and building churches was relatively new. Although the parish system survived the Penal days, as late as 1820 there was a dearth of proper church buildings in Ireland. While Catholic "chapels" existed in Dublin and in smaller towns, the situation was much more primitive in the countryside. In parts of Connacht, for example, priests offered Mass in thatched sheds or in the open air and they routinely performed marriages and baptisms in private homes. Although Catholic church-building increased dramatically in the early 1800s, the effect of this movement was not felt by much of the Catholic population, particularly in the west.[15]

Chicago's Irish population included large numbers of men and women from that part of Ireland, where church attendance was far from customary. Unlike later immigrants who adhered to strict religious practices, thousands of the Irish who settled in Chicago prior to the Civil War were Catholic in name only. That the Catholic Church quickly became the central institution in the lives of Chicago's Irish was due in no small part to priests such as Denis Dunne, who recognized that the real vitality and strength of the Church lay in its parishes.

Dunne was born in Timahoe, Queens County (Leix), Ireland, in 1823 but he grew up in New Brunswick, Canada, where his father and uncles found ready employment as ship carpenters. Dunne was ordained for the Chicago diocese in 1848 and his first assignment was as a professor at St. Mary of the Lake University. His rapid rise from assistant priest to vicar general of the diocese illustrated the vigor of the young Chicago Church and the opportunities available to talented Irish clergymen. After brief stints in country parishes in Galena and Ottawa, Illinois, Dunne returned to Chicago in 1854 to serve as rector of St. Patrick's Church on the city's West Side. Not long afterward, Bishop O'Regan appointed him vicar general, a post he continued to hold during the administration of Bishop James Duggan.

Dunne's years in Chicago spanned the period of heaviest Irish immigration and he was well aware of the need for adequate churches. Not only did he lead the drive to complete the spacious brick church of St. Patrick's, which still stands today at the corner of Adams and Desplaines streets, but he encouraged lay initiative, especially in the areas of fund-raising and charity work. Parishioners voted on contracts for the church building and in 1859 they elected men to canvass the neighborhood for funds to liquidate the $11,700 parish debt.[16] Although it appears that the rector prepared the parish's financial reports, they were approved during meetings of the congregation.

Dunne was also instrumental in forming a chapter of the St. Vincent de Paul Society, which quickly took root in Irish parishes throughout Chicago. This group, composed of prominent men from St. Patrick's, supported free schools for Catholic children and raised money for destitute parishioners. While the St. Vincent de Paul Society remained largely parish-bound, it represented the first "Catholic" attempt to deal with social problems plaguing the Irish community in the 1860s.

Under Dunne's administration, St. Patrick's emerged as a model Irish-American parish, sensitive to newly arrived immigrants as well as to prosperous families in the congregation. Like many of the Chicago Irish, Dunne had no personal memories of Ireland but he knew the painful history of his people and he understood the longing of Irish Catholics for acceptance by the larger society. Indeed, when the Civil War broke out he formed a regiment known as the 90th Volunteers.

Although many Chicago Irishmen were less than enthusiastic about fighting a war which promised the abolition of black slavery, others like Dunne seized the opportunity to demonstrate just how American Irish immigrants could be. At the first meeting at St. Patrick's on August 8, 1862, the organizers of the Irish Legion pledged their loyalty to the Union cause and they lashed out at fellow Irishmen "who have sought, or who are now seeking, the protection of the blood-stained felon flag of Great Britain, to escape their duty to the United States."[17] The 90th Volunteers' record of service gave new meaning to the term "Fighting Irish." Of the 980 men who left Chicago with the Irish Legion, only 221 returned in June 1865.[18] Participation of Irish Catholics in the Union Army did much to improve their image, establishing a patriotic pattern that later generations adopted in their struggle to become fully American.

More than any other Irish priest of his generation, Dunne tried to lay broad and deep foundations for the Catholic Church in Chicago. At a time when most pastors were wholly absorbed in building churches, Dunne devoted much of his energy to the cause of Catholic education and he remained firm in his conviction that the Church must care for the young and the needy. In addition to supporting grammar schools in St. Patrick's parish, he organized an industrial school at 2928 South Archer Avenue in Bridgeport to care for "unruly and vagabond boys of [the Catholic] faith," many of whom had been left fatherless by the Civil War.[19] Although priests and laity alike recognized the need for a Catholic reformatory, Bishop Duggan withheld his support. Undaunted by the lack of official sanction, Dunne relied on the generosity of St. Patrick's parishioners and members of the St. Vincent de Paul Society to keep the institution open.

By 1865, Dunne was Chicago's most well known Irish clergyman. His work in St. Patrick's and his support of the Irish Legion and the Bridgeport Institute had won him the respect of both Catholics and Protestants. By then his duties as vicar general placed him on a first-name basis with all the city's priests. Indeed, in terms of influence, his only rival was Arnold J. Damen, who had established the Jesuit parish of Holy Family in 1857 on the prairie just west of St. Patrick's.

With priests such as Dunne in positions of authority, the future of the Catholic Church in Chicago looked promising. Then disaster struck. In 1866 Bishop Duggan abruptly closed St. Mary of the Lake University, which had only recently been reorganized by Rev. John McMullen, chancellor of the diocese. The bishop transferred McMullen to St. Paul's, a poor Irish parish on the West Side and he turned the new university building into an orphanage. Although the seminary associated with the university survived, its precarious existence was a cause of deep concern to Rev. James J. McGovern, the president, and his professors, especially Rev. Joseph P. Roles, who also served as rector of Holy Name Church.

Not long after he closed the university, the bishop stripped Dunne of his authority as vicar general by appointing Rev. T. J. Halligan administrator of the diocese. During Duggan's extended tour of Europe in 1867, Halligan withdrew financial support for the seminary and set in motion a series of events which culminated in the removal of Bishop Duggan from office. As James P. Gaffey has shown, this little-known controversy vividly illustrated the dynamics of church authority and it had profound consequences for the structure of the Catholic Church in the upper Mississippi Valley.[20] But it was also a watershed for Chicago's Irish Catholics.

From start to finish, the Duggan controversy was almost exclusively an Irish affair, involving priests and parishioners of Irish birth and descent who opposed the arbitrary actions of their Irish-born bishop. Yet Irish identity played no role in the conflict. On the contrary, the events of 1866–68 clearly reveal that the Chicago Irish considered themselves to be American Catholics who wished to see "the checks and balances of constitutional freedom" applied to their Church.[21] Once again, priests' rights were at the heart of the matter.

Following his return from Europe in August of 1868, Bishop Duggan closed St. Mary of the Lake Seminary and dismissed the priests who had brought charges against him, namely Dunne, McMullen, McGovern, and Roles. The response of Irish Catholics was swift. Mass meetings were held in Holy Name, St. Patrick's, and St. Paul's to endorse the actions of the clergy and to raise funds for the suspended priests. Unlike the 1855 conflict in Holy Name, which had received little public attention, the Duggan controversy was chronicled in the pages of Chicago's leading daily newspapers, the *Tribune* and the *Times.* Not only were the resolutions adopted by Irish Catholics made public but week after week the columns of the Chicago papers were filled with articles which detailed the disagreements between Bishop Duggan and the clergy and parishioners.

As the controversy unfolded, readers discovered that the four Chicago priests had filed serious charges against their bishop ranging from excessive absence from the diocese to conversion of diocesan funds for personal use. What made their charges so compelling was the fact that Dunne, McMullen, and Roles were members of the bishop's council and hence his advisors on matters of policy. So public did the controversy become that when McMullen left Chicago for Rome to press his case against Duggan, the *Times* published his farewell letter to the bishop along with a forwarding address! Thus did Chicagoans learn on September 27, 1868, that McMullen was on his way to Rome, fortified by his conviction that "it is my sacred duty to God, religion, and my fellowmen, to do all that I can within the bounds of truth and justice, to remove [my superior] from the bishopric of Chicago."[22]

Throughout the fall of 1868, Dunne declined to comment about the Duggan controversy, confident in the knowledge that "When the due time comes, my friends and I will vindicate our good names, and give evidence that we have neither *lightly nor falsely* made charges at Rome."[23] For Dunne, the vindication did not come soon enough. He died on December 23, 1868, in his brother's home on Adams Street, in the shadow of St. Patrick's. Although Bishop Duggan was present at Dunne's side, no reconciliation took place. Far from giving his blessing to the dying man, the bishop demanded a retraction. But Dunne refused to yield and thus he died "with the censure of the Bishop upon his back . . . and in such poverty that the clergy and people paid for his funeral."[24]

Reports of Dunne's death and the subsequent mental breakdown of Bishop Duggan persuaded church officials in Rome to intervene in the Chicago controversy. But nearly two years elapsed before Duggan was committed to a sanitarium in St. Louis and Bishop Thomas Foley arrived from Baltimore to administer the diocese. Foley was the first American-born bishop to head the Chicago diocese and his appointment was widely interpreted as a signal that Rome had "consulted the prevailing Catholic sentiment in [America] in favor of the elevation of natives to the highest offices of the Church."[25]

Foley's quiet, unpretentious, but effective leadership quickly brought a measure of peace to the troubled Chicago Church. Indeed the bishop maintained such a low profile during his ten years in Chicago that he never "permitted a journalist to interview him . . . never participated in popular demonstrations . . . abhorred politics, never voted . . ."[26] His immediate vindication of McMullen, Roles, and McGovern won him the respect and admiration of the Chicago Irish and it signaled his desire to work with the clergy. Foley was well aware of the strong ties which existed between parishioners and their clergy and he did little to diminish the power of parish priests. But more than any of his predecessors, he realized that the parish system with its divisions along ethnic and geographic lines posed a barrier to the unity of Chicago's Catholics. Not only were the city's Catholic immigrants separated into parishes of their own, but within each ethnic group parishes were further divided along geographic lines.

That the parish system had become firmly entrenched was apparent at the time of the Chicago Fire of 1871. In announcing the formation of a citywide agency to aid victims of the disaster Foley lamented that "There has not been a sufficient union among the Catholics of the city. Dr. Whitehouse of the Episcopal Church said in a recent address that his diocese was too congregational, and I think there is something of the same kind of division among ourselves. This is due perhaps to the unfortunate geographical division of the city, but as we are all Catholics we should know no north or south or west side."[27]

While substantial numbers of the Chicago Irish thought of themselves as American Catholics, Foley's remarks indicate that they were as parochial as their German coreligionists. In 1870 the Irish controlled fifteen of the city's twenty-three parishes. Although the English-speaking parishes of the Irish were more dispersed than German parishes, they were by no means evenly distributed throughout the city. On the contrary, three distinct networks of Irish parishes had emerged, one north, one south, and one west of the Chicago River. As the number of English-speaking parishes increased during the 1870s and 1880s these sectional divisions deepened, with the result that the Irish Catholic population became even more fragmented.

In 1871 the fire destroyed St. Mary's Cathedral in the city's commercial district along with six other Catholic churches, several schools, convents, rectories, and charitable institutions. In one day Chicago's Germans lost two of their largest churches, St. Joseph's and St. Michael's, while the Irish suffered the loss of Holy Name and smaller frame churches in the parishes of St. Paul's and Immaculate Conception. Bishop Foley's decision not to rebuild St. Louis's and St. Paul's met with little opposition from Chicago's Irish Catholics because these parishes had been steadily losing members.

Irish movement away from the center of the city had accelerated in the 1850s and 1860s as housing and jobs became readily available in outlying areas. Parishes soon followed. One priest who was quick to discern the trend was Arnold Damen, S.J. In 1857 he selected a site on Twelfth Street [Roosevelt Road] just west of Halsted Street for the new parish of Holy Family, in close proximity to the lumber district and the railroad yards where Irish laborers were employed. Before long the prairie surrounding the Jesuit church became a frame-house neighborhood, and by 1871 Holy Family was the largest English-speaking parish in Chicago, with a congregation of nearly 20,000 persons. Financed in part by the Jesuit order, the parish complex was massive, encompassing a Gothic brick church, three parochial schools, a convent-academy owned by the Madames of the Sacred Heart, and St. Ignatius College, the forerunner of Loyola University. Although few Irish parishes could rival Holy Family, church-building continued to occupy the energies of even the poorest congregation.

In the wake of the Chicago Fire, Irish pastors embarked on ambitious building campaigns aimed at replacing old frame churches with brick structures. This was no small feat as fully 75 percent of the churches in Irish parishes were built of wood. Although little is known of the ability of Chicago's Irish Catholics to provide funds for such a building campaign, the total value of parish complexes in 1873 was estimated at more than $2 million.[28] While Chicago's newspapers routinely criticized the brick-and-mortar approach to Catholicism, the efforts of the Chicago Irish did not go unnoticed. Indeed newspapers began to comment favorably that the construction of Catholic churches "improves and helps to fill up the surrounding neighborhood and swells and enhances the value of property."[29]

The construction of a masonry church took on special meaning in Irish parishes in Chicago. Financed by the nickels and dimes of working men and women, the church was a powerful symbol of Irish cooperation. And its construction through voluntary contributions revealed just how American the Chicago Irish had become. While Irish churches were modest affairs in comparison with German and Polish edifices, still their existence "in the waste places of the city . . . where . . . the populace are humbly and poorly housed," was a sign that the Irish were becoming devout urban dwellers.[30]

Catholic church dedications were important events for the Chicago Irish and they turned out by the thousands to witness the ceremonies, which invariably included parades and speeches. In addition to describing the new church, contemporary newspaper accounts often commented about the changes which had taken place among Irish workers following the organization of a parish. In 1876, a Chicago *Times* reporter noted that when Rev. Thomas J. Edwards began his work among Irish immi-

grants from County Clare in the North Side Rolling Mill district in 1866
that:

> The people were largely Catholic in name, but in name only. They paid
> little or no regard to the outward ordinances of religion, and cared less for
> its principles. To a great extent they were quarrelsome and dissolute. They
> were not precisely the class of people one would care to live among . . . Father
> Edwards saw that the people in this part of the city needed the restraining
> and the purifying influences of the church, and he resolved to supply this
> need. There was no place of worship, and there were practically no
> worshipers. He undertook to build the one and supply the other. In both of
> these attempts he has been remarkably successful.[31]

At the time the new $50,000 brick church was dedicated, Annunciation
was a flourishing parish of eight hundred families. Groups such as the
Total Abstinence Society and the St. Vincent de Paul Society had contributed much to parish stability, as did the parochial school which enrolled
five hundred students in 1876. Women religious played a crucial role in
such working-class parishes. In addition to instructing the children in the
doctrines of the Catholic faith, the nuns fostered middle-class aspirations.
They encouraged children to pursue their education beyond the elementary level and they recruited talented young girls for their own religious
communities. The Sisters of Charity of the Blessed Virgin Mary who
came to Annunciation parish in 1872 also promoted vocations to the
priesthood with remarkable results: by 1916, the parish claimed ten Irish-
American priests, among them Bishop Edward Dunne of Dallas, Texas.[32]

While church-building took precedence over Catholic education in
most Irish parishes in Chicago, there were signs that this attitude was
changing. Although all but two of the city's eighteen Irish parishes
supported parochial schools in 1876, few congregations had the financial
resources to maintain schools on the scale of those in St. Patrick's or
Holy Family. Bishop Foley acknowledged the problem but stressed that
where the parochial schools were as good as the public schools, Catholic
parents had an obligation "to give their children the advantage of this
Catholic education."[33]

One South Side Irish pastor who materially advanced the cause of
parochial schools was Rev. John Waldron of St. John's at Eighteenth and
Clark streets. So great was his conviction about the necessity of Catholic
education that he provided modern quarters for the children of the
parish before allowing the construction of a permanent church. For
more than twenty years after the parish was organized, the congregation
worshipped in a plain wooden church located in the heart of a working-

class slum west of State Street. Following the fire of 1871, a number of wealthy Irish families moved into the posh Prairie Avenue district at the east end of St. John's, and they were particularly anxious to see a masonry church constructed that would rival nearby Protestant houses of worship. Not only did Waldron refuse to consider their suggestion that a new church be built near the lake, but he reminded these parishioners that his duty was almost entirely to the children of the parish. He exhorted the "thrifty and prosperous" among the five hundred families in his congregation to concern themselves with the plight of poor children in St. John's who had neither books nor boots. In a stirring sermon in 1875, reprinted in newspapers across the country and in Ireland, Waldron stated his case:

> Every day last week I was out looking up the children of the parish; finding out how many do not go to school anywhere, and getting at the reasons why they stay away and run to vice and crime in the streets. In many a house I found that not one child of the family went to school. . . . "Why don't you go, Michael?" said I to one that knew me. "Because I've got no boots," he said. He might have said, because he had no anything, for he had not enough clothes on to keep him from the chill of these cold days. You can't get children to go to either church or school without clothes and books, and that's why half the children of Chicago are not in any school. . . . What does a poor lad without boots care for your books? Give them the boots first, and then we can get them to the books afterwards. I told these boys that I would give them both if they would come to our schools, and you will keep my word for me.[34]

Waldron's conviction about the necessity of Catholic education was equaled only by his nationalist fervor. He proudly owned and displayed two pikes from the 1798 rebellion and during his twenty-seven years as pastor of St. John's he hosted many Irish groups, among them the Fenian Brotherhood, the Irish Rifles, the Clan na Gael Guards, and the Ancient Order of Hibernians. Although the Christian Brothers of De La Salle and the Sisters of Mercy who staffed St. John's school did not share the pastor's devotion to the cause of Irish freedom, they were in complete agreement that their students must become "intelligent, useful citizens, a credit at once to their country, their faith, and to themselves."[35] While not denying Irish identity, these religious orders did little to reinforce it, with the result that their students considered themselves Americans first and foremost.

Complex feelings about Irish identity were not unique to the members of St. John's. Although the nationalist cause engaged the passions of Chicago's Irish population in the coming decade, it did not alter support for Catholic education nor retard parish development. Far from diminishing in importance, Irish parishes remained powerful forces in Chicago's industrial slums as well as in middle-class residential districts.

Waldron was a pioneer of the American urban parish and like other Irish priests in nineteenth-century Chicago, his view of city life was intensely parochial. He spent his entire career as a priest within an area of less than two square miles and it became for him a world unto itself. "Kerry Patch" around St. John's was a rough-and-tumble Irish neighborhood and Waldron patrolled its streets with a blackthorn stick in hand, ready to disperse "street gangs and alley loafers."[36] Contemporary accounts portrayed him as "a powerful aid to the city government in preserving order and keeping peace among the riotously inclined."[37] Despite the location of St. John's in the midst of a working-class slum, Waldron waged a battle against the Rock Island in the 1860s when it appeared that the railroad would buy up property along Clark Street from Twelfth to Twenty-second streets. Although he was powerless to prevent the encroachment of other railroads, Waldron's efforts guaranteed the survival of St. John's long after the neighborhood's homes had disappeared.

By the late 1870s, Chicago's Irish had made significant gains in terms of parochial development and Catholic education. But many lay and clerical leaders were pessimistic about the future. Continued immigration, they believed, would threaten Irish communities already in existence.

In 1879, a group of civic-minded Irishmen organized the Irish Catholic Colonization Society to deal with the problem of Irish immigration. Bishop John Spalding of Peoria served as chairman of the board of directors and William J. Onahan, Chicago's most respected Irish Catholic, was elected secretary. Ironically, at the time Onahan was working to relocate Irish immigrants on farms in the Midwest, his countrymen in Chicago were no longer at the bottom of the economic ladder. Although the Irish were heavily represented among laborers and semiskilled workers, a middle class had been formed by those who had found employment in such diverse fields as politics, municipal government, education, brewing and distilling, importing, meatpacking, undertaking, theater, and sports. While much work remains to be done on the economic background and family patterns of the nineteenth-century Chicago Irish, it seems probable that their poverty has been overemphasized.[38]

Emmet Larkin has persuasively argued that the quality of Irish immigration steadily improved after the Great Famine. As a result of the development of the national school system in Ireland, the overwhelming majority of men and women who came to America in the 1860s and 1870s were literate and many had experienced the benefits of the "Devotional Revolution."[39] Not only were these new immigrants practicing Catholics but they were accustomed to supporting parishes through voluntary contributions.

For all his work on behalf of Irish colonization, even Onahan was forced to concede that the quality of Irish immigration to Chicago improved throughout the 1880s. He noted that "These newcomers of late years are of the better class—the young, enterprising, and as a rule fairly educated," and he agreed that they would be a valuable addition to Chicago's Irish population, estimated at 300,000 persons.[40]

In the 1880s, then, the Chicago Irish were not wholly middle class but neither were they poverty-stricken immigrants. With nearly two full generations in the city, the Irish had become a powerful force in politics and they had put their imprint on the Catholic Church. By 1885, the central committee of the Democratic party was overwhelmingly Irish and within the ranks of the Church, Irish clergymen were heavily represented as pastors and members of the archbishop's staff. Indeed, the highest administrative post in the diocese, that of chancellor, continued to be held only by priests of Irish birth or descent until 1971.

In the years between 1880 and 1910, Chicago's Irish Catholics continued to make important gains politically and economically. One of the significant developments during this period was the movement of Irish families away from congested neighborhoods to outlying areas of the city. In Holy Family and Annunciation parishes they were being displaced by new immigrants, Italians and Jews on the West Side, and Poles on the Near Northwest Side. In St. John's on the Near South Side, the Irish exodus began shortly after a new church was dedicated in 1881. Father Waldron, who had refused to build a permanent church until his congregation could afford it, now watched in sorrow as "hundreds and hundreds of his beloved poor and faithful families surrendered their humble homes to the railroads, and moved in affluence to help build up and be the first families in the many South Side parishes."[41]

While many Irish Catholics retained fond memories of life in parishes such as Holy Family, Annunciation, and St. John's, the fact remains that they left by the thousands, exchanging cold-water tenements for steam-heat "flats." Although ethnic changes played a role in the breakup of older parishes after 1880, the Irish were not so much pushed out of their old neighborhoods as they were pulled by the opportunity for better housing. Parish statistics give an idea of the magnitude of this change in Irish residential patterns. Whereas fully 75 percent of English-speaking parishes established between 1843 and 1878 had been in the city proper, after 1880 the vast majority of parishes organized by Irish Catholics were located in outlying districts. While these new parishes clearly demonstrated mobility, they also cast light on the improving economic status of Irish Catholic families.

Prior to 1880, Irish parishes in Chicago reflected the predominantly working-class origins of their members. Although parishes such as St. Patrick's, Holy Family, Holy Name, and St. John's included some of the city's wealthiest Irish families in the 1870s, by and large they drew their strength from those of limited financial means. In the 1880s, however, distinctly middle-class parishes emerged as the Irish moved to residential districts several miles from the center of the city.

Archbishop Patrick A. Feehan, who headed the Chicago archdiocese during a period of enormous growth (1880–1902), was attentive to the needs of the Irish and he was aware that they were a highly mobile group. Because of the availability of priests of Irish birth and descent, Feehan did not hesitate to form English-speaking parishes with as few as fifty families. As a result, predominantly Irish parishes were organized throughout Chicago in both industrial areas and sparsely settled residential districts.

Of the forty-three English-speaking parishes organized between 1880 and 1902, St. Bernard's stands out as an example of the kind of parish formed by upwardly mobile Irish Catholics who moved into fashionable residential districts. In July 1887, Feehan assigned his former chancellor, Rev. Bernard P. Murray, to establish a Catholic parish in Englewood, a community located eight miles south of the downtown business district. As its name suggests, Englewood was a predominantly Protestant New England Yankee settlement.

Father Murray's purchase of property on Stewart Avenue, the finest street in the area, enraged Protestant residents. A group of them offered to "repurchase the church property at a goodly advance in price," but Murray refused to sell.[42] The Protestants realized, clearly enough, that although the Irish were a minority in Englewood, the formation of a new parish would attract more Catholics to the area. Beyond anti-Catholic sentiment, however, there were other reasons to fear an Irish invasion. Already by the 1880s they held a number of appointive positions in the Town of Lake and Protestants were well aware that Irish influence in politics would increase as the Catholic population grew. Then, too, Englewood residents firmly believed that the Irish would bring with them crime and vices associated with the city, thereby disturbing the tranquility of this suburban district.

For their part, the Irish did not view themselves as destroyers of community life. On the contrary, the founding members of St. Bernard's included prominent Catholics such as P. T. Barry, a former Illinois legislator who also served as a school trustee for the towns of Lake and Hyde Park. Father Murray, like other Chicago priests of Irish birth and descent, also considered himself a Catholic community builder, and during his thirty-year pastorate he was responsible for the construction of a permanent church, school, convent-academy, and hospital.

As Protestants had feared, the Catholic population of Englewood grew steadily, and by 1895 six hundred families belonged to St. Bernard's. Considering the opposition the Irish Catholics had encountered in the formation of their parish it is understandable that they wanted a magnificent church that would compare favorably with neighboring Protestant houses of worship. Murray was well aware that St. Bernard's would be a symbol of the Irish presence in Englewood and he spared no expense in the construction of a marble edifice, said to be the only church of its kind in the Middle West.

As if to force old-line Englewood residents to acknowledge the increasing importance of his Irish Catholic community, Murray scheduled the cornerstone-laying for the same day—at the same hour—that Presbyterians were to do the same for their new church, just a stone's throw from St. Bernard's. Not only did the Catholics upstage the Presbyterians but their celebration became a demonstration of Irish religious and political power.

Contemporary accounts reveal more than five thousand Catholics from parishes all over the South Side turned out to march through Englewood. The parade included platoons of Irish-American policemen and Irish military groups such as the Seventh Regiment and the Clan na Gael Guards. In the midst of this Catholic show of strength, members of the Cumberland Presbyterian Church began their own celebration—to the strains of "Onward, Christian Soldiers."[43]

While the Irish of St. Bernard's succeeded in establishing themselves as respectable members of the community, they were never accepted by Englewood's "old guard." In time, however, anti-Catholic sentiment declined and a number of Irish attained prominent positions in local banking, politics, and business. But in many ways the Englewood neighborhood remained divided along religious lines. Indeed, these divisions deepened as the Catholic population increased and new parishes were formed, each with its own identity.

Although it is difficult to determine precisely when the Chicago Irish began to define themselves in terms of their parishes, the experience of the Irish in Englewood suggests that anti-Catholic sentiment played a crucial role in reinforcing parish identity. Just as the Irish were the pioneers of Chicago's urban ghettoes in the 1850s and 1860s, they were the first Catholic ethnic group to settle in large numbers in predominantly Protestant residential neighborhoods in the 1880s and 1890s. However American the Irish in these outlying areas considered themselves to be, their religion and ethnic heritage continued to set them apart from native-born Protestants. Irish newcomers responded by using their parishes and schools to prove just how Catholic and American they were.

In communities such as Englewood, Woodlawn, Austin, Lake View, and Rogers Park, Irish-Americans built churches that equaled or rivaled existing Protestant houses of worship and they established elementary and secondary schools that compared favorably with local public schools. Far from diminishing in importance, church-building played an even greater role in the lives of the Chicago Irish as they attained social and economic parity with native-born Protestants. Indeed, the majority of Irish-American parishes organized after 1890 were shaped more by Protestant-Catholic conflict than by ethnic rivalries.

Although the parishes formed by the Chicago Irish in the 1880s and 1890s were far more American than Irish, they were not devoid of ethnic identity. The issue of Irishness remained alive, fueled by the nationalist movement and the longing of the Irish for respectability. Despite the economic, political, and social gains made by the Chicago Irish, they had not yet achieved integration into the larger society. This lesson was painfully clear to those who moved out of industrial sections of the city where Catholics predominated and into neighborhoods which were Protestant strongholds.

Because the nationalist movement of the 1880s addressed the question of Irish-American identity, it had strong appeal for second-generation Irish Catholics as well as for newly arrived immigrants. Thousands of Chicago Irish men and women believed, rightly or wrongly, that their position in American life was directly related to Ireland's status as a dependent nation. They were convinced that only when the bonds between Ireland and England were severed would they achieve acceptance as full-fledged American citizens.

As Michael F. Funchion has shown, support for the nationalist cause cut across all segments of the Chicago Irish population, but even more important, it extended to the highest levels of the Church.[44] Neither Archbishop Feehan nor his clergy interfered in the activities of the Clan na Gael. As a result, Chicago's Irish were not forced to choose between their religion and their nationalist beliefs. Indeed, pastors such as Maurice J. Dorney of St. Gabriel's and Thomas Pope Hodnett of St. Malachy's were prominent Irish nationalists and they took an active role in the cause of Irish freedom.

Unlike the experience of Chicago's Poles, who were divided into separate parishes over the question of nationalism, no such break occurred among the city's Irish.[45] Part of the reason was that their parish system had been firmly established by the time the nationalist movement gained momentum in the 1870s. Equally important was the fact that Chicago's

Irish and Irish-American clergy did not discourage their parishioners' involvement in the campaign for Ireland's freedom. They allowed groups such as the Land League and the Ancient Order of Hibernians to meet on the same basis as the St. Vincent de Paul Society and the Catholic Order of Foresters, thereby channeling nationalist fervor and reinforcing Irish and Catholic identities. Moreover, many an Irish pastor increased his parish coffers through "popular voting contests" between representatives of different nationalist groups!

Although the Irish nationalist cause did absorb money that otherwise might have gone to church-related activities, it did not cause any significant changes in terms of parish development or formation. In the South Side working-class parish of St. Gabriel's, for example, Father Dorney and his congregation financed the construction of a massive Romanesque church in 1887–88 at the height of the Land League agitation.

Throughout Chicago the situation was much the same. While the intrigues of nationalists, especially camps of the Clan na Gael, seemed to dominate the Irish community in the 1880s and 1890s, in working-class districts and middle-class neighborhoods parish building continued on an unprecedented scale. More English-speaking parishes were organized between 1880 and 1900 than had existed since the Chicago diocese was established in 1843, in addition to which the Catholic school assumed a larger role in the lives of Chicago's Irish.

According to the federal census of 1890, the foreign-born Irish represented less than 7 percent of the city's population, which had just passed the one-million mark. Not only did the second generation outnumber immigrants, but a third generation had come of age, the grandchildren of the Famine Irish. Although American-born men and women had taken the lead in securing white-collar jobs and establishing themselves as a political power, they seemed no closer to gaining acceptance in the larger society than their foreign-born Irish relatives. To make matters worse, the machinations of Irish-American aldermen such as "Foxy Ed" Cullerton, "Hinky Dink" Kenna, and "Bathhouse John" Coughlin were a constant source of embarrassment to upwardly mobile Irish Democrats because they seemed to justify the stereotype of the Irish politician as a "boodler" and "ward heeler."

The collapse of the local nationalist movement in the 1890s found the Chicago Irish at a crossroads. No longer a predominantly immigrant community, they had become to a large extent Catholic urban dwellers who regarded themselves as more American than Irish. The resurgence of nativism in the 1890s did much to redirect the energies of the second generation away from strictly Irish causes in favor of institutions and groups that met their special needs as American Catholics. Nowhere was this change more apparent than in their attitude toward Catholic education. While approximately half of all Catholic children in Chicago attended public schools in the period between 1850 and 1900, still the drive for parochial schools made tremendous gains, especially among the Irish.[46]

Although figures from the *Official Catholic Directory* tended to underestimate Catholic school enrollment, they do give an idea of the growth of the parochial school system and its multiethnic character. In 1876, grammar schools in Chicago's Irish parishes accounted for 65 percent of the Catholic school enrollment of 15,329 students. While attendance increased substantially in German, Polish, and Bohemian Catholic schools during the next decade, the Irish continued to be in the forefront of the parochial school movement. In keeping with their role as the largest group of English-speaking Catholics in Chicago, they supported the most parochial schools in the city and they accounted for 46 percent of the overall increase in attendance between 1876 and 1890. By 1890, Chicago's Catholic schools enrolled 32,814 students, making the system one-fourth the size of the city's public schools. Although their large-scale immigration had ended, the Irish still accounted for 55 percent of the Catholic school population. The Germans ranked next with 24 percent; the Poles, 14 percent; the Bohemians, 6 percent; and the French, 1 percent.

While older established parishes such as Holy Name, St. Patrick's, and Sacred Heart continued to maintain the largest Irish parochial schools, enrollment was more evenly distributed in 1890 than it had been in 1876. This was due to the fact that parochial schools were established in new English-speaking parishes in outlying areas of the city. The second-generation Irish who moved out of Holy Family parish, for example, formed the nucleus of such West Side parishes as St. Malachy's (1882), St. Charles Borromeo (1885), Blessed Sacrament (1890), St. Matthew's (1892), St. Agatha's (1893), and Presentation (1898). Unlike Holy Family, these parishes supported smaller congregations and as a result, their schools experienced slower growth. But their very existence in new subdivisions of the city confirmed that Catholic education was not merely an immigrant phenomenon. The situation was the same on the city's South and North sides where older Irish parishes steadily lost population in the 1890s. Far from diminishing in importance, parochial schools played an important role in the development of new parishes in outlying areas. Not only did they draw upwardly mobile Irish Catholics, but for many families the parochial school eased the transition from a heavily Catholic neighborhood to a predominantly Protestant district.

Although in many ways the Irish were the most "American" of Chicago's ethnic groups, they did not feel completely at ease in the city's public

schools. The reason had more to do with religion than social or economic differences. Throughout most of the nineteenth century, Chicago's
public schools had a Protestant orientation. The majority of schoolteachers
were Protestant, readings from the King James version of the Bible were
part of the curriculum until 1875, and textbooks contained glaring
examples of anti-Catholic bigotry.

As Timothy Walch has shown, in the period from 1840 to 1890
Catholics in Chicago used the press as well as legislative methods to air
their grievances against the city's public schools. Although they failed to
secure a share of the state's school fund, their criticism of the Chicago
schools went a long way to making them truly "public." In addition, the
debate over public education forced Chicago's parochial schools to
become "as American as they were Catholic."[47]

But far from being a unified system, Chicago's Catholic schools remained
divided along national lines well into the 1930s. Not only did they vary in
size from parish to parish but there were significant differences in terms
of quality of instruction and ethnic orientation. Indeed, except for the
study of religion, the English-speaking parochial schools of the Irish had
more in common with local public schools than they did with their
German or Polish counterparts. The obvious difference, of course, was
language. Whereas other ethnic groups used parochial schools to preserve and defend ancestral language and customs, the Irish established
schools as a means of strengthening their Catholicism. While these
schools segregated Irish children from Protestants as well as from Catholics of other ethnic backgrounds, they were not ghetto institutions. On
the contrary, the English-speaking Catholic schools of the Irish promoted integration into the larger society. They also played a crucial role
in the formation of an American Catholic identity.

American-born children who came of age in the 1890s and early 1900s
swelled the ranks of Chicago's Catholic elementary schools and they
represented the first generation to enter Catholic high schools in significant numbers. Although institutions such as St. Patrick's Academy and
St. Ignatius College provided for "talented young men of scanty means,"
for the most part Catholic higher education was beyond the reach of
working-class boys.[48] The situation was somewhat better for young
women because convent academies such as Sacred Heart on Taylor
Street subsidized free schools with the tuition paid by wealthy Catholic
and Protestant parents. In the 1890s, however, the Sisters of Mercy and
the Sisters of Charity of the Blessed Virgin Mary pioneered a new
concept in Catholic education, secondary schools for girls of moderate
means. At the same time, the Christian Brothers established De La Salle
Institute to prepare young men for careers in the business world.

The success of these Catholic high schools was due in no small part to the fact that they compared favorably with local public schools. In addition to incorporating such innovations as graded classrooms, teachers' institutes, and university extension courses, the Sisters of Mercy and the BVMs patterned their curriculums after the public school course of study, down to the same textbooks.[49] In St. James's High School, for example, girls received a thorough preparation in Latin, English, history, and science, precisely the subjects required for admission to the Chicago Normal School in Englewood.

Rev. Henry W. McGuire, pastor of St. James's parish from 1883 to 1911, was a moving force behind Catholic higher education. Like other Chicago priests and nuns he believed that "the future of the Catholic Church is locked up in the school that stands beside the Church." But he went further, insisting that Catholic schools existed to "teach the best in the state with the blessing and benefit of religion."[50] McGuire used contributions from his South Side Irish congregation to finance St. James's High School, providing the Sisters of Mercy with the opportunity to demonstrate the effectiveness of their teaching methods. The pastor insisted that all graduates of St. James's take the entrance exam to the Chicago Normal School because it represented "the standard set by the educational authorities of the city."[51] Although admission to the two-year teachers' college was free, only candidates who passed a rigorous exam were admitted.

The *New World,* the archdiocesan newspaper, pointed with pride to the increasing number of Catholic girls who were preparing for careers as teachers in the city's public schools. In the summer of 1902, for example, two-thirds of the candidates who passed the Normal exam were graduates of Catholic secondary schools. And St. James's students accounted for 25 percent of the successful candidates. The *New World* hailed these statistics as a victory for Catholic schools, proof that the efficiency of teaching in parochial schools was decidedly higher than that of the public schools.[52]

So successful were Catholic students in gaining admission to the Normal School that in 1915 Superintendent Ella Flagg Young attempted to limit the number of students accepted at the teachers' college from a single high school. The plan, if adopted, would have reduced the number of Catholic school teachers in the public school system and effectively closed off job opportunities for graduates of the Sisters' schools, a high percentage of whom were Irish.

The quota system at Chicago Normal was not imposed and while it took several more years for Catholics to be promoted as principals and administrators, the Irish public school teacher became a stereotype in a

city protected by an Irish police force and fire department. While the
starting salary for Chicago teachers was less than that paid patrolmen
and firemen, it was sufficient to attract ambitious working-class and
middle-class girls who preferred teaching to secretarial work or nursing.
In 1920, Archbishop George W. Mundelein estimated the proportion of
Catholic teachers in the city's public schools at 70 percent and he
attributed the increase to the fact that Irish parents "always gave their
daughters the chance of better education."[53]

But it is no coincidence that the Catholic high schools which sent the
most candidates to Chicago Normal between 1890 and 1930 were those
staffed by Irish-American women religious. Unlike high schools affiliated with German and Polish parishes which sought to strengthen ethnic
identity, institutions such as St. James's and St. Mary's on the West Side
were Catholic versions of the public schools. Just as many Chicago Irish
parishes were shaped by Protestant-Catholic conflict, so too the schools
in English-speaking parishes reflected the larger society's preoccupation
with Americanization. This process was aided and abetted by predominantly Irish religious orders. Whereas German and Polish women
religious were powerful agents in the transmission of ethnic identity,
Irish nuns served no comparable function. Like the majority of the
American Irish they had difficulty distinguishing "between the specifically Irish and specifically Catholic aspects of their lives."[54]

Although women religious such as the Sisters of Mercy, the BVMs,
the Sisters of Providence, and the Sinsinawa Dominicans did not deni-
grate Irish identity, neither were they particularly conscious of it. Possibly because so many of their recruits were Irish and Irish-American,
the nuns felt no need to foster ethnic identity in either their convents or
their schools. Indeed, the study of Irish history was not incorporated
into Chicago's English-speaking parochial schools until 1904 and then
only because of an organized campaign by the Ancient Order of
Hibernians.

While efforts at promoting Irish history, language, music, and art
made some headway, the Gaelic movement as a whole failed to catch
on. Try as they might to "take up the work . . . which their fathers failed
to do," the Chicago Irish were fighting a losing battle.[55] Not only was the
Irish population becoming more Americanized with each decade, but
the number of its foreign born in Chicago declined steadily after 1900.
Ironically, the new immigrants brought with them a stronger sense of
ethnic identity than their relatives who had immigrated earlier. But they
came too late and in insufficient numbers to make a noticeable difference in the Chicago Irish community.

Increasingly, groups such as the Ancient Order of Hibernians, which had flourished in the 1880s, became the province of the foreign-born Irish. Mary F. McWhorter, an indefatigable promoter of Irish history and culture, noted with dismay that children of immigrants associated the AOH with "the shanty Irish."[56] Although the Chicago Irish made significant gains economically and politically by 1910, they had little inclination to preserve their ethnicity, especially when that identity carried negative connotations.

Irish history courses taught in Chicago's English-speaking parochial schools did little to remedy the situation. Not only did the courses emphasize Catholic aspects of Irish history but their subject matter was of little interest to city children, few of whom had personal memories of Ireland. Favorite essay topics ranged from "The Educational Status of Ireland in the Fifth Century" to "The Life of St. Columbkille." While this brand of history may have filled deep psychological needs, it offered no insight into the Irish-American experience. Instead of gaining an appreciation for the sacrifices and accomplishments of the Irish in urban America, children learned how their ancestors kept the Catholic faith alive during the Penal times. In scenes reminiscent of *Studs Lonigan,* thousands of Chicago Catholic children received two diplomas on graduation night, but Irish history awards meant little to these second- and third-generation Irish who regarded themselves as fully American.

By 1920, a large segment of the Chicago Irish population had repudiated an ethnic identity in favor of a strictly Catholic identity. The Knights of Columbus, the fastest-growing Irish-American organization in Chicago after 1900, is a case in point.[57] Although there were many similarities between the Knights of Columbus and the Knights of Columbanus in Ireland, Irish Catholics in the United States did not look to Ireland's past for a model on which to base a new fraternal organization. Instead they selected Christopher Columbus and the Knights of the Crusades.

Between 1896 and 1918, forty-nine councils of the Knights of Columbus were established throughout Chicago, representing a membership of 25,323. While a few councils selected Irish names, the overwhelming majority preferred Catholic titles, parish names, or neighborhood designations. The KCs drew their strength from second- and third-generation Irish men who were anxious to prove just how Catholic and American they had become. The "Caseys," as they were known, pledged to support the U.S. Constitution, preserve the integrity of the ballot, promote reverence and respect for law and order, and practice their religion "openly and consistently, but without ostentation."

Of all the social, athletic, and charitable endeavors supported by the KCs, none equaled their contribution to the war effort. As had hap-

pened during the Civil War and the Spanish American War, Chicago's
Irish viewed their participation in World War I as proof of their patriotism.
Fully 25 percent of Chicago's KCs served in the armed forces, with a
high proportion of enlistments. Chicago became the headquarters of the
Knights' war activities and council members vigorously supported the
Liberty Loan campaigns as investors and speakers. The KCs financed
the construction of recreation centers in military training camps in
America and Europe which were open to all soldiers, irrespective of
creed, and they paid the salaries and expenses of Catholic chaplains,
among them fifty-seven priests from the Archdiocese of Chicago.

Welfare work undertaken in World War I by the Knights of Columbus
compared favorably with that of established organizations such as the
Young Men's Christian Association. On a local level, virtually all councils experienced an increase in membership after 1917. The University
Council, for example, held the record for the highest percentage of
servicemen for any Chicago unit. Formed only in 1913, this council was
caught up in the patriotic energy of World War I. Therefore, 252 of its
412 members participated in the conflict. By 1921, the University Council claimed 1,311 members. Like many other KC groups, it was affiliated
with a parish—St. Ignatius in Rogers Park. It also maintained ties with
nearby Loyola Academy and University. As had happened during the
heyday of the nationalist movement, Chicago Irish pastors were quick to
recognize the Knights as an important part of parochial life. The University Council, for instance, raised $1,000 toward the construction of a
new grammar school in St. Ignatius's parish, where the number of
Catholic students had doubled between 1912 and 1921.

Although Catholic schools and new Catholic organizations did little
to reinforce ethnic identity, Irish parishes in Chicago did not disappear
for a variety of reasons. One was Irish mobility. Unlike their German,
Polish, Bohemian, and Italian coreligionists, the Irish formed few ethnic
enclaves in Chicago. By the 1890s, the Irish were moving out of quasi-
industrial neighborhoods such as Pilsen, Back of the Yards, and the
Rolling Mill district to residential neighborhoods in outlying areas. In
sharp contrast to Germans, Poles, and Lithuanians who purchased homes
and businesses in the city's older neighborhoods, the Irish remained by
and large renters. In 1906, for example, the *New World* apologized to its
readers (75 percent of whom were Irish) for calling attention to a serious
social phenomenon, namely that the Irish spurned home ownership:
"They who of all others are famed for their beautiful home life are—
many of them—content to live in flats, to move every May or October
day, to be ever on the wing like stormy petrels."[58]

Of all immigrant groups in Chicago at the turn of the century, the Irish were the most widely dispersed. Paul Cressey has calculated that between 1898 and 1930 Irish immigrants left initial areas of concentration such as Back of the Yards for "more desirable residential districts farther from the center of the city."[59] By 1930, the median distribution for foreign-born Irish was 6.4 miles from the Loop, nearly the same as for persons of native-white parentage. Such a pattern of dispersal, Cressey argued, reflected "the more complete disintegration of their group life and a greater degree of cultural assimilation."[60]

Yet for all their mobility, the Chicago Irish were still a parochial people. While they readily moved into steam-heat flats and bungalows, they did not abandon the concept of city life as parish-centered. One need look no further than the novels of James T. Farrell for confirmation that the parish continued to be the center of neighborhood life for the steam-heat Irish well into the 1930s.

Archbishop James E. Quigley, who headed the Chicago diocese from 1903 to 1915, ensured that the city's Irish would continue to find parish-centered communities wherever they moved. He believed that "a parish should be of such a size that the pastor can know personally every man, woman, and child in it."[61] Quigley advocated the one-square-mile parish and beginning in 1904 he divided older English-speaking parishes to form new parishes that were smaller in terms of both territory and population. After consulting with local pastors, the archbishop set boundaries that would "assure a prosperous parochial community from the start."[62] As a result, each new territorial parish began with approximately three hundred families, enough to support a church and school.

In conjunction with his policy of dividing older English-speaking parishes, Quigley endorsed the concept of the combination building which contained both church and school quarters. He urged pastors to delay the construction of a permanent place of worship until the parochial school was firmly established. Although most English-speaking parishes eventually did construct separate church buildings, in the early years parish revenues were used to open grammar schools that were on a par with local public schools. While Archbishop George W. Mundelein agreed with Quigley's philosophy of parish formation, he was even more insistent that pastors provide modern school quarters before building massive churches. In addition, Mundelein broke with tradition by refusing to form national parishes outside ethnic enclaves, in effect legitimizing the Irish-American model of parish over all others.

Quigley's and Mundelein's policies regarding parish formation met with wide acceptance among the Chicago Irish who were moving out of older congested neighborhoods. In many new apartment districts and bungalow belts, English-speaking parishes were present almost from the beginning and they provided structure for emerging middle-class Catholic communities. While a number of the sixty-three English-speaking parishes organized in Chicago between 1903 and 1939 were ethnically mixed, most still bore the unmistakable Irish imprint.

Although the relatively early dispersal of the Irish into new residential neighborhoods played a significant role in the persistence of predominantly Irish parishes, equally important was the role of the clergy. While the closing of St. Mary of the Lake Seminary in 1868 had slowed down the formation of an American-trained clergy, still vocations from Irish parishes in Chicago accounted for a sizeable increase in the number of English-speaking priests. Their ranks were also swelled by foreign-born Irish priests who came to Chicago at the request of Archbishop Feehan.

Irish-born and Irish-trained priests had done much to expand the network of English-speaking parishes in Chicago during the 1880s and 1890s. In addition to serving as pastors of large territorial parishes, several foreign-born Irish priests held key positions in Feehan's administration. But the archbishop did not neglect native-born priests in favor of his own countrymen. After 1887, for example, he selected as chancellor only American-born priests of Irish descent.

Feehan's reliance on Irish-American clergymen rankled foreign-born Irish priests who felt their influence diminishing. In 1900, Rev. Thomas P. Hodnett, pastor of the prosperous West Side parish of St. Malachy's, and Rev. Thomas Cashman, of nearby St. Jarlath's, joined forces with a country pastor, Rev. Jeremiah Crowley, to thwart the appointment of Rev. Peter J. Muldoon as auxiliary bishop. When Muldoon finally broke his silence about the controversy surrounding his appointment he declared: "The cause of the schism is that I am an American. It is the old story of the Irish priests against the American."[63] As Charles Shanabruch has detailed, the Crowley schism was a deep embarrassment to Chicago Catholics as well as to the American hierarchy.[64]

Unlike the Duggan controversy thirty-five years earlier, which centered on priests' rights and due process, the Crowley affair was basically an interclerical dispute pitting older foreign-born Irish priests against younger American-born clergymen. In a larger sense, however, it mirrored the tensions which existed within the Irish community between "greenhorns" and "narrowbacks." Although Archbishop Quigley and his successors accepted no more diocesan clergymen from Ireland into the Chicago archdiocese, they had little choice but to promote Irish-born priests to pastorates as they came of age. The result was that immigrant Irish priests continued to wield influence in Chicago parishes well into the 1950s.

In terms of structure, the English-speaking parishes formed in Chicago between 1880 and 1920 remained essentially unchanged. In contrast to German and Polish national parishes which aimed at institutional completeness, the parishes of the Irish were scale-down parochial communities. Far from supporting a wide range of social, ethnic, cultural, and athletic activities, Irish parishes were church and school centered. By the 1920s, however, there were signs that this concept of parochial life was changing. The South Side parish of Visitation is a case in point.

At the time this parish was organized in 1886, it embraced a fairly large district immediately south of the Union Stock Yard where Irish immigrants and their children found ready employment. Between 1890 and 1910 the construction of multifamily apartments along tree-lined Garfield Boulevard made the area attractive to upwardly mobile Irish Catholics, and for many Visitation became a stopping-off place on the trek from Bridgeport and Canaryville to South Shore and Beverly.

In the early days of the parish, the pastor and congregation concentrated on establishing a grammar school and building a Gothic church which dominated the boulevard at Peoria Street. By 1911, Visitation was a flourishing parish with an annual grade school enrollment of more than 1,300 students. And the opening of a $150,000 high school in 1915 put it in the forefront of the Catholic secondary school movement. Although the formation of new English-speaking parishes reduced Visitation's boundaries to less than one square mile by 1916, the end result was an intensification of parish identity. Moreover, the organization of the Polish parish of St. John of God at Fifty-second and Throop Street virtually guaranteed that Visitation would remain Irish.

The turning point in this parish occurred in 1924 with the arrival of Rev. T. E. O'Shea as pastor. O'Shea was a new breed of Irish priest: born in Chicago and raised in a working-class neighborhood. He understood the aspirations of Irish parents for their children and he was especially sensitive to the needs of the working-class youngsters who increasingly filled the parish school.

The most pressing need O'Shea addressed was that for recreation. Although the apartment buildings in Visitation parish offered a middle-class standard of living, unlike bungalow belts to the south there were few places where young children could play. In 1925, the pastor organized a parish social center with an ambitious sports program which became a model for the Catholic Youth Organization, formed five years later.[65] In 1926, O'Shea and his associate, Rev. Thomas Tormey, established a summer camp in Palos Hills which provided hundreds of working-class children with their first taste of country life. Visitation social center, with its organized activities and sports teams, did much to lessen the attraction of youth gangs, but even more important it represented a parochial solution to an urban problem.

O'Shea's concept of parish was dynamic and his focus on the needs of children made Visitation in the 1920s one of the most progressive parishes in the Chicago archdiocese. His efforts at forging links between parish and neighborhood were so successful that Irish Catholics who lived around Fifty-fifth and Halsted referred to the area as "Vis." Indeed, for more than two generations, this part of the Englewood neighborhood continued to be known by the parish name. But O'Shea's successor charted a different course and during his tenure Visitation became a bulwark against racial change.

Rev. Msgr. Daniel F. Byrnes, who headed Visitation from 1932 to 1952, was the last of a dying breed: an Irish-born and Irish-trained priest who had been incardinated into the Chicago diocese by Archbishop Feehan. Byrnes's policies were geared toward enhancing the role of Visitation as the center of neighborhood life. In addition to financing the construction of a new social center, he established the annual May crowning as the neighborhood's largest social event, involving virtually all of the four thousand families in the parish. Yet in the area of race relations Byrnes was unable or unwilling to provide leadership. In contrast to younger American-born priests of Irish descent who believed that parishes could do much to prepare neighborhoods for peaceful integration, Byrnes's response to racial change was largely negative. As the black population of Englewood increased after World War II, the Irish pastor reminded his congregation that they lived in the "largest and greatest parish in the diocese" and at Sunday Mass he periodically read the parish boundaries.[66] His message was clear: if Irish families remained in the neighborhood, Visitation would continue to flourish.

Msgr. Byrnes's attitudes about black immigration were shared by the bulk of his parishioners, and as a result Visitation gained a reputation as "one of the most dangerous spots in the city insofar as race relations were concerned."[67] While a number of Catholic parishes did develop siege mentalities when faced with ethnic or racial change, on the whole the Irish Catholic reaction was passive. Only a small number of the Chicago Irish took to the streets to defend their neighborhoods in the wake of racial succession. Like the Lonigans in James T. Farrell's trilogy, most Irish-American families reacted to black immigration by moving to other neighborhoods, even when it meant leaving behind massive parish complexes that were newly built or completely paid off. Indeed, Farrell's account of the Irish exodus from St. Patrick's [Anselm's] parish at Sixty-first and Michigan Avenue in the 1920s was still descriptive of many South and West Side parishes in the 1960s and 1970s.

Arnold Hirsch has estimated that between 1940 and 1960 more than 400,000 whites left Chicago.[68] Yet during the same period there was a massive movement of Catholics within the city limits, from racially changing areas such as Englewood and East Garfield Park to neighborhoods at Chicago's edge. While Irish-Americans moved to the suburbs in large numbers in the post–World War II era, a significant proportion remained in the city. Although the residency requirement for municipal workers accounted for much of this stability, the role of the Catholic Church cannot be underestimated. The existence of parishes at the city's outer fringes, coupled with a well-established system of elementary and secondary schools, ensured continuity of Catholic neighborhood life.

As early as 1915, the *New World* had admonished its readers "to sink local differences and racial antagonisms in the effort to view the Catholic Church in her entirety."[69] The newspaper also reminded its largely Irish audience that parochial boundaries were imaginary lines drawn for the sake of better ecclesiastical administration. But to no avail. Not only did the Chicago Irish continue to perceive the Church in strictly parish terms, but their concept of the city was increasingly narrow. Ironically, Catholic secondary schools, which accelerated the integration of the Irish into the middle class, played a crucial role in deepening sectional loyalties.

Although a few Catholic high schools such as St. Ignatius, St. Mary's, and Immaculata attracted students from parishes throughout Chicago, most served a distinct section of the city. Leo High School, operated by the Irish Christian Brothers at Seventy-ninth and Peoria Street, for example, drew young men from bungalow belt parishes that developed on Chicago's South Side after World War I. Although Leo technically was a central high school, in fact it was an extension of the Irish-American parish network which had blossomed in the area bounded by Fifty-fifth Street, Ninety-fifth Street, Ashland Avenue, and Halsted Street. Not only did its students share similar ethnic and economic backgrounds, but they also came from the same geographical area. The result was that even as Leo students prepared for careers that would take them downtown and into the city at large, they retained an identity as South Side Catholics.

The situation was much the same for Irish-Americans who lived on the city's North and West sides. Although Catholic secondary schools organized after World War II were more diverse in terms of ethnic makeup, their very location at the edges of the city strengthened rather than weakened sectional loyalties. As far as the Irish were concerned, sectional and parish loyalties took precedence over strictly ethnic ties.

As late as the 1960s, second- and third-generation Irish Catholics were far more conscious of belonging to a particular parish in a particular neighborhood than they were of their nationality.

To the generation of Chicago Catholics who came of age in the 1960s, parishes were a familiar part of neighborhood life and they provided stability in a city that was experiencing profound ethnic and racial changes. Like the Lonigans of an earlier era, thousands of Chicago's Irish Catholics believed that the Church would halt the resegregation of their neighborhoods. On the South and West sides of the city, progressive Irish-American priests and congregations worked with community groups to prepare their neighborhoods for racial integration. St. Philip Neri parish was a driving force behind the South Shore Commission, formed in 1953, and St. Sabina's was the headquarters of the Organization of the Southwest Community, a federation of seventy-five civic, religious, and fraternal groups established in 1959. On the West Side, St. Thomas Aquinas and Resurrection supported the Organization for a Better Austin in its campaign against slum landlords, abandoned buildings, panic peddling, and "redlining," the denial of conventional mortgages by banks to families in integrated areas.

Try as they might, parish groups were powerless to solve the economic problems associated with racially changing neighborhoods. Indeed, progressive Irish-American parishes were no more able to achieve racial stability than conservative parishes which attempted to keep blacks out of their neighborhoods altogether. The end result was a massive movement of middle-class white families from Chicago's bungalow belts and lakefront neighborhoods.

Irish-American families who left Chicago in the 1960s and 1970s swelled the Catholic population of such suburbs as Wilmette, River Forest, La Grange, Mount Prospect, Arlington Heights, Oak Lawn, and Orland Park. As Andrew Greeley has observed, many Irish Catholics who moved to the suburbs built "parish neighborhoods."[70] Oak Lawn, for example, with its five Catholic parishes, is in many ways simply an extension of Chicago's South Side neighborhoods. Although the existence of a Catholic parish eased the transition from city to suburbs for many families, others regarded suburban parishes as different from the cohesive communities they left behind. Moreover, the lack of parochial schools in new suburban areas meant that Catholics had no alternatives but to send their children to local public schools, thus accelerating the process of structural assimilation.[71]

Demographic studies indicate that the future growth of the Archdiocese of Chicago will occur outside the city proper, in suburban Cook and Lake counties. For Irish-Americans who choose to remain in Chicago, parishes provide continuity and structure in an increasingly black and Hispanic city. Although parochial schools on the city's far Northwest and Southwest sides no longer enroll as many students as they did in the 1950s and 1960s, they persist as important components of Catholic ethnic neighborhood life. And in older city neighborhoods which once were Catholic strongholds, parochial schools now serve minority populations. In 1982, for example, black and Hispanic students accounted for 40 percent of the city's Catholic school enrollment.[72]

But the dissolution of Chicago's Irish-American parishes does not necessarily mean the death knell for Irish identity. Lawrence J. McCaffrey has argued persuasively that residents of urban Irish neighborhoods were religiously and emotionally—but not culturally—Irish.[73] He contends that the vast majority of the American Irish have been severed from their historical roots by Catholic education. Not only did Irish-American Catholic educators ignore the Irish dimension of their heritage but they emphasized a Catholic culture that was devoid of ethnic identity. As the Chicago experience makes clear, the English-speaking parish system pioneered by the Irish did little to reinforce ethnic identity, Irish or otherwise.

Still, it comes as a surprise that the resurgence of interest in Irish identity places such little emphasis on Catholicism. Considering that the vast majority of Irish communities in urban America were parish-based, it is nothing short of remarkable that Irish identity has so quickly shed most of its Catholic moorings. Indeed, the generation of Irish-American Catholics who came of age in the 1960s led the way in embracing an ethnicity that has little connection with the Catholic Church and its urban working-class past.[74] Whereas the old identity was almost wholly Catholic-centered, the new one seeks its roots in Irish history, literature, music, and art. While the rekindling of Irish identity is a cause for celebration, the new version may prove to be as narrow and brief as the old.

Of all the forces which shaped the Irish community in Chicago, the Catholic Church exerted the most powerful influence. And the Irish in turn put their unmistakable imprint on it. Unlike other European immigrants who sought to recreate old-world peasant parish structures, the Irish in Chicago formed parishes and schools that met their special needs as American Catholics. Far from limiting mobility or assimilation, the parochial institutions created by the Irish hastened their integration into the larger society. Although Chicago's Irish-American parishes have all but disappeared, their parish model continues today, providing structure for emerging black and Hispanic Catholic communities.

NOTES

This chapter derives from research begun under a Youthgrant awarded by the
National Endowment for the Humanities.
    1. Jay P. Dolan, *The Immigrant Church: New York's Irish and German
Catholics, 1815-1865* (Baltimore: Johns Hopkins University Press, 1975), p. 4.
For background information on Chicago parishes, see Charles Shanabruch,
Chicago's Catholics: The Evolution of an American Identity (Notre Dame, Ind.:
University of Notre Dame Press, 1981) and James W. Sanders, *The Education of
an Urban Minority: Catholics in Chicago, 1833-1965* (New York: Oxford Univer-
sity Press, 1977).
    2. Dolan, *Immigrant Church,* p. 9.
    3. Ibid., p. 71.
    4. Chicago Catholic parish statistics in this essay are based on Rev. Msgr.
Harry C. Koenig, ed., *A History of the Parishes of the Archdiocese of Chicago,* 2
vols. (Chicago: Archdiocese of Chicago, 1980). Between 1844 and 1900, sixty-
one English-speaking (territorial) parishes were organized in Chicago. The sixty-
seven national parishes formed during the same period were divided as follows:
German, 27; Polish, 16; Bohemian, 8; French, 5; Italian, 4; Lithuanian, 3; Negro,
1; Slovak, 1; Slovene, 1; Dutch, 1.
    5. Population statistics in this essay are based on *The People of Chicago:
Who We Are and Who We Have Been* (Chicago: City of Chicago Department of
Planning, 1976), pp. 10, 11, 13, 17; and U.S. Bureau of the Census, *Eleventh
Census of the United States: 1890,* "Population," Part I (Washington: Govern-
ment Printing Office, 1895), pp. 671, 708, 714, 720, 726, 728.
    6. Bessie Louise Pierce, *A History of Chicago,* 3 vols. (New York: Alfred A.
Knopf, 1937-57), I:74.
    7. For a full treatment of nativism and the Chicago *Tribune's* anti-Catholicism,
see Thomas M. Keefe, "Chicago's Flirtation with Political Nativism, 1854-1856,"
Records of the American Catholic Historical Society of Philadelphia 82 (1971),
131-58; and "The Catholic Issue in the Chicago Tribune before the Civil War,"
Mid-America 57 (1975), 227-45.
    8. Chicago *Tribune,* Feb. 26, 1855.
    9. Chicago *Tribune,* Mar. 19, 1855.
    10. Chicago *Times,* Nov. 7, 1875.
    11. Cited by Shanabruch, *Chicago's Catholics,* p. 12.
    12. Chicago *Daily Journal,* Jan. 18, 1855. Contemporary newspaper accounts
question the bishop's financial dealings and they dispute the allegation that the
banished faculty left O'Regan with a $45,000 debt on unauthorized projects as
well as an embezzlement of $30,000. (Cited by Shanabruch, *Chicago's Catholics,*
p. 13.) Six days after his installation as bishop of Chicago, O'Regan hired the
city's leading architectural firm to design an episcopal residence at a cost in
excess of $15,000. See the *Daily Democratic Press,* Sept. 9, 1854, and the
Chicago *Tribune,* May 21, 1857; Aug. 15, 20, 25, 1857. Significantly, Kinsella,
Clowry, Breen, and Hoey all achieved prominence in the East.
    13. *Daily Democratic Press,* Nov. 2, 3, 5, 6, 1855.

14. Cited by Robert Trisco, "Bishops and Their Priests in the United States," *The Catholic Priest in the United States: Historical Investigations,* ed. John Tracy Ellis (Collegeville, Minn.: St. John's University Press, 1971), p. 128.

15. For information on the character of Catholicism in nineteenth-century Ireland see S. J. Connolly, *Priests and People in Pre-Famine Ireland, 1780-1845* (Dublin: Gill and Macmillan, 1982); James O'Shea, *Priest, Politics and Society in Post-Famine Ireland: A Study of County Tipperary, 1850-91* (Atlantic Highlands, N.J.: Humanities Press, Inc., 1983); Emmet Larkin, *The Historical Dimensions of Irish Catholicism* (Washington: Catholic University of America Press, 1984); Patrick J. Corish, *The Irish Catholic Experience* (Dublin: Gill and Macmillan, 1985); K. Theodore Hoppen, *Elections, Politics and Society in Ireland, 1832-1885* (Oxford: Oxford University Press, 1984); and Desmond J. Keenan, *The Catholic Church in Nineteenth Century Ireland* (Totowa, N.J.: Barnes and Noble, 1983).

16. *Daily Chicago Times,* July 1, 1859.

17. Chicago *Tribune,* Aug. 10, 1862.

18. The Irish Legion was one of the oldest Union regiments in the field, having joined Gen. William T. Sherman's army at Vicksburg, Miss. in 1863. The 90th Volunteers fought in campaigns from Mission Ridge, Tenn., to Resaca, Ga., and Jonesboro, Ark. Three hundred enlistees died in battle and more than four hundred succumbed to "the various casualties of war." On their return to Chicago, the *Tribune* commented that: "Their fine, soldierly bearing and bronzed appearance attracted general attention." Alfred T. Andreas, *History of Chicago,* 3 vols. (Chicago: A. T. Andreas Co., 1884-86), II:249-52; and Chicago *Tribune,* June 12, 14, 1865.

19. Chicago *Times,* Dec. 27, 1868.

20. James P. Gaffey, "Patterns of Ecclesiastical Authority: The Problem of Chicago Succession, 1865-1881," *Church History* 42 (1973), 257-70.

21. Chicago *Times,* Sept. 28, 1868.

22. Chicago *Times,* Sept. 22, 27, 1868.

23. Chicago *Tribune,* Oct. 13, 1868.

24. Eyewitness account of Rev. L. L. Laitner cited by Gaffey, "Patterns of Ecclesiastical Authority," pp. 263-64. The Chicago *Times,* Apr. 16, 1869, traced the bishop's "mental malady" to the deathbed confrontation with Dunne.

25. Chicago *Times,* Jan. 30, 1870.

26. Chicago *Tribune,* Feb. 20, 1879.

27. *New World,* Apr. 14, 1900.

28. Chicago *Times,* June 22, 1873.

29. Newspaper article, "Our Religious Orders, the Jesuits in Chicago," Mar. 27, 1875, St. Ignatius College Prep Archives.

30. Chicago *Times,* Aug. 21, 1876.

31. Chicago *Times,* Aug. 20, 1876.

32. Rev. Thomas L. Harmon, *Church of the Annunciation, a Parish History, 1866-1916* (Chicago: D. B. Hansen and Sons, 1916), p. 16.

33. *Western Catholic,* Sept. 15, 1877.

34. "More Waldrons Wanted," Chicago *Times,* Oct. 3, 1875, reprinted in *Western Catholic,* Sept. 15, 1877.

35. *Western Catholic,* Sept. 15, 1877.

36. Joseph J. Thompson, ed., *The Archdiocese of Chicago, Antecedents and Development* (Des Plaines, Ill.: St. Mary's Training School Press, 1920), p. 345.

37. Chicago *Times,* Dec. 18, 1868 and June 22, 1873.

38. Michael Funchion has argued that although most Irish immigrants in 1900 were manual laborers, if the second generation had been included in labor statistics prior to 1890 "one would have seen a gradual increase in the number of Irish white-collar workers from 1870 onward, as the children of Irish immigrants entered the work force." "Irish Chicago: Church, Homeland, Politics, and Class—The Shaping of an Ethnic Group, 1870-1900," *Ethnic Chicago,* ed. Peter d'A. Jones and Melvin G. Holli (Grand Rapids, Mich.: William B. Eerdmans Publishing Co., 1981), pp. 26-27. Indeed, according to the 1890 "foreign-stock" classification, Chicago's second-generation Irish (113,816) outnumbered foreign-born Irish (70,028).

39. Emmet Larkin, "The Devotional Revolution in Ireland, 1850-75," *American Historical Review* 77 (June 1972), 625-52, and *The Making of the Roman Catholic Church in Ireland, 1850-60* (Chapel Hill: University of North Carolina Press, 1980).

40. Chicago *Times,* June 3, 1888.

41. Thompson, *Archdiocese of Chicago,* p. 345.

42. Gerald Sullivan, ed., *The Story of Englewood, 1835-1923* (Chicago: Foster and McDonnell, 1924), p. 112.

43. Chicago *Sun,* Sept. 5, 12, 1896.

44. Michael F. Funchion, *Chicago's Irish Nationalists, 1881-1890* (New York: Arno Press, 1976), pp. 38-41.

45. For a full account of the nationalist controversy which split Chicago's Polonia, see Joseph John Parot, *Polish Catholics in Chicago, 1850-1920* (DeKalb: Northern Illinois University Press, 1981).

46. School statistics in this essay are based on Sanders, *Education of an Urban Minority,* p. 5; *Sadlier's Catholic Directory* (New York: D. J. Sadlier and Co., 1876), pp. 341-42; "Province of Chicago," published in James J. McGovern, *Souvenir of the Silver Jubilee in the Episcopacy of His Grace the Most Rev. Patrick Augustine Feehan, Archbishop of Chicago* (Chicago: privately printed, 1891), pp. 250-52; and *Chicago Daily News Almanac and Year-Book for 1907* (Chicago: Chicago Daily News Co., 1906), p. 429.

47. Timothy G. Walch, "Catholic Education in Chicago and Milwaukee, 1840-1890" (Ph.D. dissertation, Northwestern University, 1975), p. 83.

48. *New World,* June 29, 1895.

49. *New World,* May 15, 1897 and July 2, 1898. St. James's High School also claimed the distinction of having the first extension courses ever given in a Chicago school, with instructors from the University of Chicago. Extension courses from St. Ignatius College (later Loyola University) were conducted at St. Mary's High School as early as 1911.

50. *New World,* Sept. 2, 1911.

51. *Reverend Hugh McGuire: A Memorial* (Chicago: privately printed, [1911?]), n.p.

52. *New World,* July 12, 1902.

53. *New World,* June 25, 1920.

54. Thomas N. Brown makes this point about Irish identity in his classic work, *Irish-American Nationalism, 1870–1890* (Philadelphia: J. B. Lippincott Co., 1966), p. 34.

55. *New World,* Aug. 26, 1911.

56. *New World,* Feb. 17, 1906.

57. Information on the Knights of Columbus is based on Joseph J. Thompson, *A History of the Knights of Columbus of Illinois* (Chicago: Universal Press, 1922), pp. 342–45, 506, 768, 824.

58. *New World,* Sept. 22, 1906 and July 10, 1909.

59. Paul Frederick Cressey, "Population Succession in Chicago: 1898–1930," *The Social Fabric of the Metropolis,* ed. James F. Short (Chicago: University of Chicago Press, 1971), p. 116.

60. Ibid.

61. *New World,* Dec. 19, 1908.

62. Chicago *Record-Herald,* July 7, 1909.

63. Chicago *Inter-Ocean,* Mar. 13, 1902.

64. Shanabruch, *Chicago's Catholics,* pp. 99–102.

65. Based on August 1975 interview with John Jordan, a 1924 graduate of Visitation grammar school who later became head basketball coach at Notre Dame University. Rev. Thomas Tormey, an assistant at Visitation from 1924 to 1930, was first athletic director of the CYO.

66. Based on personal interviews conducted in August 1975 as part of an NEH Youthgrant.

67. ACLU report on Englewood disorder, Nov. 7, 1949, cited by Arnold Hirsch, "Making the Second Ghetto: Race and Housing in Chicago, 1940–1960" (Ph.D. dissertation, University of Illinois, 1978), p. 214.

68. Ibid., p. 30.

69. *New World,* Sept. 17, 1915.

70. Andrew M. Greeley, *The Irish Americans: The Rise to Money and Power* (New York: Harper and Row, 1981), pp. 146–47.

71. Under orders from Archbishop John P. Cody, who headed the Chicago diocese from 1965 to 1982, no new parish schools were established in the archdiocese after 1967.

72. Of 81,251 students enrolled in Chicago's Catholic elementary schools in 1982, 22,210 were black and 14,074 were Hispanic. The city's Catholic high school enrollment of 33,048 included 6,034 blacks and 3,856 Hispanics. Based on Chicago Archdiocese Office of Catholic Education, "Fall Enrollment Survey, October 1982." See also Alfredo S. Lanier, "Let Us Now Praise Catholic Schools," *Chicago,* Oct. 1982, pp. 147–53.

73. Lawrence J. McCaffrey, *The Irish Diaspora in America* (Bloomington: Indiana University Press, 1976), p. 176.

74. Although the number of Irish-American novelists is increasing, only a few such as Elizabeth Cullinan have mined what Andrew Greeley calls the rich lode of American Irish Catholicism. *Irish Americans,* pp. 183–98.

The Political and Nationalist Dimensions

Michael F. Funchion

Unlike many other immigrants, the Irish came to Chicago with some experience in politics. From the 1790s to the 1820s tenant farmers in Ireland had voted in landlord-directed blocs. More important, during the 1820s they as well as other Catholic voters had participated in Daniel O'Connell's powerful grass-roots political movement that in 1829 forced the British government to admit Catholics to political office.

While O'Connell was demonstrating to the Irish in Ireland that ordinary people, when properly organized, could wield extraordinary power, Democratic party leaders were teaching the same lesson to the relatively small, yet growing, numbers of Irish Catholic immigrants in America. Irish support for the Democrats went back to the early days of the party. Their enthusiasm is not difficult to understand; the party of Jefferson welcomed them into its ranks, while the opposition Federalists were often decidedly hostile to their interests. By 1820 some of the leaders of the infant Irish communities in cities like New York had gained a degree of influence in the Democratic party, where they looked out for Irish immigrant concerns. The Irish found the Democrats even more congenial in the 1820s and 1830s as the party of Jefferson transformed itself into the party of Jackson. Not only did the Jacksonians seem to have the interests of the common man at heart, but most of their leaders aligned themselves with the Irish against the anti-Catholic nativist movement that began to rear its ugly head in the 1830s. Relatively few Irish supported the Whigs, who seemed less concerned than the Democrats about working-class and Catholic interests.

The majority of the Irish who settled in early Chicago remained faithful to the Irish-American tradition of loyalty to the Democratic party. During the years before the Civil War they generally voted for Democratic candidates who represented their antinativist, anti-abolitionist, and antitemperance views. By contrast they seldom voted for the Whigs, the chief opposition party until the late 1840s. They virtually never voted for the various parties—Know-Nothing, Free Soil, and Temperance— that emerged in the late 1840s and early 1850s with the breakup of the regular two-party system, and rarely supported the Republican party (established in 1854).

Their considerable numbers—during the years before the Civil War the Irish accounted for roughly one-fifth of the city's population— combined with their high level of political participation gave the Irish considerable clout in Chicago elections. As early as the late 1830s complaints were voiced about undue Irish political influence. During the 1840s Irish Democratic fidelity helped them to maintain the supremacy they enjoyed in the city. In the next decade when a considerable number of native Americans left the Democratic party, largely over the slavery issue, the Irish often found themselves in a minority on election day. Yet (from an Irish point of view) there was only one really disastrous election during this decade. It was the municipal election of 1855, in which the anti-Catholic Know-Nothings captured control of the city council and elected a mayor in the person of Levi D. Boone, a grand-nephew of the famed frontiersman, Daniel Boone. They promptly passed a law barring immigrants from applying for city jobs; and in an effort to promote temperance, they raised the cost of beer licenses. In 1856, however, the Irish and Germans joined with liberal-minded Americans to elect a mayor and council that reversed the odious policies of the Boone administration.[1]

Besides exercising influence at the polls, the Irish during these years also managed to elect a fair number of their fellow countrymen to the city council, as well as picking up some of the limited number of municipal jobs. In 1860, for example, 49 of the 107 members of the police force were Irish.[2]

Although the Irish possessed political clout before 1865, it was not until the post–Civil War period that they really began to play a dominant role in the city's politics. By the late 1860s the Irish were clearly on the move. In the city council elected in November 1869, they held fifteen of the forty seats. This trend continued; in 1890, for example, twenty-three of Chicago's sixty-eight aldermen were Irish.[3]

There are two reasons why the Irish did not assume a dominant position in politics until after the Civil War. One was that prior to the late 1860s and 1870s the adult Irish population of Chicago was composed overwhelmingly of immigrants. Because they knew the English language and had some familiarity with Anglo-style politics, Irish-born Americans produced more politicians than other immigrant groups. Still they were not as able as the second generation, which was generally better educated and more familiar with American ways. Thus, it was not until significant numbers of Irish born or reared in America began to reach maturity in the late 1860s and 1870s that the number of influential Irish politicians began to increase substantially.

A second reason for the immense political thrust of the Irish during the last decades of the nineteenth century was the changing nature of Chicago politics. As the city grew from a relatively small prairie community into a large metropolis, it was faced with an enormous number of complex issues such as the allocation of franchises to transit and utility companies. Simplistic old-style politics were not capable of dealing efficiently with this new situation. Therefore a system of brokerage or machine politics developed that depended to a large extent on extralegal and illegal practices to get things done. Because of their old-country experience in circumventing the inequalities and oppression of the British legal system, the Irish were adept at operating within such a system. Also, since the Irish entered politics mainly to make money, they found the economic rewards of brokerage politics particularly attractive, and were much more inclined to participate in it than they would have been in a system where such rewards were lacking.

Up until 1915 or so Chicago's Irish politicians operated in an extremely fragmented situation. Neither the Republican nor the Democratic parties exhibited any degree of unity. Instead of being controlled by efficient, centralized machines as they were in some other cities, both were divided into a number of factions, wheeling and dealing across party lines.

The Irish, who figured prominently in all the Democratic factions and had some representation in Republican circles, were the single most important ethnic group on the local political scene.[4] Yet the two leading political personalities during the last two decades of the nineteenth century and first decade or so of the twentieth were not Irishmen but old-stock Americans—the Harrisons—Carter H. Harrison I and his son, Carter H. Harrison II, Democrats, who between them occupied the mayor's office on and off for over twenty years, from 1879 to 1915. Well-to-do, the Harrisons were in politics for power, not money. Unlike a number of other upper- and upper-middle-class old-stock Americans in Chicago, they were not known as reformers. Although they refused to sanction the more serious abuses, the Harrisons willingly participated in machine politics. They welcomed the support of ward bosses, allotting them patronage and generally bowing to their wishes concerning lax enforcement of the drinking, gambling, and prostitution laws.

The Irish were important to Carter H. Harrison I. During his first four two-year terms as mayor (1879–87) he solicited and received the backing of several leading Irish politicians, including Mike McDonald, the Irish-born saloonkeeper reputed to be the most powerful Democratic boss in Chicago during the 1880s. Irish bosses liked Harrison. He allowed them to share in the spoils of office and, if he did not encourage their illegal activities, he usually looked the other way. Because his popularity cut across ethnic and class lines he could pull in more votes than practically any other Democrat. However, in 1891 when Harrison decided to run again for mayor, after four years of retirement, he encountered strong opposition from several Irish bosses. They were backing the incumbent mayor, De Witt Cregier, a man even more tolerant of machine antics than Harrison. In the general election Harrison and Cregier split the Democratic vote and Republican Hempstead Washburne was able to win a narrow victory. In 1893 another Harrison bid for the mayor's office split the Democratic Irish bosses three ways. Some such as Johnny Powers supported Harrison, others such as John Patrick Hopkins threw in their lot with Washington Hesing, an important German Catholic Democrat, and a few backed former mayor Cregier, who never had much of a chance of winning. This time Harrison won the Democratic nomination and went on to trounce his Republican opponent. It was a Pyrrhic victory. In the following October a young and probably insane Irish-American shot and fatally wounded him.

A special election was held to choose Harrison's successor. Despite initial opposition from Powers and other Harrisonites who disliked him because of his opposition to the martyred mayor, the Democrats nominated Hopkins. In the December 1893 special election Hopkins narrowly squeaked by his Republican opponent, George B. Swift, thereby becoming the first Irish Catholic mayor of Chicago.

Hopkins's election was one of the first of several major victories for what became known as the Sullivan-Hopkins or Sullivan faction, which was top-heavy with Irishmen. Led by Roger Sullivan, a businessman and in the early 1890s clerk of the Probate Court, this faction proved to be extremely resilient in the vicissitudes of Chicago politics; after 1915 it would virtually dominate the Democratic party. Known for their boodling, the Sullivan-Hopkins faction certainly lived up to their reputation during the Hopkins administration. In cooperation with the other Democratic and Republican boodlers in the city council, the Sullivan-Hopkins aldermen pulled off one of the most daring grabs in the history of Chicago politics. They passed laws granting franchises to their own electric and gas companies, which they planned to sell later at a tidy profit.

Preferring behind-the-scenes political activity to elective office, Hopkins decided not to run for reelection in 1895 and the Democrats nominated Frank Wenter instead. Hurt by the corrupt image of the Hopkins administration, Wenter lost the election to the Republican candidate, George B. Swift. But two years later the Democrats recaptured city hall with Carter Harrison II. Elected to four consecutive two-year terms, the younger Harrison remained in office until 1905. Although more reserved than his father, he was able to draw support from several different groups. His Catholic connections—he was a graduate of St. Ignatius College (later Loyola University) and his wife and children were Catholics—no doubt added to his popularity among the Irish and other Catholic ethnics. If personal popularity does much to explain Harrison's success, so does the fact that he received the support of several important Irish political bosses, such as Tom Carey of the Stockyards and "Bathhouse John" Coughlin and Michael "Hinky Dink" Kenna of the First Ward. They liked Harrison for the same reasons that had made his father popular with many of the ward bosses: he was a winner who allowed them a share in the spoils of office and tolerated the less blatant shenanigans of the machine system. Still, not all Irish Democratic politicians liked Harrison. Sullivan, Hopkins, and their crowd resented the young mayor because he was an obstacle to their schemes to gain greater control over the local party and the city government, and because he staunchly opposed their favorite form of graft—selling city franchises.

Bitter relations between Harrison and the Sullivan-Hopkins faction intensified after Harrison vetoed a measure that would have allowed Sullivan, Hopkins, and their fellow shareholders to sell for a huge profit the gas company they had set up in 1895. In the mayoral elections of 1901 and 1903 the Sullivan-Hopkins faction, which by then had added the future leader George Brennan to their ranks, worked for the election of Harrison's Republican opponents. Although they failed in their attempts to defeat Harrison and take away his control of the Cook County Democratic Central Committee, they were gaining in power. In 1902, for example, they managed to capture control of the state organization with the help of some downstate allies.

In 1905, for only the second time in its history, the Democratic party nominated an Irish Catholic for mayor, Judge Edward F. Dunne. Harrison, who had lost some degree of his popularity because of his inability to achieve an acceptable settlement on the traction question, decided not to run when he realized that Dunne was all but unstoppable. Educated at Trinity College, Dublin, the Connecticut-born and Peoria-reared Dunne was not the machine type Irish politician familiar to Chicagoans. Instead, he was an urban populist reformer who based his campaign almost entirely on the single issue of municipal ownership of the traction lines. Supported by labor leaders, the radical Bryan-Altgeld elements of the Democratic party, and a few maverick reformers like Clarence Darrow, Dunne also received the backing of the Sullivan-Hopkins faction as well as that of the ward bosses who had supported Harrison. Despite the fact that his positions on patronage and law enforcement seemed rather vague, the machine element embraced Dunne because his traction policy, which was popular among rank-and-file Democrats, was likely to bring in votes.

If the machine politicians rallied around the Irish Catholic urban populist, the middle-class and largely Protestant "good government" reformers opposed him, for their views on what constituted reform differed from his. They were interested in efficiency in government, civil service reform, better law enforcement and the like. Dunne was concerned mainly with social reforms designed to help the common man: municipal ownership of utilities and transportation systems, higher real estate taxes for corporations, and better salaries for government workers. Good-government reformers thus felt far more comfortable supporting the Republican candidate, John Harlan, who indicated that he would push their program.

Elected by a comfortable though by no means substantial margin, Dunne brought changes to city hall. For the first time in years Chicago had an issue-oriented mayor who appointed Bryan-Altgeld radicals, social settlement workers, and labor leaders to most of the top posts in his administration. For example, he made Clarence Darrow a special corporation counsel, selected Jane Addams as a member of the school board, and made Margaret Haley, a Teachers' Federation leader, one of his kitchen cabinet. Compared to the number of radicals, social settlement people, and labor leaders, there were few businessmen and party regulars in the Dunne administration.

As Richard E. Becker has noted, Dunne and his band of urban populists "succeeded beyond any doubt in proving that the mayoral office could become something much more than the tool of bosses, vested interests, or 'goo goo' reformers."[5] During their two years in office they achieved success in a number of areas. They vigorously enforced public health and building codes; went to court to force corporations to pay higher real estate taxes; increased the salaries of teachers; cracked down on some of the more serious violations of the drinking, gambling, and vice laws; and effected moderate reforms in the police department. They were less than successful in other areas. Despite strenuous efforts, Dunne failed to convince the Republican-dominated city council to reduce gas and electric rates to levels he considered reasonable. More significantly, he did not pass his pet project: municipal ownership of the traction lines. Instead, in the waning days of his administration, the city council passed a compromise bill over his veto. It allowed the traction companies to remain in private hands, but gave the city a substantial amount of the profits as well as the right of purchase after six months' notice.

In overriding Dunne's veto on the traction bill, the Republicans in the city council received help from about two-thirds of the Democratic aldermen, who considered the mayor fanatical for opposing a reasonable bill that seemed to have fairly wide support in the city. Democratic opposition to Dunne on the traction issue was symptomatic of a broader problem that plagued the Dunne administration: the inability to gain consistent support from the Harrison and Sullivan-Hopkins factions. Although some of the ward bosses once allied with Harrison were originally friendly toward the mayor, many Harrisonites had never reconciled themselves to the new administration because of its harsh public criticism of Harrison's traction policy. They picked away at Dunne, hoping to see the return of their man to city hall in 1907. And although the Sullivan-Hopkins people were at first favorably inclined toward Dunne, they became disenchanted with him. They disliked his modest attempts to enforce the drinking, gambling, and vice laws and resented his removal of some of their friends from the city payroll, even though he had allowed the vast majority of them to retain patronage jobs. By the end of Dunne's term, the Sullivan-Hopkins people, like the Harrisonites, dearly wished to see the last of him.

Although his opponents seemed better organized, Dunne still had considerable support among many Democrats, particularly among the radical element and the rank-and-file Irish, and he was thus able to capture the Democratic nomination in 1907. But the general election was a different story. With solid Republican backing and the clandestine support of a number of Democratic bosses, who believed that he would go easy on enforcement of the drinking, gambling, and vice laws, Republican Fred Busse defeated Dunne to become Chicago's first German-American mayor.

Since before the 1907 election the mayoral term had been increased from two to four years, Chicagoans had to wait until 1911 for the next opportunity to elect a chief executive. For those who wanted an exciting, free-for-all contest, it was well worth the wait. The Democratic primary had three contenders. Both Harrison and Dunne were looking for their old jobs, while the Sullivanites were backing Andrew J. Graham. Toward the end of the primary it became clear that the real race was between

Harrison and Dunne. Realizing that Harrison was the greatest obstacle to their control of the party, the Sullivanites began to encourage their followers to vote for Dunne. Their efforts were in vain, however, as Harrison squeaked by Dunne; Graham came in a rather distant third. At the same time, Charles E. Merriam, the reform-minded professor from the University of Chicago, easily won the Republican primary.

During the general election party loyalty carried little weight. Republican machine factions headed by William Lorimer and Fred Busse worked for Harrison, fearing loss of power should a reformer from their party become mayor. For the same reason some of the Sullivanites, including Sullivan, Hopkins, and George Brennan, supported Merriam. Others like Edward Cullerton, John Brennan, and Mike McInerney, convinced that Harrison would do them less harm than an untried Republican reformer, backed the former mayor. Die-hard Dunnites backed Merriam, seemingly more out of personal hatred for Harrison than anything else. The outcome was fairly close, with Harrison defeating Merriam by some 17,000 votes.

The 1911 election proved to be Harrison's last triumph. Despite its poor showing in the mayoral primary, the well-oiled Sullivanite machine continued to make gains at Harrison's expense. The mayor's boss support dwindled during the next four years as he began to crack down on saloons and houses of prostitution. In 1914 two of his most stalwart Irish boss supporters, Coughlin and Kenna, reluctantly deserted him for the Sullivan camp. Harrison's fate as a "has-been" was sealed in 1915 when the Sullivanite candidate for mayor, Robert M. Sweitzer, the clerk of the County Court, defeated him in the Democratic primary.

In retrospect, 1915 was an important year in Chicago politics because it saw the Sullivanites in control of the local Democratic party. With his defeat, Harrison's faction was finished as a significant force. Likewise, the Dunne element exerted little influence in the county organization. Ironically, Dunne's defeat in the 1911 mayoral primary did not diminish his popularity. In 1912, he was elected governor of Illinois, the only Irish Catholic to have held that office.

Although in the years ahead they would suffer from dissension and meet with sporadic opposition from the weak Harrison and Dunne factions, the Sullivanites (led by George Brennan after 1920) managed to keep the Democrats fairly united. Anton Cermak unified the party further when he took over after Brennan's death in 1928. With a relatively high degree of unity, the Democrats were thus in a favorable position to take control of the city in 1931, a control they have maintained to the present day.

The other important development in 1915 was the emergence of

William H. Thompson to a position of preeminence in the local Republican party. A product of a powerful machine group originally headed by William Lorimer and then by Fred Lundin, Thompson won the Republican mayoral primary and then went on to defeat Sweitzer in the general election. For the next sixteen years Thompson would dominate the Republican party in the city, holding the office of mayor for twelve of those years. Although at times Thompson seemed invincible, in the long run the corruption that marked his administration did much to wreck the local Republican party.

During the half-century before 1915 the Irish were clearly the single most important ethnic group in Chicago politics. Although they occupied the mayor's office for less than four years, they held more than their share of seats in the city council and supplied the bulk of the Democratic ward committeemen.[6] Irish ward boss support was crucial to the success of the two Harrisons and it was an Irish-led faction that took over virtual control of the Democratic party in 1915.

The overwhelming majority of Chicago's Irish politicians during this period were American-reared sons of Irish immigrants. A considerable number either were born in Chicago or had come to the city as children. Others, however, had spent their childhood elsewhere and moved to Chicago as young men. Though advantageous, a Chicago upbringing certainly was not a prerequisite for a successful political career. Hopkins, Sullivan, and Brennan, for example, were neither born nor reared in the city. Whether they grew up in Chicago or not, the overwhelming majority of Chicago's Irish politicians came from working-class, and in some cases poor, families, and many had received only a modicum of education. Mayor Dunne, the well-educated son of a Peoria distiller, was clearly an exception in this regard.

Ambitious to a man, many Irish politicians did not depend solely on politics for their livelihood. Several important ward leaders like Powers, Cullerton, Coughlin, and Kenna ran profitable saloons. Some like Hopkins and John M. Smyth, an influential Republican politician, operated retail stores. Others owned construction firms, coal companies, real estate agencies, and the like. And although few of the top politicians were lawyers, certain middle-level ones pursued active legal careers.

Most of the city's Irish politicians became involved in politics as young men. They used the connections they had made through their local parishes, Irish organizations, and saloons as their original power base and then expanded their contacts as they moved up the political ladder. The majority seemed to be interested in politics primarily for its material rewards. From the late 1860s, with the emergence of McCauley's Nineteen in the city council, several Irish aldermen sold their votes to traction and utility companies looking for profitable franchises. Politicians also received money from saloonkeepers and gambling and prostitution establishments in return for using their influence with the police to ensure that the drinking, gambling, and vice laws were not rigidly enforced. Similarly, they picked up handsome dividends for their efforts to secure low real estate tax assessments and received kickbacks from building contractors in return for helping them get lucrative city contracts. In those cases where the politician himself ran a saloon or construction firm he could, of course, use his political clout to help himself directly.

Although top and middle-level Irish politicians seemed to gain the most from Chicago's system of machine politics, even such small-fry politicians as precinct captains, as well as many of the party faithful, also received economic benefits, mainly in the form of patronage jobs. Several city and county departments had more than their share of Irish on their payrolls. In 1900, for example, the federal census indicated that 43 percent of "watchmen, policemen, firemen, etc." in Chicago were first- or second-generation Irishmen, even though they made up only 14 percent of the male labor force in the city. Political influence was also used to secure jobs with companies holding municipal contracts and franchises. The 1900 census also revealed that 58 percent of gas works employees in the city were either Irish immigrants or their children.[7] Jobs, of course, were not the only economic benefits provided by the system. Chicagoans who were down and out and in need of money, food, or coal could always count on their ward organization for some assistance.

Material benefits were the main but not the only Irish political motivation. For many, particularly those who had clawed their way to the top of the ladder, the need to exercise power undoubtedly was an important factor. Several psychological studies of power seekers indicate that they seek authority as a "compensatory reaction against low estimates of the self."[8] Although one must be cautious about psychoanalyzing groups of people, this theory tends to explain, at least in part, the Irish thirst for political influence. Whether they were reared in Ireland or America, most Irish had grown up in economically disadvantaged circumstances and were often treated with contempt by the Anglo-Protestant establishment. Although the effect of such an upbringing no doubt differed from individual to individual, it seems likely that it tended to develop a sense of inferiority in a number of Irish people.

With scores of patronage workers and other individuals indebted to them for favors, ward bosses could usually count on a solid bloc of votes at election time. At times, however, this support was not sufficient to ensure victory at the polls and thus Irish machine politicians often resorted to illegal methods in an effort to win elections. Saloonkeepers provided free drinks to individuals in return for their votes. Precinct captains rounded up itinerants and marched them into polling places. Illegally naturalized aliens and even the dead often managed to vote. Toughs threatened and sometimes inflicted physical harm on opposition voters in an effort to persuade them not to vote. And if all else failed, an opponent's ballots could be "lost" or miscounted.

Elitist good-government reformers, who wanted honest and efficient municipal administration, constantly attacked election fraud as well as the whole system of machine politics. Although justified in their criticism of the abuses of machine politics, these reformers seemed oblivious to its positive aspects. Their privileged upbringing and comfortable life-styles blinded them to the fact that in providing jobs and other needed services, the machine politicians helped to improve the lives of thousands of ordinary Chicagoans. The reformers were, in short, callous about the needs of the masses whom the government was supposed to serve. Thus not only did they criticize machine politics, but most of them also opposed the policies of Dunne and other urban populist reformers that were designed to help the common man.

Although they differed on what constituted reform, the good-government and urban populist reformers had one thing in common: they were crusaders for causes. In contrast to these two groups, the Irish and other machine politicians seemed to be involved in politics largely for profit. Yet it would be a mistake to believe that Chicago's Irish machine politicians took no interest in issues. Indeed, certain matters were important to them. They consistently opposed temperance, Sunday blue laws, and other measures that tried to legislate morality. Aside from the fact that their constituents might suffer economically from blue laws, Irish politicians did not believe that the government should be the handmaiden of pietistic, Protestant crusades. Like most Catholic Americans, they felt that morality was a matter for the churches, not the government. Similarly, they opposed restrictive immigration laws and prohibitions against the use of foreign languages in public schools—legislation designed to preserve the Anglo-Protestant heritage of the United States. However, machine politicians generally supported economic and social legislation that helped ordinary people. They did so not because they were committed to some form of socialist ideology, but simply because such laws benefited their largely working-class constituencies.[9]

To repeat, although Chicago's Irish machine politicians showed concern for voter interests, the chief reason they were in politics was to make money. In this respect they were carbon copies of their counterparts in New York, Boston, and other large American cities where machine politics thrived. By the same token, they stood in sharp contrast to Ireland's politicians, who were concerned with far-reaching issues such as self-government and land reform.

How different were the Chicago Irish and other American Irish machine politicians from their political counterparts in Ireland? Did the Irish political nature undergo a substantial transformation on crossing the Atlantic? Not really. Rather the differences between the Irish and the American Irish politicians can be attributed to the strikingly different situations in which each group operated. A foreign power ruled Ireland and an alien establishment held most of the land. Considering these circumstances it was inconceivable that Irish politicians could be anything other than issue-oriented. If the Irish in late nineteenth-century Chicago or New York had had to deal with matters of similar magnitude, they probably would have produced considerably more idealistic politicians. Indeed, during the antebellum period, when the Protestant nativist crusade seemed to threaten the very existence of the Irish community in the United States, Irish-American politicians directed much of their energies to this issue. As anti-Catholicism declined after 1860 and the Irish began to feel more secure as Americans, they could afford to move away from purpose politics and turn their attention to the politics of profit, which began to flourish in the rapidly growing cities of America.

Despite the fact that the Irish at home and those in Chicago and other American cities practiced different forms of politics, both groups had much in common.[10] The deeply rooted Gaelic tradition of personal loyalty was as important among Chicago's ward politicians as it was among the members of the Irish Parliamentary party. Both the Irish in Ireland and those in America were less than staunch supporters of the concept of civil service. Although Irish local governments never developed the type of patronage system that flourished in Chicago and other American cities, personal connections with members of local government bodies often played a crucial part in getting jobs. Finally, although their rhetoric tended to obscure the fact, the members of the Irish Parliamentary party shared some of the pragmatism of Irish American politicians. Home Rule was in essence a practical compromise between the Irish republican demand for an independent Ireland and the Unionist desire to maintain the status quo. And on the land issue, it is noteworthy that the Irish Parliamentary party refused to endorse doctrinaire solutions like land nationalization. Instead, the party supported peasant ownership, a position conservative enough that it eventually won the support of British Tories. After most of Ireland became an independent state the nonideological nature of Irish politics became even more apparent. Ireland's two major parties, Fianna Fail and Fine

Gael, have been practical in their approach to economic and social problems, while the weaker Labour party has been one of the least doctrinaire left-wing parties in Western Europe.

Besides parliamentary politics Ireland had another political tradition, that of revolutionary republicanism. Although it gained the support of the majority of the Irish nationalist population during the period 1918–21 and succeeded in achieving independence for most of the country in 1921, revolutionary republicanism was relatively weak throughout practically all of modern Irish history. Without Irish-American support it might not have survived.

Chicago's first recorded Irish nationalist organization, founded in 1842, was a branch of Daniel O'Connell's Repeal Association. Far from being a revolutionary group, O'Connell's organization sought to repeal the union between Great Britain and Ireland through peaceful agitation. However, after the collapse in Ireland of the Repeal movement and its replacement by the more militant Young Ireland movement, Chicago's Irish flocked to various revolutionary organizations. The most important of these was the Fenian Brotherhood.

Established in New York in 1858 as an affiliate of the newly formed Irish Republican Brotherhood (IRB), the Fenians rapidly gained strength in Irish America. Although the brotherhood showed early promise, by the mid-1860s it was in serious trouble. British spy infiltration of the IRB destroyed whatever chances it had to stage a successful revolution and greatly undermined Fenian morale. Even more destructive was the 1865–66 split within the American wing of the republican movement. One group, led by the former Young Irelander John O'Mahony, wanted to concentrate on helping the IRB fight the British in Ireland, while the other, led by Colonel William B. Roberts, advocated an invasion of Canada. Roberts's faction, known as the Senate wing, believed that such an effort might touch off an Anglo-American war, which conceivably might force the British to give up Ireland. Most Fenians in Chicago lined up with the Senate wing and some joined the military contingents that invaded Canada. Ending in utter failure, these forays made the brotherhood look foolish and did much to undermine its support among Irish Americans.[11]

Although it survived in one form or another until 1886, American Fenianism was finished as an effective nationalist advocate by the end of the 1860s. As it withered, the Clan na Gael, a new and more cautious revolutionary organization, began to fill the void. Founded in New York in 1867, the Clan emerged as the leading Irish-American nationalist voice by the mid-1870s. Chicago's first Clan na Gael camp was founded in 1869.[12] Others soon followed and for the next three decades the Clan, though never large in numbers, was at the center of Irish nationalist activity in the city. Acting through the United Irish Societies of Chicago, the Clan helped to sponsor most of the Irish nationalist rallies, some of which drew crowds in the thousands. The Clan also controlled the other major Irish organizations like the Ancient Order of Hibernians, the Irish National Land League of America, and the Irish National League of America. As support groups for the Irish Parliamentary party, these latter two organizations officially championed a peaceful solution to the Irish national question. In practice, however, Chicago branches supported the policy of the Clan na Gael. Although willing to assist the Irish party's nonviolent campaign for Irish Home Rule, they were prepared, should the occasion arise, to support a rebellion to liberate Ireland.

Chicago Clan na Gael members did not limit their interests to Irish matters; they also were actively involved in the local political scene. From the mid-1870s until the end of the century, the Clan, under the leadership of a crafty and rather unscrupulous lawyer, Alexander Sullivan, took advantage of the city's decentralized political system to establish itself as a mini-machine that secured patronage jobs for its members. Although the Clan did not have a majority of the local Irish politicians in its ranks, several members held influential positions in the Democratic party and some, though to a lesser extent, in the GOP. Among the Clan members active in politics were Mike McInerney, the Democratic boss of the Stockyards district; Daniel Corkery, a coal dealer who was a political force in Bridgeport; Frank Agnew, a building contractor who served for a time as chairman of the Cook County Democratic Central Committee; and John M. Smyth, a furniture dealer who was a Near West Side Republican power broker. These and other Clan na Gael politicians naturally helped rank-and-file members of the organization to get patronage jobs. The Clan also made deals with other politicians, promising them its support on election day in return for a share of the spoils of office. In the early 1880s, for example, Mayor Carter Harrison I rewarded Alexander Sullivan for his support by allowing him to recommend several Clan na Gaelers for positions on the police force.

Although certain Clan na Gael camps in other cities also engaged in politics, in no other city was the Clan so deeply entrenched in the machine system as in Chicago. Such involvement disturbed revolutionary purists, for they felt that it weakened and tainted the Clan. Yet prior to the mid-1880s there was little local or national censure of Sullivan and his political activities. And it is likely that such criticism would have remained low key had it not been for the fact that Sullivan's practices and policies as national leader brought him into disrepute with a significant minority of Clan na Gaelers throughout the United States.

In August 1881 Sullivan became chairman of the Clan na Gael Executive Committee. During the next few years, he and two other members of the executive—the Triangle—managed the organization in a high-handed manner. They either embezzled or misused nationalist funds, and began a futile two-year bombing campaign in Britain without the approval of the Irish Republican Brotherhood, the Clan's ally, with jurisdiction over revolutionary activities in the British Isles. By the end of 1884 a group of New York Clan na Gaelers led by John Devoy had denounced Sullivan and demanded his ouster as national leader. In early 1885 they gained the support of a group of Chicago Clan na Gaelers, including Dr. Patrick H. Cronin and Patrick Dunne. Both Cronin and Dunne were leaders in the campaign against Sullivan, charging him with the misuse of nationalist funds.

From the mid-1880s until the end of the century, Devoy's Chicago allies battled the Sullivanites. The struggle became especially bitter in May 1889, when a few of Sullivan's followers murdered Cronin. Cooperating with Devoyites in other cities, anti-Sullivanites established a rival Clan na Gael and supported the Ancient Order of Hibernians, Board of Erin, which had split from the AOH in 1884 because individuals friendly to Sullivan ran the parent body. Through these organizations and a short-lived umbrella group, the Confederated Irish Societies of Chicago, the Chicago Devoyites sponsored their own nationalist rallies during which they denounced Sullivan and his followers. They also used the columns of local newspapers to assail their enemies and teamed up with anti-Sullivan politicians in an effort to wreck him and his political allies. Yet despite this campaign, the vast majority of Clan na Gaelers in Chicago remained loyal to Alexander Sullivan. Unlike the followers of John Devoy, the Sullivanites did more than cater to the nationalism of the American Irish. By participating in machine politics, they satisfied the bread-and-butter needs of Irish Chicagoans.

In July 1900, after months of negotiations, the two warring factions of the Clan na Gael agreed to reunite at a convention in Atlantic City. The majority of the Sullivanites in Chicago enthusiastically supported the reunion, although Sullivan himself, whose influence in the Clan had declined, played no part in the merger and was probably against it. Ironically, no sooner had the national Clan na Gael achieved reunion than the Clan in Chicago suffered a serious schism.

The Chicago trouble had actually started sometime prior to the Atlantic City convention. At issue was John Finerty's control of the United Irish Societies of Chicago. Finerty edited the Chicago *Citizen,* an influential

Irish weekly. His critics demanded that he give up his position as UIS president. John T. Keating was Finerty's major opponent. He headed a group that comprised two-thirds of the Sullivanite camp of the Clan na Gael. The remaining members loyally stood by Finerty, supporting his claim that Keating and his clique sought to control the UIS for political reasons. After the Clan was reunited, its national executive committee came out in support of Keating and expelled the pro-Finerty camps from the organization.[13]

Although the Clan's influence in local politics declined around the time of this schism, it remained an important Irish nationalist organization.[14] From 1900 up until his death in 1915, Keating was one of the most influential Clan na Gaelers in the United States. He served as chairman of the national executive committee as well as being a member of the Revolutionary Directory, the body that coordinated the activities of the Clan and its affiliate, the Irish Republican Brotherhood.

While Keating worked on behalf of the Clan na Gael, Finerty became involved in a new Irish constitutional nationalist organization, the United Irish League of America, a support group for the recently reunited Irish Parliamentary party. Chicago's Irish did much to get the league off the ground. In 1901 the United Irish Societies of Chicago sponsored one of the first major meetings of the UILA and Finerty served as the organization's first president.[15] Because the Clan na Gael now refused to participate in or cooperate with constitutional nationalist organizations as it had in the 1880s, Chicago had for the first time a distinctive Irish constitutional nationalist movement. But the nationalist philosophy of the vast majority of Irish Chicagoans probably did not change. As in the past they were probably willing to support Home Rule as a step in the right direction, but would eagerly back a rebellion for an independent Ireland at an appropriate time.

During the first decade of the present century, UILA members in Chicago had little to cheer about as the Irish Parliamentary party's campaign for Home Rule made little progress. But their spirits rose in 1912 when the British Liberal party introduced the third Home Rule bill in the House of Commons. Because the anti–Home Rule House of Lords in 1911 had lost its right to block such bills permanently, and could now only delay them for a couple of years, most Irish-Americans were confident that the Home Rule measure would become law in 1914. This, of course, did not happen. Ulster Protestant threats of revolution convinced the timid Liberal government that it would have to make concessions to the Orange minority. Before an agreement could be worked out, World War I started. Although Home Rule technically became law, it was immediately suspended and never was implemented.

The Irish Parliamentary party's failure to achieve Home Rule, coupled with its support for the British war effort, dampened Irish-American enthusiasm for the constitutional brand of Irish nationalism. By the end of 1914 the UILA was a shadow of its former self. Meanwhile, support for revolutionary Irish nationalism was growing. The Easter Rising of 1916, the arrests and executions of its leaders, the inability to arrive at a Home Rule settlement, and Parliament's decision to pass a law authorizing the conscription of Irishmen further strengthened the revolutionary cause in the United States. Whatever support was left for the Irish Parliamentary party among Irish-Americans virtually disappeared in 1919. Following the defeat of the Irish Parliamentary party in the December 1918 general election, Sinn Fein set up an independent Irish parliament (Dáil Éireann) in Dublin and declared Ireland a republic. Shortly after, the Anglo-Irish war began.

The Chicago Irish held mass meetings and collected money on behalf of the rebel cause. Chicago had several branches of the Friends of Irish Freedom, a militant organization founded in early 1916. However, when Eamon de Valera broke with the leadership of the Friends in 1920 and set up his own American support group, the American Association for the Recognition of the Irish Republic, a number of Chicagoans left the Friends for the new organization. Of all the Chicagoans active in the Irish struggle, none was more prominent than former governor and mayor Edward F. Dunne. As one of the members of the three-man American Commission on Irish Independence, Dunne traveled to Paris in 1919 in an unsuccessful effort to bring the question of Irish independence before the peace conference. Later on, he helped launch the bond-certificate campaign on behalf of the Irish Republic.[16]

Dáil Éireann's ratification in January 1922 of the December 1921 Anglo-Irish treaty gave virtual independence to over four-fifths of Ireland. It also brought to an end the intense Irish nationalist activity that Chicago had witnessed during the previous years. Yet for the next year or so a number of Irish-Americans in the city actively supported the anti-treaty forces fighting against the new Irish Free State government because dominion status fell short of their Republican hopes.

From 1923, when the Irish civil war ended, until the late 1960s, the Chicago Irish showed relatively little interest in the Irish nationalist movement which focused on ending the partition that divided six Ulster counties from the rest of Ireland. In addition to the existence of a free though truncated Irish nation, the declining strength of the Irish community also weakened Irish nationalism in in the city. Few new immigrants entered Chicago and many of the American-born Irish were becoming less and less conscious of their Irish heritage. Nonetheless, during this period Irish nationalist organizations did generate a certain degree of Chicago enthusiasm.

Irish-American nationalism has made somewhat of a comeback since the recent troubles erupted in Northern Ireland in 1968. Chapters of the Irish National Caucus, a political lobbying group, and the Irish Northern Aid Committee, a controversial organization that collects money for the families of imprisoned members of the Provisional IRA, were formed in the 1970s. Yet the present movement is pitifully weak in comparison to the nationalist activity prior to the creation of the Irish Free State. Although persons of Irish descent in Chicago generally sympathize with the plight of Northern Ireland's 600,000 Catholics and would like to see a united Ireland, most are too removed from Ireland to have a deep abiding interest in the struggle. Even among those who are Irish in a significant way the northern cause has not received the support one might expect. Some are put off by IRA violence, others by the seeming inability of Irish-America to change materially the situation in the Six Counties. Thus, unlike the Chicago Irish of the late nineteenth and early twentieth centuries who gave substantial material and moral support to the Irish nationalist struggle, the present-day Chicago Irish have done relatively little to help the cause. There is little likelihood that this will change.

Irish-Americans, particularly in Chicago, never invested as much enthusiasm or talent in nationalism as they did in Catholicism or politics. But at first glance the period from 1915 to 1928 appeared dismal for Chicago's Democrats. They lost three out of four mayoral races, never managed to elect a governor or senator, and saw the city go Republican in every presidential election. Yet on closer examination the Democrats' situation was not so bleak. Not only did they usually control the city council and often win a number of key local offices, but more important, after 1920 they were far more unified than the Republicans. Thus, with a fairly high degree of party solidarity the Democrats were in a good position to take control of the city in 1931.

Roger Sullivan continued to serve as the Democratic boss up until his death in 1920, when he was replaced by his urbane protégé George Brennan. Several other Irishmen—Paddy Carr, Thomas Nash, Patrick Nash, John Clark, and Jimmy Quinn—also held important positions in the party. On the whole Chicago's Irish politicians of the 1920s were an improvement over their counterparts at the turn of the century. For the most part they abstained from the more blatant forms of corruption and by education and background were professionally better equipped to deal with the city's affairs.[17]

Although Brennan lacked the power of future party leaders like

Anton Cermak, Edward Kelly, and Richard Daley, he was by most standards an extremely capable leader who did much to solidify the party. He won over some former rivals, while at the same time managing to keep most of the party regulars happy.

Unlike Sullivan, Brennan succeeded in getting a Democrat elected mayor, although the results of this election for the local party were mixed. In 1923, after eight years of Republican rule, Brennan and his colleagues were eager to see a Democrat in city hall. Instead of picking a party regular, however, they turned to William E. Dever, an Irish Catholic reformer with a long record of public service. As an alderman and judge, Dever's credentials as an honest public servant were above reproach. Convinced that Thompson would run again, Brennan apparently believed that a reform candidate was needed to defeat the Republican incumbent. Not only would Dever get most of the regular Democratic vote, but he also would likely pick up the votes of Republican reformers disgusted with Thompson's corrupt administration. As it turned out Thompson decided not to run again and Dever easily defeated the less well known Republican candidate, Arthur Lueder. Thus, for the second time in its history Chicago had an Irish Catholic mayor who did not come from the machine tradition.

As far as patronage was concerned, Dever's administration worked out fairly well for the Brennan machine. Although personally choosing most of the high-ranking officials in his administration, the mayor permitted the Democratic machine control over the vast majority of patronage jobs. Yet in another important area—enforcement of prohibition—Dever antagonized a number of Democratic leaders as well as countless numbers of rank-and-file Democrats who wanted a plentiful supply of liquor. Although he personally was against prohibition, once in office Dever found it impossible to tolerate the illegal, gangster-dominated liquor trade. His police squads closed breweries and speakeasies and even raided private homes. By 1927 a number of Democratic leaders had their fill of Dever and when Thompson decided to run against him in the mayoral election of that year, many secretly worked on the Republican's behalf. Dever, like Dunne twenty years earlier, lost his bid for reelection.

Dever was clearly both a blessing and a curse for the Brennan machine. He strengthened the party by giving it a considerable amount of patronage during his four years in office. On the other hand, his unpopular policy of strict enforcement of prohibition allowed the Republicans once again to capture city hall. Dever's policy caused dissention within the ranks of the machine, which made Brennan's job of building a strong and unified party more difficult. Nonetheless, the party weathered the storm and remained in far better shape than the factionalized Republicans.

As it turned out, the Dever-Thompson race of 1927 was the last mayoral contest Brennan would see. In the summer of 1928 he died following a brief illness. After a certain amount of infighting the leadership of the party passed into the hands of Anton Cermak, a Bohemian who had served as majority leader of the city council and who in 1928 was president of the Cook County Board of Commissioners.

Some accounts of his takeover give Cermak credit for changing the direction of the Democratic party in Chicago. According to these accounts Cermak curbed Irish power and opened up city politics to other ethnics. This thesis holds that Cermak created a machine that completely controlled the city, unlike the previous two Irish administrations. Cermak deserves high marks as a politician, but he did have Irish allies and he did not drastically alter the party.[18]

Although an expert ethnic coalition builder, Cermak was certainly not an innovator in this regard. Irish ward bosses who dominated the decentralized Democratic party in the years between the end of the Civil War and the turn of the century were in certain respects even better practitioners of this art. Not only did old-stock Americans, Germans, and Swedes represent four-fifths of the electorate, but they were predominantly Republican. As a result, even though the Irish dominated the Democratic party and elected a considerable number of Irish aldermen, they could not expect to win city- and countywide offices if they slated too many Irish candidates. Thus out of sheer self-interest, if nothing else, Irish ward bosses supported ethnically balanced tickets. In the 1880s, for example, when roughly three-fourths of the Democratic ward committeemen were Irish, the Democrats usually nominated two old-stock Americans, one German, and one Irishman for the four major elective citywide offices.

Irish bosses seemed particularly reluctant to consider the nomination of one of their own as mayor. Many of them supported the Harrisons, while those that were anti-Harrison almost always backed a non-Irish candidate. Only once, in 1893, was an Irishman nominated for mayor. This practice worked out well for the Irish. Because their party usually controlled city hall, they benefited from the spoils of office. At the same time their power in their own wards was not diminished.

Irish politicians' relationship with the largely Catholic eastern and southern European immigrants was somewhat different than it was with the older groups. The new immigrants, who began to arrive in Chicago in substantial numbers in the 1890s, enhanced Irish political power in one respect but menaced it in another. They strengthened it because, unlike the older groups, they were largely Democratic in local politics. On the whole, they found Irish ward bosses sympathetic to their economic needs. Moreover, they viewed the Democrats as the "Catholic" party, one that was more in tune with their views on personal liberty issues.

At the same time, the new immigrants threatened the Irish by moving in large numbers into Irish-controlled wards, something old-stock Americans and Germans never had done. As their numbers grew and they became naturalized citizens, they sought greater recognition from the ward organizations, thus endangering the ascendancy of some of the old Irish war-horses.

The general tendency was for the Irish to hold on to power as long as possible. Johnny Powers, who managed to remain for years as alderman from an Italian ward that once had considerable numbers of Irish, is perhaps the best example of Irish tenacity. Irish hunger for office naturally antagonized other ethnic leaders and the ethnic press at times criticized the Irish for their undue political influence. Yet most of the new ethnics remained Democrats—an indication the Irish could not have been all that bad—and as time went on they gradually began to gain some degree of influence in the party. In 1918, for example, 15 percent of the Democratic candidates were of new immigrant stock.[19]

When Brennan took over control of the party in 1920, the eastern and southern European ethnic groups represented over one-third of the city's population. Realizing that for its own well-being the Democratic party had to grant these groups greater recognition, he made an effort to come up with slates that were more representative of the diverse ethnic makeup of the party. At times Irishmen were denied nominations in order to achieve more balanced tickets. In 1922, for example, Dan Ryan, Jr., the incumbent president of the Cook County Board of Commissioners, was passed over as the Democratic nominee for that position in favor of Cermak. A significant number of Irish leaders supported Brennan's efforts to reduce Irish influence; others were less than enthusiastic. The need to placate these individuals, coupled with the fact that it was impossible, and indeed undesirable, to make sweeping changes overnight, meant that the effort to open up the party moved slowly. In 1924, for example, only 13 percent of the Democratic candidates came from southern and eastern European backgrounds; two years later 66 percent of the Democratic ward committeemen were still Irish. Yet by 1928, the last year Brennan had a hand in selecting nominees, the efforts of the Democratic boss and his colleagues began to bear fruit. In that year 21 percent of the Democratic candidates were of new immigrant stock.[20]

Some Irish politicians who supported Brennan's drive for more ethnically balanced slates readily backed Cermak in his campaign to secure the party leadership. Although some of these individuals may have preferred one of their own, they supported the Bohemian leader because it was in their own political interest to do so or because they were convinced that he could provide the party with the best possible leadership. Other Irish politicians opposed Cermak, some because he was non-Irish, but most because he was a threat to their political prospects. In short Irish opinion on Cermak was divided.[21]

For his part, Cermak showed little animosity toward the Irish as a group. Indeed he valued and appreciated the support he received from Irish allies, support that was crucial in his takeover of the party. And while he curbed the power of certain politicians like Timothy J. Crowe and Michael Igoe, he did so for pragmatic political reasons and not because they were Irish.[22]

As party leader Cermak supported greater representation for the new immigrant groups, but the changes that occurred were not drastic. During his time the party did not witness any substantial increase in the number of ward committeemen of southern and eastern European stock. In 1927, for example, while Brennan was still leader, there were five Slavs, two Jews, and one Italian among the fifty Democratic ward committeemen, whereas five years later under Cermak there were seven Slavs, three Jews, and one Italian. Such changes were certainly less than revolutionary. Similarly there seems to have been no dramatic jump in the numbers of candidates of southern and eastern European stock nominated by the party. In 1928, 21 percent of the Democratic candidates were of southern and eastern European origin; four years later when Cermak controlled the party this figure had increased only to 26 percent.[23] Furthermore, when Cermak became mayor in 1931, he handed over two of the important jobs he held to his faithful Irish allies; Pat Nash became chairman of the Democratic Central Committee, while Emmet Whealan became president of the Cook County Board of Commissioners.[24]

If accounts of Cermak as an inveterate foe of the Irish distort reality, so to a lesser extent do those that portray him as the great hero of the new immigrants. While he certainly received considerable support from these groups, he was not necessarily more popular with some of them than were certain Irish politicians. Although Cermak received a greater percentage of Bohemian, Yugoslavian, and Jewish votes when he ran for mayor in 1931 than had Dever in 1923, he did not do as well as Dever had among Poles, Lithuanians, and Italians.[25]

Although Cermak's image as the great ethnic hero needs some modification, his reputation as the most effective Democratic boss in Chicago up to that time is deserved. Pursuing a carrot-and-stick policy with dissident Irish politicians, Cermak gradually took over the Democratic leadership during the two years following Brennan's death. By the end of 1930 Chicago's Democrats were more unified than they ever had been. If unity enhanced their power, so did Cermak's ability to field winning candidates. Once in office, these Democrats were able to supply the machine with plenty of patronage jobs, thereby adding to its power. The machine did amazingly well in the county elections of 1930 and in 1931 Cermak himself defeated Thompson for mayor. In 1932 Chicago went Democratic in a presidential election for the first time since 1892. Moreover, the Democrats captured most of the local offices and elected a Chicago Jewish Democrat, Henry Horner, as governor. While the victories of Cermak and his machine caused the virtual collapse of the Republican party in Chicago, the Republicans certainly contributed to their own demise. Bitter intraparty factionalism, Thompson's corruption and his anti-ethnic slurs during the 1931 campaign, and a "Republican" depression all combined to erode the power of the GOP.[26]

By the beginning of 1933 Cermak was riding high. He had firm control of the local party machinery as well as the city council, and most of the important city and county offices were in Democratic hands. On the state level the Chicago machine controlled the Democratic State Committee, two of the mayor's loyal Irish colleagues served as the Democratic leaders in the senate and assembly, and Horner had been elected governor. And in Washington, D.C., Franklin D. Roosevelt was about to enter the White House. However, because Cermak had been a die-hard Al Smith supporter at the 1932 Democratic convention, he was concerned that the machine might not be able to reap the full benefits of the new Roosevelt administration in Washington. In an effort to improve his relationship with the president-elect, he decided to visit him in Florida. The trip, of course, ended in tragedy. On February 15, a deranged Italian immigrant tried to shoot Roosevelt but hit Cermak instead. On March 6 he died.[27]

Shortly after Cermak's death the city council named Alderman Francis J. Corr temporary mayor and petitioned the Illinois legislature to pass a special law allowing it to select a mayor from inside or outside the council. The legislature readily complied and on April 14, 1933, the aldermen elected Edward J. Kelly, chief engineer of the Sanitary District and president of the South Park Board. Kelly was the handpicked candidate of Patrick A. Nash, chairman of the Democratic Central Committee, who had taken over the party reins following Cermak's death. Nash chose his longtime friend Kelly for two reasons: he had not been in the thick of the political fray and thus had made few important enemies, and he was an experienced administrator. No doubt the fact that Kelly was Irish (his father was an Irish immigrant, his mother German), also carried weight.

Reelected three more times, Kelly remained in city hall for the next fourteen years.[28] Unlike Cermak, who had served as top boss of the Cook County Democrats, Kelly shared the party leadership with Nash. They worked well together. Nash was a back-room politician who had run for elected office only twice in his career. As chairman of the Democratic Central Committee, Nash was content to shape general party strategy, allowing Kelly a free hand to run the city. Furthermore, Nash was a conciliator. In contrast to Kelly, whose high-handed tactics tended to alienate allies, Nash got along well with his fellow politicians. Kelly would have been considerably weaker without Nash and it is probably no coincidence that he was forced from office within four years of his friend's death in 1943.

As in Cermak's time, the Irish continued to dominate the party hierarchy during the Kelly-Nash years, though there were several important non-Irish leaders. While ethnic considerations were important in appealing to voters, they were not as significant in the various power struggles that occurred within the party. In 1936, for example, Kelly tried unsuccessfully to deny renomination to Governor Horner. He was backed by Jacob M. Arvey, the most powerful Jewish ward leader in the city. Meanwhile, the Jewish governor garnered support from maverick Irish politicians such as James Whalen, Martin J. O'Brien, and Al Horan. Similarly, in 1938, Kelly decided to slate another Pole in the primary race for county judge against the popular Polish incumbent, Edmund K. Jarecki. Although Kelly's candidate received the support of the Polish-American Democratic Organization, certain Irish politicians like Thomas Courtney endorsed Jarecki, who won the April primary and was reelected in November.

Although the Kelly-Nash machine suffered from a certain amount of dissension and from the declining popularity of Kelly during the latter years of his administration, the two Irish leaders kept intact the structure they inherited from Cermak and expanded its power and vitality in two important ways.

First of all, contrary to the popular notion that the New Deal weakened urban machines, the Kelly-Nash machine gained strength from the programs of the Roosevelt administration. Federal funds allowed the city to build a subway and new highways, improve roads and sewage systems, enlarge its airport and construct ten public housing projects, all of which redounded to the credit of the Kelly administration and the local Democratic machine. Second, although there does not appear to have been any considerable degree of political favoritism used in determining who received federally funded jobs and relief, local politicians benefited at election time. While some recipients believed that benefits depended on political loyalties, many were simply grateful to politicians for cutting the red tape involved in federal programs. Third, and perhaps most important, federal monies allowed the machine to keep the patronage system alive and well. Without these funds the city would have been forced to cut back on the less essential patronage jobs in order to pay for relief programs and other needed services. Finally, the machine's prestige grew as a result of the close relationship that developed between Kelly and President Roosevelt. FDR solicited the mayor's advice and referred to him in glowing terms. Kelly, for his part, strongly supported Roosevelt's decision to run for third and fourth terms, made sure that the machine produced handsome majorities for the president at each election, and loyally backed his policies, even his unpopular scheme to pack the Supreme Court.

If the New Deal bolstered the fortunes of the Kelly-Nash machine, so did the mass movement of the city's blacks from the Republican to the Democratic party. During the 1920s Chicago's blacks were solidly Republican, not only because of their historic allegiance to the party of Abraham Lincoln, but also because Mayor Thompson actively sought their support and catered to their needs. In contrast, Brennan's Democrats manifested a decided prejudice against them. On becoming mayor in 1931, Cermak made some effort to win over the black vote. He began to build up Democratic organizations in their wards, and he also used strong-arm tactics—firing black Republican patronage workers en masse and cracking down on black gambling operations. Despite this strategy, Chicago's black population was still overwhelmingly Republican at the time of his death.

Kelly helped to change this situation by taking a decidedly positive approach. Shortly after becoming mayor he reversed Cermak's policy on black gambling operations. He appointed some blacks to influential positions in city government and he dispensed patronage jobs to them in greater numbers than any previous Chicago mayor, including Thompson. At the same time he made a strenuous effort to establish effective Democratic organizations in the black wards. These efforts soon began to pay off. In 1934 Arthur Mitchell, a black Democratic candidate for Congress, defeated his black Republican opponent. In the mayoral election of 1935 Kelly picked up the majority of black votes, as he did again in 1939 and 1944. Meanwhile, the number of black Democratic ward committeemen and aldermen began to grow. In 1939, the mayor pulled off what turned out to be a major coup when he convinced Republican Alderman William Dawson to switch parties. Not only did

Dawson build up a strong Democratic organization in his own second ward, he also gained a dominant influence over other black wards. In effect he created a black Democratic machine whose unfailing loyalty considerably enhanced the power of the citywide Democratic organization.

Although his policy toward blacks was motivated mainly by pragmatic political considerations, it should be noted that Kelly had a genuine commitment to civil rights. He continually pressed for integrated schools and open public housing, even though this caused an erosion of his support in the white community.

Finally, it needs to be mentioned that with or without Kelly, blacks in Chicago as in other American cities would have moved to the Democratic party because of New Deal policies and Republican insensitivity to their needs. What Kelly did, and did brilliantly, was to insure that this new and large bloc of Democratic converts solidified rather than weakened the power of the local machine. Had Brennan with his prejudiced attitude toward blacks or Cermak with his intimidating policy been at the helm of the Democratic party during the mid- and late 1930s, one can envision a much different scenario taking place.

Like his use of New Deal programs, Kelly's gestures toward blacks benefited not only the machine but the city as a whole. In other areas, however, he pursued policies that enhanced the machine's power at the public's expense. For example, his willingness to allow the patronage system to be used in hiring principals and teachers and his appointment of political hacks to the school board did much to undermine the quality of the city's public school system. Worse still was the cozy relationship that existed between the machine and organized crime, which ran a vast network of gambling operations throughout the city. In return for about half the profits, ward bosses ensured that the police looked the other way when it came to enforcing the law. The machine collected millions each year, but the city was left with a tarnished police force and a criminal element in the streets.

The public school mess, police corruption, and official tolerance of organized crime began to catch up to the Kelly administration during the mayor's last term. Increasing numbers of ordinary Chicagoans joined with reformers, who had long been after Kelly's head, in demanding that the abuses of the machine be curbed. At the same time several influential machine politicians, most of whom were Irish, were becoming more and more dissatisfied with Kelly. They resented his high-handed tactics (Nash was no longer around to smooth ruffled feathers), disliked his commitment to open public housing, a policy that was most unpopular with their white constituents, and felt that his performances as mayor and party chieftain left much to be desired. When in early 1946 Kelly put together a weak slate of candidates for the upcoming November election, several party leaders decided that he had lost his touch. In July they convinced him to resign as party leader and replaced him with Jacob Arvey, a man who, though personally loyal to Kelly, was acceptable to the anti-Kelly people. After the November elections, in which the Democrats did indeed suffer major defeats, Arvey in conjunction with ward committeemen Joseph Gill and Al Horan conducted a public opinion survey to get some idea of how Kelly would fare if he ran for another term in 1947. When the results proved negative, Kelly was prevailed upon to bow out. Following the advice of chairman Arvey, the Democratic Central Committee selected another Irishman, the millionaire businessman Martin J. Kennelly, as their party's candidate.

Kennelly was an ideal choice for a machine in desperate need of a quick face-lift.[29] A reform Democrat with a record of opposition to the Kelly-Nash machine, he was likely to appeal to rank-and-file Democrats who had become disgusted with Kelly's shenanigans. In addition, he might win the support of reformers like Professor Paul Douglas, who threatened a primary contest should Kelly be renominated by the machine. At the same time, Kennelly seemed politically naive. Although he had actively worked for anti-Kelly candidates such as Horner, Jarecki, and Courtney, he had remained on the periphery of politics. All things considered, it was unlikely that Kennelly would do any serious damage to the machine's interests.

In the following April Kennelly defeated his lackluster Republican opponent, Russell Root, by a comfortable margin. Reelected in 1951 in a somewhat closer race, Kennelly served as mayor for a total of eight years. During this period he tried to provide the city with honest, efficient, and effective government. The results of his efforts were mixed. On the positive side, his administration freed the public school system from political influence and therefore did much to improve its quality as well as its image. It also sponsored housing, urban renewal, and highway construction projects, and reorganized certain city departments in an effort to provide better and lower-cost service. On the negative side, Kennelly showed no real concern for the interests of the city's growing black minority; and despite some short-lived attempts to root out organized crime, his administration failed to sever the link between it and certain machine politicians and policemen.

Although a reform mayor occupied city hall, the machine remained intact during the Kennelly years. Like Dever, Kennelly kept his distance from the machine but made no attempt to build up a rival organization. A believer in the separation of powers, Kennelly did not try to exert any significant influence over the machine-controlled city council. Because

Chicago had a strong council-weak mayor system of government, the machine's aldermen were in the driver's seat. During these years a certain number of aldermen received kickbacks from businesses in return for special favors. Yet, as in the case of Dever, Kennelly came into conflict with the machine on one major issue. In Dever's case it was prohibition, in Kennelly's, patronage. A strong believer in the civil service system, Kennelly gradually began to transfer jobs from the patronage to the civil service rolls. By the beginning of the last year of his administration, some 10,000 patronage jobs had been placed under civil service; only 3,000 patronage positions remained. This policy naturally weakened the machine and indeed might have proved fatal had it been allowed to continue.

Upset with Kennelly's policy regarding civil service, the Democratic machine decided to replace him with Cook County Clerk Richard J. Daley, who had been chairman of the Central Democratic Committee since 1953. Unlike Kelly, who agreed, albeit reluctantly, not to run again in 1947, Kennelly decided to challenge Daley in the primary. It became a three-way race when the maverick reformer Ben Adamowski entered the fray. Because he failed to clamp down on organized crime and clean up the police department, Kennelly's reform support dissipated and he was easily beaten by Daley in the April 1955 primary.

In the November general election Daley defeated his Republican opponent, the reformer Robert Merriam. He thus became Chicago's sixth Irish Catholic mayor. Reelected for five more terms, Daley served as mayor until his death in December 1976. His tenure of twenty-one plus years in office was longer than that of any of his predecessors.

Daley was by far the most powerful mayor and political boss in the history of Chicago.[30] A hard worker, with a flair for organization and details and an ability to get the best from his subordinates, Daley provided both the city and the Democratic machine with strong, effective leadership. The Daley administration furnished Chicagoans with city services—garbage collection, snow removal, street lighting and repair, etc.—that were superior to those in most major American cities. It maintained a decent public transportation system, built needed expressways, sponsored urban renewal projects, kept the city financially solvent, and kept taxes at reasonable levels. In short, Chicago by and large lived up to its reputation as "the city that works." For this Daley won the support of the business community as well as most ordinary citizens.

If the city worked, so did the machine, a remarkable feat in a day and age when all other similar institutions had fallen by the wayside. Daley and the inner circle of the Democratic Central Committee generally nominated winning candidates for city and county offices. The patronage jobs that went along with these offices as well as those from city hall meant that the machine had at its disposal perhaps as many as 30,000 patronage positions. Doled out to ward committeemen and precinct captains as well as to members of the party faithful, these jobs were the oil that kept the machine running. In return for their keep, Democrats paid back the machine with their votes, financial contributions, and political work. In addition to lubricating the machine, Daley and his colleagues ensured that its parts were in good working order. They promoted competent individuals in the party hierarchy and demoted or dumped those whose performance was inadequate.

Daley was careful to keep his role as mayor distinct from his position as party boss. For example, he did not consult ward committeemen on nonpolitical city business. Neither did city bureaucrats play a part in formulating party policy. Yet each position enhanced Daley's effectiveness in handling the other. Control of city hall, for example, enabled Daley to help the machine by providing its members with patronage jobs and city contracts. On the other hand, by controlling the machine he was able to have a dominant influence over the city council, since the overwhelming majority of the aldermen were machine Democrats. Similarly, the Daley administration could make use of the precinct captains to provide better city services and thus increase machine popularity. A person with a particular problem, say poor garbage collection, could go to his precinct captain, who would call the "right people" and have the matter taken care of promptly.

Although it accomplished much good, the Daley regime had negative qualities. For one thing, although Daley was not an absolute monarch, too much power was concentrated in the hands of one man for too long a period for a healthy democratic society. Second, while Daley himself and many of his colleagues were personally honest, there was far too much corruption in the machine. During the early 1970s, for example, Daley's press secretary Earl Bush and Alderman Tom Keane were convicted of mail fraud; Cook County Clerk Edward J. Barrett of bribery; and Alderman Paul Wigoda of federal income-tax evasion.

Another serious deficiency of the Daley administration was its failure to deal adequately with the needs of the black community in regard to housing and education. It was no secret, for example, that the Daley administration did not oppose segregation in schools and public housing. Yet although some civil rights groups assailed the administration for being anti-black, the vast majority of blacks in the city loyally supported the machine. Despite its negative aspects, the Democratic organization provided them with concrete benefits. It gave blacks a share of the

patronage jobs, while its precinct organizations provided them with
useful services such as assistance in applying for various government
benefits.

Aware that blacks were 40 percent of the city's population and that
retention of their support was vital, Daley and his colleagues nominated
an increasing number of black candidates for public office. After the
1971 election, the city treasurer and sixteen of the fifty aldermen were
blacks. Yet despite growing black representation, white ethnics still held
the overwhelming majority of the really influential party positions.

Among the white ethnics, the Irish continued to exert an influence far
in excess of their numbers. As their population in the city declined, their
influence did slip. When Daley became mayor they were only about 10
percent of Chicagoans. Still, 33 percent of the aldermen were Irish. In
1970, with probably no more than 5 percent of the population, they
represented 16 percent of the aldermen, 34 percent of the Democratic
ward committeemen, and at least 38 percent of the Cook County circuit
court judges. They also held a staggering number of important city and
county offices, many of which were rich in patronage.[31]

In many respects the Irish politicians of the Daley and post-Daley
years have been cut from the same cloth as their counterparts of the late
nineteenth and early twentieth centuries. Patronage obviously is as
important as it was in the past, and recent politicians, like their
predecessors, have looked upon politics as a career. Very few have
entered the political arena out of a sense of civic duty, as the reformers
like to claim for themselves. Similarly, ideology continues to mean little
to Chicago's Irish politicians. They make pragmatic political decisions
based on what they think is good for the machine as well as their
constituents, without reference to any particular social or economic
philosophy.

Although much alike in their basic political attitudes, recent Irish
politicians have differed from their forerunners in certain respects. In
contrast to those of the past, Irish politicians of recent years have been
fairly well educated and virtually all of them have been reared in
Chicago. A Chicago upbringing now seems to be almost a prerequisite
for a successful career in local politics. Furthermore, money no longer
seems to be the major reason the Irish enter politics. Indeed, considering their educational background, some probably could have done
better financially in the private sector. They mainly enter politics today
in search of power or because of family tradition. For example, Chicago's
Irish lawyer-politicians include Alderman Edward Burke and Illinois
representative John Cullerton, scions of famous political families.[32]

Up until Daley's death in December 1976, Chicago's Irish had enjoyed a consistency in politics that their earlier counterparts never experienced. Daley's successor, Michael Bilandic, a Croatian, became the first non-Irish mayor in over forty-four years. Although experienced and hard working, Bilandic lacked his predecessor's powers and administrative ability and thus did not last long. Renominated by the machine, he was defeated in the 1979 Democratic primary by Jane Byrne, who, despite her past association with the Daley administration, ran as a reformer. Byrne easily won the general election to become Chicago's first woman and seventh Irish Catholic mayor. Although she had battled the machine, she soon made peace with it and tried to govern the city in the Daley tradition. However, like Bilandic she failed to measure up to Richard J. In February 1983 she was challenged in the Democratic primary by Daley's son, State's Attorney Richard M. Daley, and by black Congressman Harold Washington, who ran as an antimachine reformer. The majority of white machine politicians supported Byrne, but a substantial minority backed Daley. Washington enjoyed the support of the black community, including its machine politicians, as well as the backing of some white liberals. He narrowly won the three-way race with about 34 percent of the vote.

In the following general election, Washington squeaked by his little-known Republican opponent Bernard Epton, who had the open support of some white Democratic ward leaders and the clandestine support of others. In an election where race was a major issue Washington received 97 percent of the black vote and Epton 80 percent of the white. At the present time Washington, wearing the mantle of reformer, is quarreling with the white machine politicians on the city council. What the final outcome will be is difficult to say, though it seems clear that the days of Daley will never be repeated.

From the very early days of Chicago the Irish have played a major role in the political life of the city. During the first quarter-century or so of the city's history, though old-stock Americans dominated the leadership of various parties, the Irish exhibited clout at the polls. In the post–Civil War period Irish political power grew tremendously as the more Americanized Irish community produced several influential politicians who were well adept at playing the game of machine politics. After the turn of the century the new immigrants began to make inroads on Irish power as the blacks did some decades later. Yet the erosion of Irish power was extremely slow, a fact that is perhaps best demonstrated by their continuous occupation of city hall from 1933 to 1976.

Several reasons account for the persistence of Irish political power in Chicago. First of all the Irish entered politics in larger numbers than did other groups. Lacking the opportunities in the private sector that were available to old-stock Americans and to a lesser extent Germans, ambitious young Irish-Americans in the nineteenth century gravitated toward political careers as a way of economic and social advancement. Although the later economic condition of the Irish improved considerably, they still entered politics in sizeable numbers because by then it had become traditional, practically hereditary, to do so.

Not only did significant numbers of Irish Chicagoans choose political careers, but they also came well equipped for the vocation. A knowledge of the English language and a familiarity with the English system of government, from which the American was derived, enabled more Irish immigrants to participate effectively in politics than otherwise would have been the case. Moreover, the Irish political tradition with its emphasis on personal contacts and getting things done outside the formal framework of government was ideally suited to the political environment of Chicago.

Another factor that contributed to Irish political success was their ability to build ethnic coalitions. Since they only accounted for roughly one-fifth of the electorate during the first few decades of the city's history, the Irish learned early on the need for multiethnic cooperation. Thus during the last decades of the nineteenth century Irish ward bosses made sure that citywide Democratic tickets were not top-heavy with Irish candidates. When the new immigrants began to gain voting power in the early twentieth century, Irish leaders gradually began to support the nomination of their candidates for public office, as they did with blacks from the 1930s on. Although other groups often resented them for taking more than their share of the nominations and patronage, the Irish usually allowed other ethnics enough of the spoils of office to keep them loyal to the Democratic party.

In their effort to retain political power the Irish benefited immensely from the population mix of Chicago. Except for the early years when the old-stock Americans accounted for more than 40 percent of the city's population and the recent years when blacks have reached about the same percentage, no single ethnic group in Chicago was ever numerically strong enough to challenge the Irish on their own. Nor were two or more groups ever compatible enough to team up against them. Furthermore, the Irish benefited from the fact that from the late nineteenth century up until the end of World War II or so the Catholic population of the city was rising. Although German, Polish, Bohemian, Italian, Lithuanian, and Croatian Catholics might not have viewed the Irish always with friendly eyes, they shared their basic political attitudes and thus found the Irish-dominated Democratic party compatible with their goals and aspirations. It was their support in combination with other factors that helped make the Democrats the perpetual majority party in the city, which greatly furthered Irish power.

Finally, it should be emphasized that the Chicago Irish have been concerned almost entirely with local government. They have shown little interest in state and national politics except insofar as they might affect the local situation. There has been only one Irish governor of Illinois and no Irishman has ever been elected to the U.S. Senate from the state. Although some Irish Chicagoans have served in the U.S. House of Representatives, few have remained long enough to gain much seniority and influence.

One cannot explain this parochialism by saying it is part of the Irish-American political tradition, for the Irish in other states have produced presidential candidates, governors, senators, and influential congressmen. Rather the answer lies in the great cultural and religious gulf that has separated Chicago from the rest of the state.[33] Unlike Chicago, downstate Illinois has been overwhelmingly rural or small town and Protestant, with a considerable Southern evangelical culture element in the lower part of the state. Consequently the Chicago Irish have viewed the rest of Illinois as alien territory whose representatives in Springfield might encroach further on their already limited form of home rule and whose voters would not countenance the election of an Irish Catholic to an important office like governor or senator. When occasionally Irish Chicagoans did run for such offices their suspicions were largely confirmed. Although Dunne was elected governor in 1912, he lost his bid for reelection in 1916, and both Sullivan in 1914 and Brennan in 1924 lost their senatorial contests.

Because what political opportunities existed beyond Chicago were risky at best, the Irish concentrated on maintaining the power they had in the city, an "almost single-minded concentration" that helped them preserve their machine when the Irish in other cities had lost theirs.[34] Even though anti-Catholicism has diminished, narrowing the culture gap between Cook County and downstate, the Irish still look with distrust on those beyond Chicago's metropolitan borders. In the future, however, as Irish power in Chicago continues to decline, more Irish politicians may be inclined to look beyond the city. Then the Chicago Irish may begin to bring forth national leaders of the caliber that the Irish in other states have produced.[35]

NOTES

1. The discussion of pre-1866 Irish politics is based on Bessie Louise Pierce, *A History of Chicago,* 3 vols. (New York: Alfred A. Knopf, 1937-57); Ruth M. Piper, "The Irish in Chicago, 1848-1871" (M.A. thesis, University of Chicago, 1936); and the Chicago *Tribune,* Apr. 19, 1874.

2. George Potter, *To the Golden Door: The Story of the Irish in Ireland and America* (Boston: Little, Brown, 1960), p. 530.

3. Based on the lists of aldermen in Alfred T. Andreas, *History of Chicago,* 3 vols. (Chicago: A. T. Andreas Co., 1884-86), 2:50; and *Chicago Daily News Almanac for 1890,* p. 84.

4. My discussion of Irish politics in Chicago, 1866-1915, is based upon the following: Pierce, *History of Chicago;* Lloyd Wendt and Herman Kogan, *Lords of the Levee: The Story of Bathhouse John and Hinky Dink* (New York: Garden City Publishing Co., 1944); Carter H. Harrison II, *Stormy Years: The Autobiography of Carter H. Harrison, Five Times Mayor of Chicago* (Indianapolis: Bobbs-Merrill Co., 1935); Joel Arthur Tarr, *A Study in Boss Politics: William Lorimer of Chicago* (Urbana: University of Illinois Press, 1971); Paul Michael Green, "Irish Chicago: The Multiethnic Road to Machine Success," in *Ethnic Chicago,* ed. Peter d'A. Jones and Melvin G. Holli (Grand Rapids, Mich.: William B. Eerdmans Publishing Co., 1981); Ralph R. Tingley, "From Carter Harrison II to Fred Busse: A Study of Chicago Political Parties and Personages from 1896 to 1907" (Ph.D. dissertation, University of Chicago, 1950); Charles Edward Merriam, *Chicago: A More Intimate View of Urban Politics* (New York: Macmillan Co., 1929); Ralph Arthur Straetz, "The Progressive Movement in Illinois, 1910-1916" (Ph.D. dissertation, University of Illinois, 1951); Alex Gottfried, *Boss Cermak of Chicago: A Study of Political Leadership* (Seattle: University of Washington Press, 1962); Edward R. Kantowicz, *Polish-American Politics in Chicago, 1888-1940* (Chicago: University of Chicago Press, 1975); Charles Fanning, Ellen Skerrett, and John Corrigan, *Nineteenth Century Chicago Irish* (Chicago: Center for Urban Policy, Loyola University of Chicago, 1980); Perry R. Duis, *The Saloon: Public Drinking in Chicago and Boston, 1880-1920* (Urbana: University of Illinois Press, 1983); Richard Edward Becker, "Edward Dunne, Reform Mayor of Chicago, 1905-1907" (Ph.D. dissertation, University of Chicago, 1971); and John D. Buenker, *Urban Liberalism and Progressive Reform* (New York: Charles Scribner's Sons, 1973).

5. Becker, "Edward Dunne," p. 217.

6. As late as 1914, 69 percent of the Democratic ward committeemen were Irish. Green, "Irish Chicago," p. 231.

7. *U.S. Twelfth Census, 1900,* "Special Reports: Occupations," pp. 516-20.

8. Harold P. Lasswell, *Power and Personality* (New York: W. W. Norton, 1948), p. 53, cited by Gottfried, *Boss Cermak,* p. 337.

9. Irish opposition to temperance laws and so on was a typical "ritualistic" position shared by other Catholic ethnics and some Protestants. For an analysis of ethno-religious factors in the politics of the period see Paul Kleppner, *The Cross of Culture: A Social Analysis of Midwestern Politics, 1850-1900* (New

York: Free Press, 1970); and Richard Jensen, *The Winning of the Midwest: Social and Political Conflict, 1888-1896* (Chicago: University of Chicago Press, 1971).

10. Although not always agreeing with his interpretations I found the following useful in my analysis of Irish history in its relationship to the Irish-American political experience: Thomas N. Brown, "The Political Irish: Politicians and Rebels," in *America and Ireland, 1776-1976: The American Identity and the Irish Connection,* ed. David Noel Doyle and Owen Dudley Edwards (Westport, Conn.: Greenwood Press, 1980).

11. William D'Arcy, *The Fenian Movement in the United States: 1858-1886* (New York: Russell and Russell, 1971); Piper, "Irish in Chicago," pp. 18-28; and Pierce, *History of Chicago,* 2:14-16.

12. For the history of the Clan in Chicago see Michael F. Funchion, *Chicago's Irish Nationalists, 1881-1890* (New York: Arno Press, 1976).

13. *Gaelic American,* Apr. 4, 11, 18, 25, May 2, 30, June 6, 13, 1925; John Corrigan, "United Irish Societies of Chicago," in *Irish American Voluntary Organizations,* ed. Michael F. Funchion (Westport, Conn.: Greenwood Press, 1983), p. 280.

14. The reasons for the decline of the Clan's political influence are not clear. For Clan involvement in late 1890s local politics, see John Devoy's Diary, Devoy Papers, MSS 9820, National Library of Ireland; Harrison, *Stormy Years,* pp. 106-7; Carter H. Harrison II, *Growing Up with Chicago* (Chicago: Ralph Fletcher Seymour, 1944), pp. 283-84.

15. Francis M. Carroll, "United Irish League of America," in Funchion, ed., *Irish American Voluntary Organizations,* p. 272.

16. For the Irish-American contribution to the liberation of Ireland, 1910-23, see Francis M. Carroll, *American Opinion and the Irish Question, 1910-23* (Dublin: Gill and Macmillan, 1978).

17. The material on Irish politics, 1920-28, is based on Arthur W. Thurner, "The Impact of Ethnic Groups on the Democratic Party in Chicago, 1920-28" (Ph.D. dissertation, University of Chicago, 1966); Green, "Irish Chicago"; Gottfried, *Boss Cermak;* John M. Allswang, *A House for All Peoples: Ethnic Politics in Chicago, 1890-1936* (Lexington: University Press of Kentucky, 1971); Merriam, *Chicago;* Kantowicz, *Polish-American Politics;* and Humbert S. Nelli, *The Italians in Chicago, 1880-1930: A Study in Ethnic Mobility* (New York: Oxford University Press, 1970).

18. Gottfried, *Boss Cermak;* Nelli, *Italians in Chicago;* and Len O'Connor, *Clout: Mayor Daley and His City* (New York: Avon Books, 1976) credit Cermak with new ethnic coalition politics. Others disagree with or modify this claim. Allswang, *House for All Peoples,* views Cermak as more ethnically oriented than the Irish but notes that Sullivan and Brennan appealed to many groups in gathering votes and constructing tickets. Kantowicz, *Polish-American Politics,* asserts that Cermak united "all the newer ethnic groups who were dissatisfied with Irish dominance of the Democratic party," but argues that Cermak's influence over the Polish vote has been exaggerated. Finally Thurner, "Impact of Ethnic Groups," and Green, "Irish Chicago," give Brennan and his associates

the chief credit for assembling a multiethnic party. Green insists that Cermak was not anti-Irish.

19. For ethnic voting patterns from 1890 to 1920 and statistical information on 1918 ethnic percentages of Democratic candidates see Allswang, *House for All Peoples,* pp. 31-33, 42, 85, 218-19.

20. Thurner, "Impact of Ethnic Groups"; Green, "Irish Chicago." Statistics based on Allswang, *House for All Peoples,* pp. 85-86; and Gottfried, *Boss Cermak,* p. 175. Gottfried notes that in 1926 twenty-five of the forty-two candidates on the Democratic county slate were Irish.

21. For information on individual Irish politicians see Green, "Irish Chicago," and Gottfried. Gottfried's evidence (*Boss Cermak,* pp. 170-203) supports Green's argument that Cermak was not anti-Irish.

22. Gottfried, *Boss Cermak,* pp. 179-80, notes that Pat Nash's support for Cermak was most crucial.

23. For the ethnic composition of the Democratic slates and ward committeemen from 1918 to 1932 see Allswang, *House for All Peoples,* pp. 85-86. His survey includes all the ward committeemen but not all party candidates. See also Gottfried, *Boss Cermak,* pp. 175, 294-95, 310.

24. Green, "Irish Chicago," p. 250.

25. Allswang, *House for All Peoples,* p. 42; Kantowicz, *Polish-American Politics,* p. 153; Nelli, *Italians in Chicago,* pp. 229, 234.

26. Information on the Democratic machine is based on Gottfried, *Boss Cermak;* Allswang, *House for All Peoples;* Green, "Irish Chicago"; Thurner, "Impact of Ethnic Groups"; Kantowicz, *Polish-American Politics;* Nelli, *Italians in Chicago;* Merriam, *Chicago;* and Harold F. Gosnell, *Machine Politics: Chicago Model,* 2d ed. (Chicago: University of Chicago Press, 1968).

27. In addition to Gottfried, *Boss Cermak;* Gosnell, *Machine Politics;* and Green, "Irish Chicago," see Lyle W. Dorsett, *Franklin D. Roosevelt and the City Bosses* (Port Washington, N.Y.: Kennikat Press, 1977).

28. The material on the Kelly years is based on Roger Biles, *Big City Boss in Depression and War: Mayor Edward J. Kelly of Chicago* (DeKalb: Northern Illinois University Press, 1984); Gene Delon Jones, "The Local Political Significance of the New Deal Relief Legislation in Chicago: 1933-1940" (Ph.D. dissertation, Northwestern University, 1970); Edward Mazur, "Jewish Chicago: From Diversity to Community," in *The Ethnic Frontier,* ed. Peter d'A. Jones and Melvin G. Holli (Grand Rapids, Mich.: William B. Eerdmans Publishing Co., 1977), pp. 263-91; James Q. Wilson, *Negro Politics: The Search for Leadership* (Glencoe, Ill.: Free Press, 1960); and Peter J. O'Malley, "Mayor Martin H. Kennelly of Chicago: A Political Biography" (Ph.D. dissertation, University of Illinois at Chicago, 1980). See also Allswang, *House for All Peoples;* Dorsett, *Franklin D. Roosevelt;* Gosnell, *Machine Politics;* Gottfried, *Boss Cermak;* Green, "Irish Chicago"; Kantowicz, *Polish-American Politics;* Merriam, *Chicago;* Nelli, *Italians in Chicago;* and Thurner, "Impact of Ethnic Groups."

29. Material on the Kennelly years is based on Biles, *Big City Boss;* O'Connor,

Clout; O'Malley, "Mayor Martin H. Kennelly"; Wilson, *Negro Politics;* William Russell Gable, "The Chicago City Council: A Study of Urban Politics and Legislation" (Ph.D. dissertation, University of Chicago, 1953); R. Gene Geisler, "Chicago Democratic Voting, 1947-57" (Ph.D. dissertation, University of Chicago, 1958); and Mike Royko, *Boss: Richard J. Daley of Chicago* (New York: New American Library, 1971).

30. The Daley years material is based on Geisler, "Chicago Democratic Voting"; O'Connor, *Clout;* Royko, *Boss;* Wilson, *Negro Politics;* Milton J. Rakove, *Don't Make No Waves—Don't Back No Losers: An Insider's Analysis of the Daley Machine* (Bloomington: Indiana University Press, 1975); and Leo M. Snowiss, "Chicago and Congress: A Study of Metropolitan Representation" (Ph.D. dissertation, University of Chicago, 1965).

31. Rakove, *Don't Make No Waves,* pp. 34-40.

32. For recent Chicago Irish politicians see Edward M. Levine, *The Irish and Irish Politicians* (Notre Dame, Ind.: University of Notre Dame Press, 1966); Rakove, *Don't Make No Waves;* Gable, "Chicago City Council"; and Andrew M. Greeley, *That Most Distressful Nation: The Taming of the American Irish* (Chicago: Quadrangle Books, 1972).

33. Such a wide gulf did not exist between other cities where the Irish settled and the rest of the state.

34. Rakove, *Don't Make No Waves,* pp. 6-7.

35. During the past two decades, one Chicago Irishman, William Clark, ran for the United States Senate (1968) and another, Michael Howlett, ran for governor (1976). Both lost contests where their chances of victory were small.

The Literary Dimension

Charles Fanning

The Chicago Irish have been uniquely blessed in the quality and inclusiveness of the literary record of their existence as an urban ethnic group. The blessings are largely attributable to the fact that the two main contributors to that record, Finley Peter Dunne (1867–1936) and James T. Farrell (1904–79), were also the first American writers of genius to emerge from Irish ethnic backgrounds. The legacy of these two Chicago Irishmen is an unbroken narrative of the Irish-American experience stretching from Dunne's treatments of the Famine immigration of the late 1840s to Farrell's depiction of the dying days in 1946 of an Irish-American matriarch. Here, I provide an outline of that major narrative accomplishment, and also introduce two additional Chicago Irish writers, Kate McPhelim Cleary (1863–1905) and Clara E. Laughlin (1873–1941), whose turn-of-the-century fiction forms a bridge from Dunne to Farrell.

The world of American big-city journalism in the last quarter of the nineteenth century was one of the most exciting places in the history of communications. Because of exploding immigrant populations and rapidly expanding industrialization, cities were where the action was, and of course Chicago had a lion's share. Between her two defining spectacles, the Great Fire of 1871 and the World's Fair of 1893, the city grew from 300,000 to 1,300,000 people, many of them immigrants, and became a world leader in meat-packing, grain and lumber distribution, banking, manufacturing, and merchandising. During these hectic years, Chicago had as many as thirty-two competing daily papers at one time, and in June 1884 one of these, the *Telegram,* hired a sixteen-year-old boy to cover the police beat. This was Peter Dunne, the son of Irish immigrants, born in the shadow of St. Patrick's Church at West Adams and Desplaines streets, and fresh out of the West Division High School, where he had managed to graduate last in his class of fifty. Over the next eight years Dunne worked for six different newspapers and moved up fast. At nineteen he was covering the White Sox for the *Daily News,* at twenty-five he arrived as editorial page chairman at the *Evening Post,* where he soon imagined himself into the character of Mr. Martin Dooley, the aging barkeep/philosopher of Archer Avenue in the South Side Irish neighborhood of Bridgeport. (Actually, Mr. Dooley was Dunne's third Irish newspaper creation. The first had been Colonel Thomas Jefferson Dolan, a political hack used to satirize the doings of the Chicago city council in 1890, and the second was Colonel Malachi McNeery, invented in December 1892 and modeled on a friend who kept a saloon in the Loop.)

The *Evening Post* of October 7, 1893, contained the first appearance of Mr. Dooley, who spoke with a pronounced brogue from behind the bar of his working-class Bridgeport saloon. In the course of this first 750-word column, mention was made of Charles Stewart Parnell, "Carey, th' informer," the "gr-rand ma-arch in Finucane's Hall," led by John McKenna ten years earlier, and the recent arrest of Pat Riley, "the big, strappin' kid iv Dominick Riley, that lived beyant the rollin' mills." Immediately apparent are the seeds of Peter Dunne's accomplishment in the three hundred weekly Dooley columns that followed—the imaginative creation of Bridgeport, the first fully realized Irish ethnic neighborhood in American literature.[1]

Before Dunne, no Irish-American writer had honestly scrutinized his own background in a sustained body of work. The first cluster of Irish-Americans to show signs of becoming a group literary force had been John Boyle O'Reilly and his staff at the *Boston Pilot* in the 1880s. Without exception, they all went in the opposite direction from Dunne: away from early realistic tendencies, and toward an embrace of the contemporary literary standard of genteel idealism. O'Reilly himself led the way. His first novel, *Moondyne Joe* (1879), was a fairly straightforward attempt to fictionalize his own experience as a transported convict in Australia, but by the time of his early death in 1890, he had become a conventional genteel poet. Similarly, O'Reilly's assistant editor, Katherine Conway, published a promising autobiographical novel, *Lalor's Maples,* in 1901, but followed it with an increasingly romantic corpus of short stories and poems. James Jeffrey Roche, who edited the *Pilot* after O'Reilly, and Louise Imogen Guiney, a frequent contributor of poems, began as genteel idealists and never looked back. Such, presumably, was the grip of Boston's literary establishment, that none of these writers could bring themselves to forge a career in which he or she dealt realistically with the heritage they all shared—being Irish in an American city. Perhaps because he was a journalist, with few ambitions toward "litrachoor," and because he lived in Chicago, without Oliver Wendell Holmes looking over his shoulder, Finley Peter Dunne was able to place Martin Dooley on Archer Avenue and keep him there until 1900, when he moved to New York and a different sort of career as a nationally syndicated humorist.

In his earlier Chicago setting, Mr. Dooley provides many riches unavailable elsewhere. First of all, it must be said that in contrast to his later manifestation as the purveyor of comic perspective on national issues, Mr. Dooley is funny in only half of the Chicago pieces. This is important because of the tradition of Irish dialect writing that he emerged from and repudiates. A familiar figure of fun in American drama and journalism throughout the nineteenth century was the "stage Irishman," a condescending portrayal of broad-brush stereotypes—for example, the wily, blarneying politician and the ignorant immigrant, tripping over his own feet in a vain attempt to understand the New World. But even when he is being funny, Mr. Dooley provokes laughter not because he knows so little, but because he knows so much. He is witty, satirical, cutting—he exposes delusions rather than being victimized by them. Furthermore, the three hundred Chicago Dooley pieces, funny and serious both, add up to something new and of great value to students of American ethnic literature and history.

Through Mr. Dooley, Dunne made three contributions to the development of American literary realism. As an urban local colorist, he described the life and customs of Bridgeport in the 1890s. As a creator of character sketches of Irish immigrants, he affirmed that the lives of common people were worthy of serious literary consideration. And because both of these contributions came through the medium of Irish dialect, he expanded the possibilities for literature of the vernacular voice, in the same way that Mark Twain had done ten years earlier, when he let Huck Finn tell his own story. As for the historical contribution, Mr. Dooley takes us as close as we are likely to come to the circumstances, customs, and attitudes of a nineteenth-century Irish-American neighborhood. He measures up very well to his own standard of what history ought to be:

> I know histhry isn't thrue, Hinnissy, because it ain't like what I see ivry day in Halsted Sthreet. If any wan comes along with a histhry iv Greece or Rome that'll show me th' people fightin', gettin' dhrunk, makin' love, gettin' married, owin' th' grocery man an bein' without hard-coal, I'll believe they

was a Greece or Rome, but not befure. Historyans is like doctors. They are always lookin' f'r symptoms. Those iv them that writes about their own times examines th' tongue an' feels th' pulse an' makes a wrong dygnosis. Th' other kind iv histhry is a post-mortem examination. It tells ye what a counthry died iv. But I'd like to know what it lived iv.[2]

Dunne's Dooley columns are cameo etchings, with the precision and vividness of illuminated corners of the Book of Kells, of the archetypal Irish immigrant themes and characters. The themes include memories of the Great Hunger, the turbulent voyage out to America, the shattered dream of gold in the streets, the hard life of manual labor, the sufferings of the destitute, the pains of assimilation, the gulf between immigrants and their American children, and the slow rise to respectability. And the characters include Civil War veterans, heroic firemen, stoic, exploited mill workers, rack-renting, miserly landlords, failed politicians who lose their money, successful ones who forget their friends, lace-curtain social climbers with pianos in the parlor, and compassionate, overworked parish priests. And, of course, presiding over all is the bartender—Mr. Dooley, himself: satirist, social critic, and philosopher, generally cynical but specifically kind; at the least (in his own words) "a post to hitch ye'er silences to," at the most, a provider of companionship and solace to bone weary working people.

By accretion of the weekly Dooley columns, a whole picture emerges, and Dunne has stitched this world together with locating landmark references throughout the series. All movement for Mr. Dooley is defined in relation to the "red bridge" that joins Bridgeport to the rest of Chicago. Archer Road is a lively main street, extending from Dooley's saloon to his rival Schwartzmeister's "down th' way" to the political capital of Bridgeport at Finucane's Hall. Social position is measured by the proximity of one's home to the rolling mills and the gas house. And meandering backdrops for many scenes are provided by the Chicago River and its swampy runoff, Healey's Slough. It is no wonder that Mr. Dooley laments the takeover by newer immigrant groups of Bridgeport's "sacred sites." Thus firmly placed in the imagination, Bridgeport blossoms before us as a believable ethnic subculture with its own customs and ceremonies, a social hierarchy rooted in ancestry, family, and occupation, and a shared perspective on the world. That culture takes shape when Dunne's columns are arranged in thematic groups.

When he first appeared in the *Evening Post* in 1893, Martin Dooley was already over sixty. In the course of the Chicago pieces, Dunne provided him with a plausible, detailed past, stretching back to a childhood Christmas in Ireland, when "th' lads that 'd been away 'd come thrampin' in fr'm Gawd knows where, big lads far fr'm home in Cork an' Limerick an' th' City iv Dublin—come thrampin' home stick in hand to ate their Christmas dinner with th' ol' folks." Mr. Dooley recalls the Famine, when "thim that was scrapin' th' sod f'r a bare livin' fr'm day to day perished like th' cattle in th' field." To demonstrate "the necessity of modesty among the rich," he tells of one tenant farmer "that had thramped acrost th' hills fr'm Galway just in time to rent f'r th' potato rot," and who is maddened by the contrast between his own starving family and that of the lavishly self-indulgent landlord. Goaded to desperation by music and dancing at the big house, the tenant rises up and murders his landlord and is hanged "so fast it med even th' judge smile." Dooley also remembers his own emigration ("We watched th' little ol' island fadin' away behind us, with th' sun sthrikin' th' white house-tops iv Queenstown an' lightin' up th' chimbleys iv Martin Hogan's liquor store"), the storm at sea after which a baby is found dead, and his youthful illusions about America as the place where "all ye had to do was to hold ye'er hat an' th' goold guineas 'd dhrop into it." Arriving in Chicago, he finds that "there was mud to be shoveled an' dhrays to be druv an' beats to be walked. I chose th' dhray; f'r I was niver cut out f'r a copper, an' I'd had me fill iv excavatin'." Other memories include employment restrictions due to Irish county rivalries between Limerick "butthermilks" and Dublin "jackeens," fights and strikes along the old Bridgeport canal during its heyday as a busy artery, and the effects on Chicago's Irish of the Civil War, an 1867 cholera epidemic, and the notorious fire of '71 that "desthroyed old buildin's so that new wans cud be put up."

Mr. Dooley also gives us in unprecedented detail the colors of the Bridgeport passing scene in the 1890s. Social life centers naturally around the Catholic Church. The annual parish fair boasts a shooting gallery, gambling games, "Roddy's Hibernyun band playin' on th' corner," and booths selling everything from prayerbooks to oyster stew. A church production of "The Doomed Markey" stars Denny Hogan in the title role. The parochial school graduation of "Hennessy's youngest" features music by the "St. Ignatius Quintet" and a recitation of "th' speech that Robert Immitt made whin they was goin' to hang him," and an experimental "temperance saloon" closes on its opening night, after the patrons have "dhrunk thimsilves into chollery morbus with coold limonade." Mr. Dooley attends secular events as well. A genealogy lecture in the school hall erupts into a brawl over whose ancestors were kings and whose only dukes. (Dooley declares that, "f'r mesilf I'd as lave have a plastherer f'r a grandfather—me own was marrid to th' niece iv th' parish priest.") At a benefit raffle for an ailing bartender, big O'Malley rolls fifty-four, then swallows the dice to ensure victory. During a family reunion, the emotional climate shifts from nostalgia to name-calling, until "they wasn't two Dooleys in th' hall 'd speak whin th' meetin' broke up." And for the kids, there are football games between the "young Parnells" and the "young Sarsfields," and skating parties on a flooded, iced-over vacant lot. The crooked course of love on Archey Road is the theme of several pieces which corroborate Mr. Dooley's opinion that "f'r an impetchoos an' darin' people th' Irish is th' mos' cowardly whin it comes to mathrimony that iver I heerd tell iv." One example is "Dacey th' plumber, who'd niver 'v marrid if he hadn't got into th' wrong buildin' whin he wint to take out a license f'r his dog, an' got a marridge license instid." For balance, there is the story of young Felix Pendergast, who courts a girl with singular lack of success by playing "Th' Vale iv Avoca" on the cornet under her window at midnight.

Politics was, of course, the most visible and controversial career opportunity for the Irish in American cities in the late nineteenth century. As an experienced political reporter who had been close to the action in Chicago since the 1880s, Dunne was well qualified to describe the Irish contribution to his city's government, and the Dooley political pieces constitute a valuable inside narrative of the Irish-American pursuit of power, and a vivid microcosm of the urban political machine. In addition, because bosses made reluctant historians, Dooley gives us much new information about the electoral process and the workings of ward politics. Several pieces provide insight into an important Chicago tribal rite, the election of aldermen. Dooley recalls with relish his own service as precinct captain in his corner of Ward Six: "I mind th' time whin we r-rolled up twenty-siven hundred dimocratic votes in this wan precinct an' th' on'y wans that voted was th' judges iv election an' th' captains." Or again, "I mind whin McInerney was a-runnin' f'r county clark. Th' lads at th' ya-ards set up all night tuckin' tickets into th' box f'r him. They voted all iv Calvary Symmitry an' was makin' inroads on th' potther's-field." During one election, ten votes for the Republican candidate appear mysteriously, and to avoid disgrace Dorsey feeds them to his favorite goat, Monica. Further reminiscences of rioting between rival torchlight parades, brick-throwing incidents, and bone-bruising nomination procedures support Dooley's judgment that "politics ain't bean-bag. 'Tis a man's game, an' women, childer, cripples an' prohibitionists 'd do well to keep out iv it."

Mr. Dooley also gives us privileged glimpses of the operations of the mayor's office and the city council. To dissuade Hogan's son from becoming a priest, he lists the advantages of being an alderman: "Ye have nowthin' to worry ye. Whin ye'er hungry ye go to a bankit. Whin ye'er broke all ye have to do is to give something away that don't belong to ye. . . . Did ye iver hear iv an aldherman bein' arristed? By gar, I believe th' polisman that 'd arrist an aldherman wouldn't get off short iv tin years." To illustrate cooperation on legislation between the mayor and the council, Dooley relates an exchange between Mayor Carter Harrison and Bridgeport's Billy O'Brien on the issue of installing a garbage dump on the South Side. The quality of appointments made by the spoils system is questioned in the story of Hannigan, the water inspector, who avoided his job to the extent that "he used beer as th' chaser." And the mechanics of dispensing graft become clear in the career of Alderman Dochney, who "was expelled fr'm th' St. Vincent de Pauls, an' ilicted a director iv a bank th' same day."

Dooley also provides several capsule political biographies in which sympathy for the hardships of deprived childhood is tempered by his feeling that nothing so qualifies a man for political life as a talent for roughhouse bullying. One young tough with "th' smell iv Castle Garden [the New York immigrant reception center before Ellis Island] on him" rises from a brawler to the boss of the ward, then commits the unpardonable sin of betraying his community. He moves up to Michigan Avenue and leads the citizen's committee formed to prosecute his old supporters. In other vignettes, political aspiration ruins the lives of decent men. Convinced by self-serving friends that he can win a seat in the state legislature, little Flanagan throws away his savings, job, and house, then loses the election. A similar fate confronts Slattery, "a dacint, quite little lad," who parlays a successful saloon into an aldermanic seat, then sacrifices his reputation to the lure of easy money. Defeated for reelection and deserted by his customers, "all he had left was his champagne thirst." The "education" of an alderman is the theme of another piece, expressive of Dunne's skepticism about the possibility of political reform in Chicago: "Jawny Powers . . . didn't meet so manny men that'd steal a ham an' thin shoot a polisman over it. But he met a lot that'd steal th' whole West Side iv Chicago an' thin fix a gr-rand jury to get away with it."

Mr. Dooley also provides healthy perspective on the American contribution to the Irish freedom movement. He recalls his Uncle Mike's participation in that most bizarre of nationalist events, the 1866 Fenian invasion of Canada: " 'Uncle Mike,' says I to him, 'what's war like, annyhow?' 'Well,' says he, 'in some rayspicts it is like missin' th' last car,' he says; 'an' in other rayspicts 'tis like gettin' gay in front iv a polis station,' he says." Dooley also remembers the printing and dispensing of Irish Republic bonds in the old days, and the talk at meetings of the Clan na Gael, the secret revolutionary organization in the 1880s, about sending dynamiters to England to help "the cause." As a lapsed Clansman, a onetime believer in violent revolution who now espouses a milder view, he takes satiric advantage of the Clan's alphabetical codes, secret handshakes, and elaborate structure of officers and "camps."

Nationalist events in Dunne's own time also evoked immediate responses. The passage of the second Home Rule bill in the House of Commons in 1893, Gladstone's retirement in 1894, and the British cabinet crisis of 1895 are all noted by Mr. Dooley, who refuses to be stampeded into believing that Irish freedom is close at hand: "ye can't grow flowers in a granite block, . . . much less whin th' first shoot 'd be thrampled under foot without pity. 'Tis aisy f'r us over here with our bellies full, to talk iv th' cowardice iv th' Irish; but what would ye have wan man iv thim do again a rig'mint? . . . No, faith, Jawn, there's no soil in Ireland f'r th' greatness iv th' race." About the contributions of the Chicago Irish to the cause, Mr. Dooley has mixed emotions: sympathy for the rank-and-file nationalists, and suspicion for the motives of their leaders. "Did ye iver," he asks in 1895, "see a man that wanted to free Ireland th' day afther to-morrah that didn't run f'r aldherman soon or late"? He carefully scrutinizes the cluster of nationalist commemorations in his community, including the annual August 15th picnic of Chicago's United Irish Societies and the St. Patrick's Day parade. Invariably, he finds these events to be riddled with hypocrisy and self-delusion and his reports often include parodies of the excesses and simplifications of nationalist oratory. With these columns, Dunne made enemies among Irish nationalist editors, including Chicago's John Finerty, who frequently lambasted him editorially, and New York's Patrick Ford, who refused to advertise collections of the Dooley pieces. But to those who listened, Mr. Dooley offered clear, rational commentary on matters that more often stirred the fanatic heart.

To my mind, Dunne's greatest contribution to Chicago and American history and literature is his solid and sympathetic characterization of Mr. Dooley's working-class-immigrant clientele. In column after column, he created characters and situations corroborating the faith of the literary realists in the possibility of dignity, heroism, and tragedy in the common lives of common people. There is, for example, the story of the old widower Shaughnessy, "a quite [quiet] man that come into th' road befure th' fire," who "wurruked f'r Larkin, th' conthractor, f'r near twenty years without skip or break, an' seen th' fam'ly grow up be candle-light." His family history reads like an O'Neill tragedy in miniature. Driven reluctantly toward the priesthood, the oldest boy dies bitterly of consumption. The second son is a charming ne'er-do-well who burns himself out and also dies young. As for the first daughter, Mr. Dooley says only that "she didn't die; but, th' less said, th' sooner mended."

Further deaths and desertions leave Shaughnessy with one child, Theresa, who "thought on'y iv th' ol' man, an' he leaned on her as if she was a crutch. She was out to meet him in th' avnin'; an' in th' mornin' he, th' simple ol' man, 'd stop to blow a kiss at her an' wave his dinner-pail, lookin' up an' down th' r-road to see that no wan was watchin' him." In time, Theresa makes a good marriage — to the "prisident iv th' sodality" — but in relieving the weight of the family's accumulated social failure, she leaves her father with a worse burden. After the wedding reception, Mr. Dooley waits up for a time with the old man, and leaves with us a simple and powerful image of his loneliness: "Him an' me sat a long time smokin' across th' stove. Fin'lly, says I, 'Well,' I says, 'I must be movin'.' 'What's th' hurry?' says he. 'I've got to go,' says I. 'Wait a moment,' says he. 'Theresa 'll' — He stopped right there f'r a minyit, holdin' to th' back iv th' chair. 'Well,' says he, 'if ye've got to go, ye must,' he says. 'I'll show ye out,' he says. An' he come with me to th' dure, holdin' th' lamp over his head. I looked back at him as I wint by; an' he was settin' be th' stove, with his elbows on his knees an' th' empty pipe between his teeth."

Dunne had begun this piece with a reflection on the nature of heroism that reveals his purpose: "Jawn, . . . whin ye come to think iv it, th' heroes iv th' wurruld, — an' be thim I mean th' lads that've buckled on th' gloves, an' gone out to do th' best they cud, — they ain't in it with th' quite people nayether you nor me hears tell iv fr'm wan end iv th' year to another." That Dunne is consciously revising accepted notions of heroism in these pieces is also clear in the Memorial Day column of 1894, where Mr. Dooley remarks that "th' sojers has thim that'll fire salutes over their graves an' la-ads to talk about thim, but there's none but th' widdy f'r to break her hear-rt above th' poor soul that died afther his hands had tur-rned to leather fr'm handlin' a pick." Other quiet heroes in the Dooley pantheon include little Tim Clancy, "the Optimist," who copes cheerfully with the problems of supporting a family of ten on "wan twinty-five a day — whin he wurruks" in the steel mill, and Pat Doherty, a legitimate Civil War hero who has returned quietly to his job at the mill, while blowhards who never left Chicago wave the bloody shirt. Infuriated by the Memorial Day mouthings of a political hack in Dooley's saloon, Doherty delivers a withering blast against war and hypocrisy:

> Doherty was movin' up to him. "What rig'ment?" says he. "What's that?" says O'Toole. "Did ye inlist in th' army, brave man?" says Pat. "I swore him over age," says I. "Was ye dhrafted in?" says th' little man. "No," says O'Toole. "Him an' me was in th' same cellar," says I. "Did ye iver hear iv Ree-saca, 'r Vicksburg, 'r Lookout Mountain?" th' little man wint on. "Did

anny man iver shoot at ye with annything but a siltzer bottle? Did ye iver have to lay on ye'er stummick with ye'er nose burrid in th' Lord knows what while things was whistlin' over ye that, if they iver stopped whistlin', 'd make ye'er backbone look like a broom? Did ye iver see a man that ye'd slept with th' night befure cough, an' go out with his hooks ahead iv his face? Did ye iver have to wipe ye'er most intimate frinds off ye'er clothes, whin ye wint home at night? Where was he durin' th' war?" he says. "He was dhrivin' a grocery wagon f'r Philip Reidy," says th' little man. "He don't want anny wan to get onto him," says I.

Dunne also extends the literary potential of the common life into the dimension of tragedy. Exemplary here are his stories of Chicago firemen, who risked their lives daily in their tinder-box city, "consthructed," in Mr. Dooley's words, "f'r poor people out iv nice varnished pine an' cotton waste." The most admired man in Bridgeport, fireman Mike Clancy performs feats of great and irrational courage that smack of hubris. He drives the hose cart around corners on one wheel, dives into falling buildings, and rescues people by descending the ladder head first, because "I seen a man do it at th' Lyceem whin I was a kid." Clancy is flawed in that he doesn't know when to quit. Promising his wife that he will retire after "wan more good fire . . . a rale good ol' hot wan," the fireman goes off to his death. The piece ends with a memorable image of the common man as tragic hero, one of the few such images indigenous to the Irish-American community in the nineteenth century: " 'Oh,' he says, bringin' his fist down, 'wan more an' I'll quit.' An' he did, Jawn. Th' day th' Carpenter Brothers' box factory burnt. 'Twas wan iv thim big, fine-lookin' buildings that pious men built out iv celluloid an' plasther iv Paris. An' Clancy was wan iv th' men undher whin th' wall fell. I seen thim bringin' him home; an' th' little woman met him at th' dure, rumplin' her apron in her hands."

Remarkable in these sketches is Dunne's ability to sympathize, through Mr. Dooley, with the situations of the Bridgeport heroes and victims. And the key to that sympathy, as to the realism of the pieces, is in Dunne's fully imagined conception of Dooley as a member of the community he describes. That conception comes through clearly in two sketches of the lives of young Bridgeport criminals. Jack Carey, "the idle apprentice," is "a thief at tin year," in the city jail at twelve, and "up to anny game" from then on. Branded a chronic troublemaker, Carey is hounded by the police, and a bitter feud develops between him and a fellow Bridgeporter, Officer Clancy, who succeeds in getting Carey sent "over th' road" to the state penitentiary. Upon his release, Carey murders Clancy in broad daylight in the middle of Archer Avenue, and is himself shot down by a squad of police. For Dooley's patron John

McKenna, the moral is clear: "It served him right." But Mr. Dooley is not so sure: "Who? . . . Carey or Clancy?" is his ending question. The spectacle of two Bridgeporters turning against and destroying each other has left him too disturbed to be able to sort out causes and assign blame. A similar story is that of a child of religious parents, Petey Scanlan, who "growed up fr'm bein' a curly-haired angel f'r to be th' toughest villyun in th' r-road." His career ends after he had robbed a store, terrorized Bridgeport, and fled to his parents' home. Having berated Lt. Cassidy for making a scandal before her neighbors, Mrs. Scanlan leads Petey to the patrol wagon on her arm, and is left "settin' in a big chair with her apron in her hands an' th' picture iv th' lad th' day he made his first c'munion in her lap." Again, Mr. Dooley can only shake his head in bewilderment: "What was it at all, at all? Sometimes I think they'se poison in th' life iv a big city. Th' flowers won't grow here no more thin they wud in a tannery, an' th' bur-rds have no song; an' th' childher iv dacint men an' women come up hard in th' mouth an' with their hands raised again their kind."

These are not the reactions of Finley Peter Dunne, a sophisticated city editor with progressive leanings, but of Martin Dooley, an aging Irish immigrant, puzzled, pained, and apprehensive at these signs that his own community is dissolving.

Despite its distinctive coloration, Bridgeport in the 1890s was not a stable community. Many forces for change were operating, most of them related to the complex process known to that time as "melting" into American life. Like other immigrant groups, the Irish found themselves caught between two worlds, and forced to make uncomfortable compromises in order to become "assimilated." By the nineties, the children of the Famine immigrants (those who, as Mr. Dooley remarks, had been "born away from home") were making it into the American middle class in large numbers—but not without cost to their sense of identity as individuals and as an ethnic group. The stairway of upward mobility was strewn with cases of swallowed pride and stifled traditions, and the Dooley pieces embody the peculiar mixture of fulfillment and frustration that went along with being Irish in America at that time. In the first place, the city itself would not hold still. In keeping with the familiar rhythm of neighborhood invasion by poorer groups while the older residents move up and out, the ethnic makeup of Bridgeport was changing rapidly in the nineties. Mr. Dooley contrasts the "fightin' tinth precint" in the old days, when it was the stronghold of "ancient Hellenic" heroes from Mayo and Tipperary, and the same precinct in 1897, by which time "th' Hannigans an' Leonidases an' Caseys" have moved out, "havin' made their pile," and "Polish Jews an' Swedes an' Germans an'

Hollanders" have "swarmed in, settlin' down on th' sacred sites." A particularly disturbing sign of "change an' decay" is the appointment of "a Polacker" as tender of the strategic "red bridge," which takes control of the gate to Bridgeport out of Irish hands.

The American dream of success also drove damaging wedges into the immigrant community, as Mr. Dooley notes in stories about hardhearted Irish landlords, one of whom "had acres an' acres on Halsted Sthreet, an' tinants be th' scoor that prayed at nights f'r him that he might live long an' taste sorrow." In several pieces Irish landlords evict Irish tenants, which illustrates how land- and money-hunger are breaking up Bridgeport. (Mr. Dooley explains that a career in real estate "includes near ivrything fr'm vagrancy to manslaughter.") Another force for change is the epidemic disease of galloping respectability, and the Dooley pieces are full of references to the disappearance of the old rough-and-tumble in favor of the more insidious scramble for genteel status. For example, in Mr. Dooley's youth, only people who were under arrest got their names in the paper; now, "I see hard wurrukin' men thrampin' down to the newspaper offices with little items about a christenin' or a wake an' havin' it read to thim in th' mornin' at breakfuss befure they start to th' mills." Another case in point is the running debate between Mr. and Mrs. Hogan on the subject of naming their children: " 'Ye'll be namin' no more children iv mine out iv dime novels,' says Hogan. 'An' ye'll name no more iv mine out iv th' payroll iv th' bridge departmint,' says she. 'D'ye think I'm going to sind th' child out into th' wurruld with a name that'll keep him from anny employment but goin' on th' polis foorce?' " At the end of this piece, Mr. Dooley is on hand to watch the tenth Hogan child christened—Augustus.

Signs of dissolving cultural unity naturally appeared early among Bridgeport's young people, and Dunne created a group of characters who reveal the problems of a generation gap compounded by immigration. Most visible here is Molly Donahue, a lively, fad-conscious Bridgeport girl who squares off against her Irish father in a half-dozen Dooley pieces. She first scandalizes the neighborhood by riding a bicycle down Archer Avenue in bloomers, after which she is sent off to church, where she receives "a pinance th' like iv which ain't been knowed in Bridgeport since Cassidy said Char-les Stewart Parnell was a bigger man thin th' pope." In succeeding appearances, Molly campaigns for the vote, for Elizabeth Cady Stanton's revised "Woman's" Bible, and for the liberation of "the new woman." Her piano lessons cause a cultural disagreement in the family about the relative merits of "Choochooski" and "The Rambler from Clare," and the latter is condemned as a "low chune" by Mrs. Donahue, who tells her husband, "if ye want to hear that kind iv chune, ye can go down to Finucane's Hall an' call in Crowley, th' blind piper."

Higher education also begins to be possible for the Irish in the nineties, and Bridgeport boys come trooping home from Notre Dame with bicycles, long hair, and delusions of superiority. In one essay, an educated son so intimidates his father that "he wore his shoes afther supper an' had to r-roll th' growler f'r a pint in a handbag." [To "roll the growler" was to fetch beer in a bucket from a saloon.] A last, ironic word on the crumbling of ties between the generations is the story of miserly landlord Ahearn, who "bought pieces iv th' prairie, an' starved an' bought more, an' starved an' starved till his heart was shrivelled up like a washerwoman's hand." All that he denies himself and his tenants, Ahearn lavishes on his poor-spirited only son, "a slow, tired, aisy-goin', shamblin' la-ad,—th' sort that'd wrench th' heart iv a father like Ahearn." After a final disappointment, Ahearn "tur-rned like a tiger on th' boy an' sthruck him with his ol' leathery hand." The son walks out of the house for good, leaving his father "standin' there, as we used to say iv th' fox in th' ol' counthry, cornered between th' river an' th' wall."

The greatest force against community in Bridgeport in the nineties was poverty. The national depression of 1893–98 was aggravated in Chicago by an exploding immigrant population, labor unrest, and bitter-cold winters. The suffering of Bridgeport's poor is a frequent Dooley topic, and he faces it, not with the detachment of a social scientist, but with the mingled anger, frustration, and compassion of a member of the afflicted culture. The result is a chunk of living social history available nowhere else.

An important theme is the difference between heartless, humiliating organized relief programs and personal charity, dispensed with consideration for the pride of the recipient. Out-of-work laborer Callaghan tells the sanctimonious St. Vincent de Pauls to "take ye'er charity, an' shove it down ye'er throats," even though the cost of refusal is his family's health. And Mrs. Hagan, the wife of a blacklisted railroad worker, drives the Ladies' Aid Society from her door, even though "some iv thim was f'r foorcin' their way in an' takin' an invintory." On the other hand, Dooley, himself, provides examples of the tactful practice of personal charity. He buys Christmas presents for a mother and children who have just been deserted, John McKenna finds him taking care of a baby in the saloon's back room, and when the little Grady girl comes into the shop in a snowstorm to fetch beer for her alcoholic father, Dooley puts five dollars in his pocket, closes up early, and sets off "to lick Grady."

Several pieces underscore the contrast, at its most blatant in American cities in the nineties, between the lives of the rich and the poor. Mrs.

Mulligan takes her sick baby to the lake for a change of air, but is refused passage through the Illinois Central Railroad's toll gate, which prompts Hennessy to suggest "a new caddychism. It'll go like this: 'Who made ye?' 'Th' Illinye Cinthral made me.' . . . They's naw use teachin' th' childher what ain't thrue. What's th' good iv tellin' thim that th' Lord made th' wurruld whin they'll grow up an' find it in th' possission iv th' Illinye Cinthral?' " The piece ends grimly, with Mr. Dooley's prediction that "they'll be another sthring iv crape on Mulligan's dure tomo-rah mornin'." In another column, the contrasting funerals of wealthy "Gran'pah Grogan" and a poor "Connock man up back iv th' dumps" lead Dooley to a meditation on the possible effects of price-fixing by the Beef Trust on the Connacht man's children: "Spring's come on. Th' grass is growin' good; an', if th' Connock man's children back iv th' dumps can't get meat, they can eat hay." During the famous Pullman strike of 1894, Dooley criticizes George Pullman's callousness with a harsh analogy between Chicago during the strike and Ireland in the famine years: "Musha, but 'tis a sound to dhrive ye'er heart cold whin a woman sobs an' th' young wans cries, an' both because there's no bread in th' house." Meanwhile, Pullman sits up in his mansion, ordering "a bottle iv champagne an' a piece iv crambree pie. . . . He cares no more f'r thim little matthers iv life an' death thin I do f'r O'Connor's tab."

Dunne brought a Swiftian savage indignation to his strongest poverty pieces, many of which were written during the winter of 1896–97, the fourth in a row of hard times in Chicago, and the worst. In one, a laid-off immigrant mill worker, Sobieski, is driven by desperation and his eight freezing children to pick up bits of coal on the railroad tracks, a "far worse" crime, says Mr. Dooley, "thin breakin' th' intherstate commerce act." Surprised by a watchman and frightened of his gun, Sobieski starts to run away, and is shot in the back. Then he "pitched over on his face, thried to further injure th' comp'ny be pullin' up th' rails with his hands, an' thin passed to where—him bein' a Pole, an' dyin' in such a horrible sin—they'se no need iv coal iv anny kind." Had he been properly "educated," Dooley suggests, Sobieski would not have been in the railroad yard at all, but "comfortably joltin' th' watchman's boss in a dark alley downtown. Idyacation is a gr-reat thing." The biting cynicism here indicates the gravity of the crisis in Chicago, and Dunne's frustration concerning its alleviation. Another memorable piece is the haunting story of Mother Clancy, a "black" Galway woman "from bechune mountain and sea," who finds herself destitute on Bridgeport's alien soil. For remaining stoically aloof, she is feared by her neighbors. For speaking Gaelic to herself and her fatherless son, she is branded a witch, and her house is stoned. During the terrible winter, with the mills shut down and smallpox sweeping the city, Mother Clancy holds out fiercely against going on relief, but finally appears one day at the Society for the Relief of the Deserving Poor, looking "tin feet tall an' all white cheek bones an' burnin' black eyes." She is received by society chairman Dougherty, who cuts her to the quick: " 'Well, me good woman,' says he, 'ye'll undherstand that th' comity is much besieged be th' imporchunities iv th' poor,' he says. 'We can't do anything f'r ye on ye're own say so, but we'll sind a man to invistigate ye're case, an',' he says, 'we'll attind to ye.' " A few days later, Dougherty remembers the case, and drops around to the poor woman's home, where he meets the county undertaker's wagon and the priest, who steers him away with the judgment that "we were both late." Mother Clancy dies through a combination of her own pride and community neglect, and, as Mr. Dooley recognizes, the great tragedy here is that everyone in this story is Irish. Sometimes, the price of respectability was very high indeed. Dunne chose not to republish these poverty pieces, for he seems to have bridled at their biting social criticism. While preparing the 1899 collection, *Mr. Dooley in the Hearts of His Countrymen,* he wrote his publisher that "I have piled up my old Dooleys—enough for ten books—none of which could be read by a taxpayer."[3] Still, in spite of Dunne's own misgivings, this group of columns is a moving testament of concern for the urban poor, and our only firsthand account of a crisis potentially as destructive to the Chicago Irish community as the Famine had been to the peasants of Ireland.

All through the 1890s, Mr. Dooley provided Chicagoans with weekly examples of the appropriateness for serious literature of the common speech and everyday life of Irish immigrants and their children. Had Finley Peter Dunne pursued a career in Chicago fiction instead of turning to New York and national commentary, Petey Scanlan might, I suppose, have become the Studs Lonigan of his generation. We should certainly, however, be grateful for small blessings—for the three hundred columns in which with stunning conciseness Dunne has given us the Irish of Bridgeport.

Born a few years on either side of Finley Peter Dunne, Kate McPhelim Cleary and Clara E. Laughlin were the first women to contribute significantly to the literature of Irish Chicago. Because their best work is a body of fiction that was published in the first decade of the twentieth century, Cleary and Laughlin fill the void left by Mr. Dooley's abdication to New York in 1900 and point ahead to the culminating accomplishment of James T. Farrell's novels.

Kate McPhelim was the daughter of Irish immigrants who met and married in New Brunswick. Widowed with three small children, her mother took the family back to Ireland for a time, then to Philadelphia, and finally to Chicago, where Kate attended St. Xavier's Convent School and began selling her poems to periodicals at the age of thirteen. As with Finley Peter Dunne, Chicago journalism was important to her development as a writer. In fact, at one time her whole family was working for the Chicago *Tribune* — Mrs. McPhelim contributing poems and essays; her son Edward, dramatic criticism; son Frank, general reporting; and Kate, short stories. In 1884, at the age of twenty-one, Kate married Michael T. Cleary and accompanied him to the Nebraska prairie town of Hubbell to set up in the lumber business. There, Kate Cleary had six children, became a legendary cook (contributing to *Good Housekeeping* magazine), kept a hospitable, book-laden home (known throughout the area as a cultural haven), and continued to publish fiction and poetry. In 1898, the family returned to Chicago, where business reverses forced her to turn out potboilers, sometimes at the rate of a short story a day. Cleary's better fiction was, however, published widely in respected journals such as *Century, Cosmopolitan, Harper's, Lippincott's,* and *McClure's* magazines, and she was negotiating with Houghton, Mifflin Company to publish a collection of her stories before she died in 1905 at age forty-two.[4]

Reflecting her own odyssey, Cleary's best fiction deals with the lives of Irish-Americans in Chicago and in rural Nebraska. A typical Chicago story is "The Mission of Kitty Malone," published in *McClure's* in 1901, which describes a destitute couple from Tipperary, forty-nine years married, who are living in a cheap one-room apartment on Blue Island Avenue in the old Nineteenth Ward.[5] Weakened by pneumonia, Dennis Malone can hardly be left alone, and his wife Kitty is forced to go up to city hall to get a relief ticket in order to purchase a side of bacon for Thanksgiving dinner. In a scene reminiscent of Mr. Dooley's story of Mother Clancy, the Galway woman, the questions of the city social worker made Kitty Malone burn with shame. The experience so disturbs her that she is bumped by a passing streetcar, and her food purchases are dropped and ruined. She returns, defeated, to the apartment, but the Malones are saved by the return of their son from the Philippine war with money, a turkey, and a happy Thanksgiving. Although this ending edges it into the potboiling category, the story is nonetheless notable for its moving description of the devoted immigrant couple, the dilemma of their poverty, and the shame of going on relief.

The Nebraska stories provide an effective antidote to the anti-urban pastoralism of such groups as the Irish Catholic Colonization Society, who believed that moving to the country would solve all of Irish-America's problems. Cleary's depiction of the midwest rural alternative

has the powerful bleakness of Hamlin Garland's *Main-Traveled Roads,*
that 1891 collection of fictional revisions of the agrarian myth.

In "Feet of Clay," a light-hearted young city girl marries a western
farmer and goes out to Kansas with him, unprepared for the hard, lonely
life and her vindictive mother-in-law: "always alert were those sharp
black eyes of hers; always curved in a sneering smile her thin white lips.
She was not to be won over or conciliated." After his mother's death, the
farmer turns callous and brutal, and the wife, driven beyond strength
and hope, goes mad. She begins to hear "the voices of the corn, . . . a
tawny, turbulent ocean through which she could not battle," murmuring,
"Forever, ever, ever." When she is taken away, the neighbors conclude
that "there had been nothing in her life to cause insanity. It must have
been hereditary." Cleary began this powerful story with a chilling interior monologue: "Sometimes it seemed to her that she could endure
everything save the silence. That was terrible. Days when Barret was too
far in the corn for the rattle of the machine he drove to reach her, she
could feel the silence settling down upon her like a heavy cloud. Then, if
she were washing the dishes, she used to clatter them needlessly to make
some sound. But all that was before she began to hear the voices of the
corn."

In "The Stepmother," another powerful story, first published in
McClure's in 1901, Cleary's focus is the second wife of Oliver Carney, a
luckless, lazy, and selfish farmer who has fled business failures in the
East to try his hand at farming in Nebraska, and who now fills his empty
days with drinking steady enough to mitigate his sense of failure. A
former schoolteacher with lively, hopeful ideas, the second Mrs. Carney
has been drained by years of drudgery and loneliness. The story takes
place on Memorial Day, which Mrs. Carney is resigned to spending
alone, as her courting stepson Dan has elected to take a neighboring
farm girl to town for the festivities, thereby ignoring the fact that no one
has visited the farm since Christmas, and his stepmother hasn't been to
town for over a year. (Sleeping off a morning drunk in a chair, Oliver
Carney isn't about to go anywhere.) A terrifying dust storm at the end of
the story reinforces the picture here of the hard life on this Nebraska
farm, which seems an alien place, inimical to normal social intercourse,
and Cleary also evokes the emotional impoverishment that follows from
the bleak physical setting. She notes that these "prairie people" are
ashamed of emotional display, giving "perfunctory kisses . . . at the marriage feast or before the funeral," and avoiding expressions of affection
in daily life. Certainly, there is little communication in the Carney
family, and when his stepmother has one of her "heart spells," Dan
Carney first helps and soothes her, and then feels "ashamed of the

compassionate impulse which had temporarily mastered him." Her husband asleep, her sons in town, Mrs. Carney has a final stroke while trying to take the cows in during the dust storm. Before dying, she has time only to bless her son Dan and admonish him not to be too hard on his intended wife, for life itself is hard enough on the prairie. Cleary has not mitigated her sense of the bleakness of this woman's life and death.

Though set in Nebraska, Cleary's compassionate portrayals of the sufferings of Irish-American women have wider relevance as well. Her presentations of harsh, repetitive labor and lonely isolation even within the family also ring true for ethnic women in urban settings such as Chicago. Indeed, Cleary's Nebraska stories contain early examples of an important theme in later fiction about the Chicago Irish, notably the novels of James T. Farrell, where the absence of communicated feeling within families leads to crippling emotional impoverishment.

In a much lighter vein are Cleary's several treatments of the familiar second-generation-ethnic theme of the perils of respectability. Like King Lear, old Jimmy Nelson in "How Jimmy Ran Away" has bequeathed his property too soon to his thankless son and daughter. After twelve years of inconsiderate insults, life with the daughter becomes too painful, and Jimmy, now seventy, takes off across Nebraska to seek refuge with his son. But Samuel Nelson has become a successful grain dealer, and his snobbish wife and children are scandalized by Jimmy's old clothes and rough ways. When Samuel gets his father a furnished room in the town, the old man decides to return to his daughter's house, as the lesser of two evils. There is a happier ending to "Jim Peterson's Pension," in which an injured worker finally gets fifteen years' back pension in 1895. His wife, who has been scrubbing floors since 1880, immediately comes down with an attack of gentility. Mrs. Peterson arrays her whole family in Kansas City finery, makes a special trip to Chicago for pictures (chosen for their heavy gilt frames), demands that her daughter Mary be addressed as Marie, and throws ice-cream socials through the boiling Nebraska summer. The money is soon gone, however, and Mrs. Peterson returns to normal, sadder but wiser.

Cleary takes a humorous backward look at her own convent education in "An Ornament to Society." To keep a promise to his dead wife, Jack Harrowsby tries to turn their only child, Cleopatra, into "an ornament to sassiety" by forcing her to take lessons in music, painting, and rickrack. A dismal failure at all three, poor Cleo would much rather be out on the farm breaking horses and milking the cows. She is then sent to a convent, not for the religious training, but because a neighbor has declared that the nuns "transmogrified" her daughter: "When it comes to genteel manners, an' the kind of behavior Queens has when they switches their trains straight an' stands up to receive their courtiers and penitentiaries," says the neighbor, "then I say, give me a convent." Like Mrs. Peterson, Jack Harrowsby also finally sees the light, and allows the unhappy Cleo to quit the convent school and return to the life she loves on the farm.

In her brief, active, and assiduous life, Kate Cleary published hundreds of stories, sketches, poems, and essays. She even had time for a novel, *Like a Gallant Lady,* which appeared in Chicago in 1897. In it, a romantic adventure plot is laid against a realistic background of the desolate Nebraska prairie. "The only people who associate solitude, romance and all that sort of thing with the plains," declares one character at the end of the novel, "are those who write about them without having had any personal experience."[6] Her best work establishes Kate Cleary as an Irish-American, Chicago-bred literary realist of great promise—unfulfilled because of her family commitments, the economic troubles that drove her to write romantic formula fiction, and her early death. She deserves to be remembered as a good writer and a courageous woman.

The second bridging figure between Dunne and Farrell was also the daughter of immigrants. Clara Laughlin's father was born at Ballymena, near Belfast, in 1841. There, he married a woman named McKee in 1870, and shortly after the newlyweds emigrated to Milwaukee. Her family in America was fairly well off for most of Clara's childhood, which was spent in New York City, where she was born in 1873, in Milwaukee, and in Chicago, where she attended the North Division High School for four years. After her father's death in 1891, Clara's mother rented a large house on Fullerton Avenue on the North Side and began to take in boarders. The following year, Clara Laughlin got her first job in Chicago journalism, at the Protestant weekly, the *Interior.* From there, she began to have essays and stories accepted more widely, and later in the 1890s she landed an editorial position at *McClure's Magazine.* Laughlin became a popular sentimental/genteel writer with her first published novels, *The Evolution of a Girl's Ideal* (1902), *When Joy Begins* ("A Little Story of the Woman-Heart," 1905), and *Felicity* (1907), and she went on to write a number of successful travel books as well.

Her one foray into realistic fiction was the 1910 novel, *"Just Folks",* which constitutes Laughlin's contribution to the literary chronicle of Irish Chicago.[7] The novel describes the poverty-stricken Casey family, whose situation was based on a real Irish family of Laughlin's acquaintance, who lived in a back basement in the old Nineteenth Ward, not far from Hull-House. Published first as a series of stories in *McClure's* and *Ainslie's* magazines between 1907 and 1910, the novel adds the unifying consciousness of a narrator, young Beth Tully, an idealistic juvenile court probation officer for the ward, who rents a room above Monahan's Grocery on Maxwell Street, not far from Hull-House. In the line of duty, Beth soon meets Mary Casey, who lives in a back basement on Henry Street with her unemployed, sometimes drinking husband and seven surviving children. (Two others have died.) Like several Dooley pieces and Farrell novels, *"Just Folks"* documents the shifting character of Chicago neighborhoods. The Caseys have been left behind in the Irish march to better, middle-class communities, and, thanks to the new immigration, their neighbors are now mostly Jewish.

By exposure to the Casey family's many troubles, Beth Tully learns the complexity of human and urban relations and her limits as an aid to alleviating social problems. The problems begin with "Pa"—Patrick Casey, who is presented with realistic depth as a charming ne'er-do-well who also loves and is loved by his family. With Mr. Micawber, Pa believes that something—specifically a new job in his trade of stonecutter— will turn up. Even Beth Tully, infuriated by his drinking and apparent shiftlessness, comes to realize that the man is not a hypocrite: he believes his own disarmingly earnest plans for the future; what he lacks is the ability to follow through. Mary Casey, on the other hand, is a true matriarch, holding her family together by hard work, sheer determination, and prayers to the Blessed Virgin. (The ultimate such character will be Mary O'Flaherty in Farrell's O'Neill-O'Flaherty series of five novels.) Beth Tully gets close to Mary Casey through a coincidence: Mary Keegan had "worked out" in the Tully family twenty years earlier, just before her marriage to Patrick Casey. Mary's blind spot, but also the cornerstone of her sustaining faith, is her love for her husband, and in another example of realistic complexity, Laughlin is careful to present their relationship as a bittersweet affair.

The sweetness emerges in the contrast between Mary Casey and her respectable, middle-class sister, Mrs. Foley, who "lived beyond the confines of the Ghetto and felt frank commiseration for her poor relations." Like the Dooley characters who always lose more than they gain in becoming "ginteel," Mrs. Foley is a "sickly, broken-spirited, little dyspeptic," a hypochondriac, and married to a cold man who "had wished she would die and have done with her sickly wails." In addition, the rise of the Foleys to a "swell establishment" on West Lake Street has been marred by the deaths of their ten children, most of them in infancy. Laughlin presents the Caseys' teeming cellar as clearly preferable to the moribund Foley apartment, with its "front parlor with a 'stuffed suit,' and a patent rocker and a mantel-shelf shrouded in a voluminous purple 'drape' and burdened with innumerable fancy cups and vases." The difference between the two families is reinforced when Mary Casey finds herself expecting another child. The news disturbs Beth Tully until Mary explains her feelings: "I ain't had much happiness, be your way o' t'inkin', Miss Tully, but whin I look back an' misure it all up, I wouldn' trade me hard life wid its baby fingers clutchin' at me brist, fer the aisiest single life anny woman iver lived. An' I can't be sorry 'bout the new wan. I know we'll git along, some way." Moreover, so pleased is Patrick Casey that with a characteristic stroke, he goes out and buys an encyclopedia on time, starts one child on "A" and another on "M," and looks forward eagerly to when "the new wan git so he kin rade."

The dark side of this hard life soon intrudes, though. The new baby dies after only a few days of life. Waked on a bier of yellow kitchen chairs, he gets to share for free an expensive funeral, thanks to the kindness of the priest and the other bereaved family, and "to ride to Calvary in the rich young man's hearse." Mary Casey says tearfully of her lost son, "Seem like he was born t' be lucky, an' he died before he had a chance t' find it out." In fact, the Casey children suffer the most from their family's poverty, and Laughlin certainly avoids indulging in a romanticized view of slum life in telling their stories. Eldest son Mikey had gone to work at eleven "in a wall-paper factory, where he worked in a steaming room whose temperature averaged 110 degrees." As a result, he contracted paint poisoning and became "quare in the head," and a series of small scrapes with the law has landed him in reform school. Eldest daughter Angela Ann had started work at twelve as a cash-girl, and her subsequent jobs have included bundle-wrapping, pasting labels on medicine bottles, and working in a mail-order business for thirty-nine-cent gold rings. Presently sixteen and a bundle-wrapper again, "she had no ability, no prospects—she drifted from job to job, squeezing in, unchallenged, at rush seasons and being remorselessly let off the moment it became possible to weed the unfit from the fit." And all this time, she dutifully brings her pay envelopes home untouched: "she had never bought a dress, nor even a shirt-waist."

Angela Ann is trapped. With no clothes to attract them and no place to entertain, she has no boyfriends. Without money, she cannot go out to have girlish fun. She is bitterly aware of the difference between her situation and that of "the belle of Henry Street," Gertie O'Malley, a policeman's daughter with a parlor, a pretty silk dress, "and a whole court of Nineteenth Ward beaus." A moral dilemma comes when Angela Ann accepts a red dress from a lecherous fellow worker. Beth Tully persuades her to return the dress, but the experience is a crisis for her as well, for Beth realizes that although she believes in "the rewards of virtue," it may be "asking too much of Angela to believe in them too."

Although she tells Angela that "if you keep sweet and good, *some* fine young man'll come along and make you a good husband," Beth is silenced by the girl's reply: "It's in the plays an' the story-books an' the Advice to the Lovelorn; but it ain't so! The girls that's free an' aisy wid the min gits the most beaus—an' thim that tries to do right gits laughed at, an' called fools."

Laughlin thus presents realistically the "starvation of many sorts" that ultimately drives Angela Ann to leave home. The last straw is the news that her mother is expecting again, and Angela answers the advertisement of an unscrupulous dramatic agent, who packs her off to the downstate coal-mining area in a singing, dancing, and carousing "road company." Ironically, Patrick Casey is scandalized by the blow to the family's reputation, declaring that "She 've disgraced us, an' she be dead t' me," and Mary Casey alone voices parental concern: "If I could only know she had a roof over her head an' a fire t' kape her warm!" Several months later, Angela Ann returns, ill and contrite; and although she cannot answer her mother's question, "Tell me ye've kep' dacint, gyurl," she is nonetheless forgiven and taken back into the family. Again, the "respectable" values are called into question. Beth Tully comes to see, without judging, that "expediency" governs "many people's morals," and Mary Casey's heartfelt sympathy for her daughter is presented as clearly preferable to her husband's hypocritical moralizing. Now this is strong stuff for a woman writer in 1910. Laughlin's position here has much in common with the pioneering, piercing critique of genteel values in Kate O'Flaherty Chopin's astonishing novel of 1899, *The Awakening,* in which the heroine refutes hypocrisy and boredom with her own suicide.

In *"Just Folks"* the prodigal's return is facilitated by the sad, surprising news that greets her: her father has died—a hero. Having picked up a stonecutting job in a mining town, Patrick Casey had gone off to southern Illinois. When a mine cave-in trapped four hundred men, he had volunteered for the rescue attempt and had been killed. Mary Casey's reaction is, I think, a peculiarly Irish combination of fatalism and hopefulness about death. She had dreamed her husband a hero, and now her faith in him has been vindicated. By dying, Patrick has bequeathed his children "a name ye kin be proud of." And Mary's last word on the subject is unambiguous: "Thank God fer your *chance,* Patsy b'y!"

Mary Casey is an archetypal Irish-American matriarch, and her honest reactions are to be trusted: joy at the birth of a new child, grief at her baby's death and her daughter's desertion, forgiveness at her daughter's return, and even the mixture of sadness and pride at her husband's martyrdom. It is she who keeps the false standards of genteel respectability at bay, for, as Beth Tully recognizes, she is the reality principle of

Laughlin's novel: "Mary Casey lived too deeply and truly to miss any essential element of life. There was nothing more splendidly real about her than the way shade and shine played on each other's heels in her days." Unfortunately, the character of Mary Casey and the realistic picture of life among the urban poor in *"Just Folks"* are unique in the Laughlin canon, which is otherwise populated with a parade of cardboard gentlefolk in idealized, romantic settings. For a writer committed to telling their whole story, the Chicago Irish had twenty years more to wait.

At the beginning of his own first novel, *Young Lonigan: A Boyhood in Chicago Streets* (1932), James T. Farrell forges a link with his great fellow chronicler of Chicago Irish life. The occasion is the front-porch revery of Studs Lonigan's father on the evening of his son's graduation from St. Patrick's grammar school:

> Nope, his family had not turned out so well. They hadn't had, none of them, the persistence that he had. He had stuck to his job and nearly killed himself working. But now he was reaping his rewards. . . . Well, Pat Lonigan had gone through the mill, and he had pulled himself up by his own bootstraps, and while he was not exactly sitting in the plush on Easy Street, he was a boss painter, and had his own business, and pretty soon maybe he'd even be worth a cool hundred thousand berries. But life was a funny thing, all right. It was like Mr. Dooley said, and he had never forgotten that remark, because Dooley, that is Finley Peter Dunne, was a real philosopher. Who'll tell what makes wan man a thief, and another man a saint?[8]

The son and grandson of Irish Catholic working-class laborers, James T. Farrell was born in 1904 and raised in a South Side Chicago neighborhood that became the setting for much of his remarkable body of work, which constitutes the greatest sustained production in twentieth-century America of quality fiction in the realistic tradition. Filling to date over fifty volumes, this corpus includes hundreds of stories and four large fictional cycles, which are further connected as progressive explorations of their main characters' varying responses to an urban environment similar to Farrell's. These related groups are the Studs Lonigan trilogy, the O'Neill-O'Flaherty pentalogy, the Bernard Carr trilogy, and the "Universe of Time" sequence, of which nine volumes (of a projected thirty) were published before Farrell's death in 1979.

The first two groups, the three Lonigan and five O'Neill novels, share a setting (the South Side neighborhood around Washington Park where Farrell himself grew up), a time frame (roughly 1900 to 1930), and several characters. I believe that these eight "Washington Park" novels should be seen as comprising one grand design, with two contrasting movements: the downward, negative alternative embodied in Studs Lonigan, who dies pointlessly, and the upward, positive possibility embodied in Danny O'Neill, who lives to become a writer. The great tragedy of the mostly inadequate critical response to Farrell's work, it seems to me, is that *Studs Lonigan* has been seen as the whole story, when, in fact, it isn't half of the story—not even about Washington Park.[9]

Farrell's own childhood in Washington Park had much more in common with Danny O'Neill's experience than Studs's. However, with a wisdom unusual in young writers, Farrell knew that in order to deal objectively with his own youthful, exaggerated feelings of hatred and rejection of his background, he had to tell Studs's story first. Thus, in part *Studs Lonigan* is the exorcism desired by Danny O'Neill when, in the middle of the Lonigan trilogy, in which he is a minor figure, he vows that "Some day he would drive this neighborhood and all his memories of it out of his consciousness with a book."

Instead of the tight, fatalistic narrative drive of the Lonigan trilogy, the five O'Neill-O'Flaherty novels are diffused and episodic, and in this looser structure is embodied a broader, more open-ended, but still unsentimentalized view of urban society. I wish to focus on the Washington Park novels because in them Farrell has provided the most thoroughly realized embodiment in American literature of three generations of Irish-Americans—from nineteenth-century immigrant laborers to Depression-era intellectuals. This body of work forms the bulk of the first, amazingly prolific, phase of Farrell's career. Between 1932 and 1943, he published the *Studs Lonigan* trilogy, four of the five O'Neill-O'Flaherty novels, two other Chicago-based novels (*Gas-House McGinty* and *Ellen Rogers*), and over fifty Chicago stories. *Studs Lonigan* was completed with *The Young Manhood of Studs Lonigan* (1934) and *Judgment Day* (1935), and the O'Neill series is as follows: *A World I Never Made* (1936), *No Star Is Lost* (1938), *Father and Son* (1940), *My Days of Anger* (1943), and, ten years later, *The Face of Time* (1953).[10]

As Dunne did in Mr. Dooley's Bridgeport, Farrell presents Washington Park as a world in itself, with four clear reference points like the markings on a compass: the Street, the Park, the Church, the Home. This is especially true for his young protagonists, Studs Lonigan and Danny O'Neill, who seldom leave the neighborhood and for whom these perceptions of urban life are fresh and crucially formative. (As an epigraph for *Young Lonigan,* Farrell quotes Plato: "except in the case of some rarely gifted nature there never will be a good man who has not from his childhood been used to play amid things of beauty and make of them a joy and a study.")

Much more than simply a choice of locale for unsupervised leisure time, the Street and the Park emerge in Farrell's fiction as archetypal opposing options for the city child. Each represents a possible way of growing up, a style of life, and each has its own pantheon of heroes, ideal models to engage a child's imagination. In the course of the Washington Park novels, Farrell embodies this powerful opposition in the contrasting development of Studs and Danny. The Street is the destructive element, characterized by gang life with its brutalization of finer instincts by pressures to conform: to fight, drink, dissipate energy and time, all in the service of an ideal of being "tough and the real stuff." The center of street life in Washington Park is Charley Bathcellar's poolroom on Fifty-eighth Street near the El station; its heroes are the gamblers, drinkers, and loafers who congregate there. The Park, on the other hand, is the creative and liberating element, the setting for a pastoral dream of release from the disorder of the streets and the claustrophobia of apartment living. The center of park life is the athletic field, which is to the city child a kind of paradise—a lined-out grassy place where rules are clear and enforced and success and failure unambiguous. Its heroes are sports figures, from park league stars to the Chicago White Sox, the pride of the South Side.

Danny O'Neill's most vivid childhood memory involves having watched a no-hitter pitched by Chicago's Ed Walsh in 1911. This thing of athletic beauty is his first exposure to art, and it sinks in. Danny chooses the Park and single-mindedly resolves to become a professional baseball player; he practices by the hour through his childhood years, mostly alone with a rubber ball and his imagination. Baseball is at once the most beautiful sport to watch and the least team-oriented of team sports. Thus it is not surprising that it so fascinates this young Chicago boy who is something of a lonely dreamer, with the detachment of a developing artist. It is no more surprising that Studs Lonigan chooses the Street. A normally inquisitive boy, he shows signs of intelligence, even imagination, in early scenes of *Young Lonigan.* And yet he is weak-willed and easily led, and he assumes the facile and corrupting "tough guy" values of the street-corner society to which he is drawn after graduation from eighth grade. He joins the Fifty-eighth Street Gang and takes his models from the poolroom and the silver-screen gangsters at the Michigan Theater. It is significant that the recurrent, ever-receding dream of Studs's short, unhappy adulthood is of his one afternoon in the Park with Lucy Scanlan during their eighth-grade summer. So the twig is bent for both boys, and the opposition of Street and Park is central to Farrell's delineation of the complex mixture of character and environment that brings Danny to his vocation as an artist and Studs to his grave at twenty-nine.

Even their characteristic daydreams are telling. Studs walks the Street in his mind, acting out his dream of himself as a tough guy; Danny drifts lazily across the Park, catching imaginary fly balls for the White Sox.

For Farrell's Irish Catholic characters, the familiar world is an even smaller unit than the Washington Park neighborhood—it is the parish. Providing both continuity with Ireland and help toward adjustment in America, as well as religion's traditional gifts of meaning and solace, the immigrant/ethnic Catholic Church is crucial to Farrell's full evocation of Chicago Irish life. The Washington Park novels describe this sophisticated cultural complex in full swing, and they also illustrate the various attitudes toward the Church among three generations of Irish-Americans. For immigrants such as Tom and Mary O'Flaherty, Danny O'Neill's grandparents, Catholicism remains the tacitly accepted center of life. As he nears death, Old Tom is genuinely comforted by conversations with the understanding Father Hunt, one of several sympathetic priests in Farrell's novels. Mary's faith also brings her through the grief of her husband's death and the thousand subsequent crises of her unquiet old age.

One step removed from the losses and alienation of immigration, Farrell's second-generation-American characters are affected by their religion in many different ways. Studs's mother Mary Lonigan is a self-righteous Catholic in the "holier than thou" mold. Lizz O'Flaherty O'Neill comes closest to picking up her parents' values, although she exaggerates them by retreating into a concentrated piety and staking everything on the positive nature of suffering as preparation for Heaven. Her fatalistic attitude clashes with her husband Jim's pragmatism, and they often fight bitterly about her incessant visits and donations to the Church, which come at the expense of personal hygiene, housekeeping, and sometimes meat for the table. Lizz walks the world in a dirty-faced daze, seeing visions of dead relatives and Satan under the bed, wishing that she had become a nun, and responding to every difficulty with blind faith in "God's will." Still, her Catholicism does sustain her through years of terrible poverty, continual pregnancies, stillbirths and infant mortality, and the death of her husband. Quite simply, Catholicism works for Lizz, and she is at once the craziest O'Flaherty and the most secure. Her sister Margaret, on the other hand, is the most insecure, troubled, and miserable of the children. Attractive and desirous of love, money, and a "good time," Margaret is torn between two philosophies and two worlds: the puritanical Catholic morality of her training in the parish and the Jazz Age hedonism all around her in the downtown hotel where she works. An affair with a wealthy married man exacerbates her problem. Unable to resolve the contradictions in her life, she storms through a frenetic, confused young womanhood, marked by excessive drinking, a persecution complex, and attempted suicide. The men of the second generation take religion more lightly than the women. Studs's father Patrick Lonigan and Tom's son Al O'Flaherty are unquestioning but no more than nominal participants in Catholicism, while Al's brother Ned has rejected the Church outright and substituted "New Thought," a hazy collection of self-help ideas whose main tenet is the "power of the wish," roughly translatable as "all things come to him who wishes for them."

As for the third generation, Studs Lonigan and Danny O'Neill also go different ways in their attitudes toward the religion in which they are raised and educated. For all his flirtations with street life, Studs remains a conventional Catholic, never questioning the teachings and prohibitions of the Church, and reacting typically right up to his last illness. Studs's fevered death-bed dreams reveal him as a believer in Heaven and Hell and the Catholic way of deciding who goes where. Moreover, he twice attempts to pull his sinking life together by joining parish groups— the young people's association at St. Patrick's Church and the Order of Christopher (modeled on the Catholic fraternal organization, the Knights of Columbus).

Given his greater intelligence and the artistic bent, Danny O'Neill's reactions to the Church are understandably more complex. As a sensitive, highly imaginative child, he is terrorized by the fear of hell instilled by his family and the nuns of Crucifixion School. (When he first appears, at the beginning of *A World I Never Made*, Danny is thinking about Hell, and whether missing Mass will put him there. He is seven years old.) Danny agonizes for years under the load of guilt imposed by what he considers to have been an imperfect first confession and communion. And later he tries to force a vocation to the priesthood to please the nuns and his grandmother. And yet, there are positive aspects to Danny's exposure to the Catholic culture. His seventh-grade nun is the first person to push him toward the intellectual life, and some of his priest-teachers at St. Stanislaus High School encourage him further toward learning and writing. Thus, Catholicism does provide Danny with models of educated and ideologically dedicated men and women. In addition, the Church gives him other things unavailable to him elsewhere in Washington Park: a sense of order, of historical continuity, and of mystery. And it is these gifts that inspire Danny to harness his imagination with words, for his first successful piece of creative writing is the romantic tale of a priest's martyrdom in Ireland during Elizabethan times.

So it is that, although he ultimately repudiates Catholicism, the Church and parochial schooling do have some salutary influence on Danny O'Neill's intellectual and imaginative growth. This aspect of his development combines with the efficacious faith of the immigrant O'Flahertys and Lizz O'Neill to mitigate the many examples of the Church's negative effects in the Washington Park novels. These include the fear and trembling of Danny's and Studs's guilt-ridden adolescences, the wilder flights of Lizz's hysterical religiosity, at its height in her performances at wakes, the pompous and hackneyed rhetoric of Father Gilhooley's sermons at St. Patrick's, and the heartless verbal bludgeoning of Studs's pregnant fiancée by his mother (in the name of moral rectitude) as Studs lies dying. In short, Farrell's view of Catholicism is ambiguous and mixed—true to life and to his commitment to an aesthetic of realism. Though it cannot save Studs from an early death or sustain Danny into adulthood, the Church is a powerful presence throughout these novels, from Studs's graduation from St. Patrick's grammar school at the beginning of *Young Lonigan* to Mary O'Flaherty's black rosary beads at the end of both *My Days of Anger* and *The Face of Time,* marking her own death and her husband's.

After the Street, the Park, and the Church, the fourth cardinal point in the world of Washington Park is the Home, which for most residents of the neighborhood meant, and still means, apartment life. Through the three main families of his eight Washington Park novels, Farrell describes an inclusive range of South Side styles of apartment living: from the struggling O'Neills to the comfortably middle-class Lonigans, with the O'Flahertys fluctuating somewhere in between. Their homes and homelives appear in meticulous, day-by-day detail, of interest to anyone who wants to know how ordinary people lived in Chicago in the 1910s and 1920s.

Jim O'Neill's slow fight toward a better life for his large family is measured in terms of the three homes they inhabit over the course of the five O'Neill-O'Flaherty novels. In 1909, they are living in a cold-water tenement flat at Twenty-fifth and LaSalle streets, in a polyglot working-class neighborhood with poor Irish, Germans, Italians, Poles, Jews, and blacks. There is a wood-burning stove in the kitchen for heat and cooking both, and a ramshackle outhouse in the backyard, shared among several families. The place is dirty, crowded, comfortless—but it is all Jim can afford, as an underpaid teamster working backbreaking six-day weeks, and with a new child coming every year.

By 1914, the O'Neills have moved south to a small cottage at Forty-fifth and Wells. The only substantive improvement over the LaSalle Street apartment is the fact that this is a single-family dwelling. Plumbing and heating are still inadequate; on cold days, the children "take turns sticking their feet in the oven to get warm." However, the family also feels somewhat better off because their cottage is in an all-white, mostly Irish neighborhood, and stands right across the street from "St. Martha's" Church. (St. Cecilia's Church marked the spot, and Farrell's parents, brothers, and sisters lived in such a cottage from 1914 to 1918.) That the family is still very poor is underscored in the harrowing conclusion of *No Star Is Lost,* when two-year-old Artie O'Neill dies of diphtheria, unattended by a doctor who has ignored the O'Neills because he knows they can't pay him. "There's only one crime in this world, Lizz," says the heartbroken Jim, "to be a poor man." And on the day of Artie's funeral another O'Neill child is born—dead.

In 1918, following Jim's promotion to night dispatcher at the express company, the O'Neills move further south—to Fifty-eighth and Calumet in Washington Park, which looks like heaven after what they have been through. On the opening page of *Father and Son,* Jim is surveying their new apartment, which has "a bathroom inside, running hot and cold water, steam heat, gas and electricity." He is proud to have caught up with the O'Flahertys, who live only a block away, at 5816½ South Park Avenue.

The O'Flahertys have arrived here after a series of moves that also shed light on the migratory pattern of typical South Side apartment dwellers during these years. Like so many Irish couples, Tom and Mary O'Flaherty begin their life in Chicago in an old immigrant neighborhood near the Chicago River. (As Tom lies dying of cancer, Mary recalls him "sitting in the kitchen in Blue Island Avenue," wondering "what time . . . it would be in the old country.") In telling their story, Farrell also documents the means by which the majority of marginally middle-class families with immigrant parents got ahead—pooling resources. Young adults lived at home until they married, and they were expected to contribute their earnings to the family. Thus, by the time old Tom O'Flaherty retires from his job as a teamster (an unusual thing in itself; most immigrant laborers worked until they dropped), his children Al, Ned, Margaret, and Louise are earning enough to maintain a decent standard of living. So it is that extra money from Al's job as a shoe salesman allows the family to move from a crowded apartment on Twelfth Street to a "big apartment" in the 4700 block of Indiana Avenue, in "a good neighborhood," Grand Boulevard, just north of Washington Park. From this point on, the O'Flahertys qualify as what Lizz O'Neill, with mingled jealousy and derision, labels "steam-heat Irish." It is to this apartment on Indiana that five-year-old Danny O'Neill comes to live with his grandparents in 1909, because his father doesn't make enough money to support the growing O'Neill family.

After old Tom O'Flaherty's death near Christmas of 1910, the

O'Flahertys move further south—to Fiftieth and Calumet, near "Crucifixion" Church and School, where Danny O'Neill's education begins in September, 1911. Crucifixion is Farrell's name for the Corpus Christi parish complex at Forty-ninth and Grand Boulevard (now Dr. Martin Luther King Drive) where his own schooling began. Founded in 1901, this parish served the "gold coast" Irish, who built mansions along Grand Boulevard in the 1890s, and contributed generously to the construction of one of Chicago's most impressive churches, which was completed in 1915. Louise O'Flaherty dies of consumption while the family is living on Calumet, and this sad event, combined with complaints about Margaret's noisy drinking, sets the family moving again in 1912, to 5137½ Prairie Avenue, one block further south. They are still in Crucifixion parish, and Danny continues to attend school there.

The O'Flahertys live on Prairie through 1914, when Margaret, jilted by her married lover, has a terrifying month-long drinking bout punctuated by two suicide attempts. Farrell's descriptions of her anguish and that of the family are interwoven with the story of Artie O'Neill's death to make *No Star Is Lost* an unforgettably powerful novel. At its conclusion, the spring or summer of 1915, the O'Flahertys move again—to Fifty-seventh and Indiana, in "St. Patrick's" parish, Washington Park. On moving day, walking along Fifty-eighth Street for the first time, eleven-year-old Danny O'Neill is challenged by two older boys who are checking him out as a newcomer to their territory. Their names are Johnny O'Brien and Studs Lonigan. By 1918, when *Father and Son* opens, the O'Flahertys have made their last move in the series—south again, to 5816½ South Park Avenue. The view out over Washington Park makes this their most attractive apartment.

Farrell's chronicle of the migratory pattern of the Chicago South Side Irish community is no less detailed, and even more important thematically, in the *Studs Lonigan* trilogy. Although their rationale remained mostly unstated, the O'Neills and O'Flahertys always moved south in order to keep ahead of the influx of black people to the South Side after World War I. However, the issue of white flight to avoid neighborhood integration looms as a large and central theme in all three Lonigan novels.

Chicago's South Side began to change during World War I, when thousands of black people arrived in the city from southern states, seeking jobs and escaping Jim Crow laws. At first these migrants settled in the clearly defined "Black Belt" that stretched south along both sides of State Street from the old black ghetto around Sixteenth Street. (In 1910 the center of black Chicago had been at Thirty-first and State, and blacks constituted 2 percent of the city's population.) As their numbers grew, however, blacks moved east and south from the increasingly congested Black Belt into adjoining neighborhoods which had previously been all white. The terrible race riots of July 1919 were the first overt and unignorable sign of white opposition to this movement. Also, neighborhood groups were formed or redirected for the purpose of keeping out the blacks.

One such attempt was made by Washington Park's Ridgeway Club around 1920, for blacks had begun moving into apartment buildings south of Garfield Boulevard and east of State Street in 1915. (There had been blacks in the area since the 1880s, but these early settlers had stayed west of State, which had been considered by all concerned a natural boundary line between the races.) Of course, riots and neighborhood actions could not divert the flow of what was a major migratory movement, and so it was that the whites of Washington Park and other South Side communities, confused and frightened by the threat to their established way of life, elected to abandon their homes and to flee wholesale to new neighborhoods further south. Many from Washington Park went over to Hyde Park, hoping (not without cause) that the University of Chicago would help shelter them from integrated living. Others went south and east to the new and somewhat fancier area known as South Shore, which boasted a country club and proximity to Lake Michigan. In the wake of this mass exodus, black people moved in and took over the old neighborhoods. The census figures are dramatic. In 1920, the Washington Park area had 38,076 residents, 15 percent of them black; in 1930, 92 percent of the area's larger population of 44,016 were black. Equally dramatic are the figures for the smaller square of territory bounded by Garfield Boulevard, South Park Avenue, Fifty-ninth Street, and State Street, within which the Lonigans, O'Neills, and O'Flahertys were all living in the twenties. In 1920, this area housed 11,825 whites and 848 blacks; in 1930, there were 426 whites and 14,475 blacks.

Also relevant here is the story of Farrell's own childhood parish of St. Anselm's, whose boundaries were Fifty-seventh, St. Lawrence, Sixty-third, and State, and its pastor Irish-born Father Michael S. Gilmartin. After serving twelve years as an assistant at the Irish parish of Holy Angels on Oakwood Boulevard and four years as a country pastor, Father Gilmartin got his opportunity to organize a city parish of his own. His territory was the new residential district adjoining Washington Park. Within a year of having celebrated the first mass in his new parish on July 4, 1909, Father Gilmartin had financed the construction of a school, convent, rectory, and parish hall. As the number of parishioners continued to grow, he paid off the parish debt and began to save for a new church. By 1924, when ground was finally broken for St. Anselm's

Church at the corner of Sixty-first and Michigan, many of Father Gilmartin's parishioners had already moved further south to escape the burgeoning black population. When the handsome new church was dedicated in December 1925, St. Anselm's School had four hundred students. In 1930, that number was down to one hundred, and two years later Father Gilmartin was transferred and St. Anselm's was given over to the Divine Word Fathers, under whom it became a thriving black parish. (The first Divine Word pastor baptized more than fifteen hundred black converts between 1932 and 1940.)[11]

Nowhere is this important complex of events in Chicago history more clearly described than in the *Studs Lonigan* trilogy. Farrell adheres to his credo of literary realism in keeping his narrative close to the actual events of those years, while, at the same time, through the novelist's art, he shows us what it felt like to be a man such as Patrick Lonigan, who believed that Washington Park would be his last home in Chicago. In doing so, Farrell contributes much to our understanding of the origins of interracial tensions in Chicago in the years following World War I. Among other things, *Studs Lonigan* is a study of forced displacement, and, as such, the dislocation of the Lonigan family is analogous to that of their ancestors in Ireland.

As the trilogy opens, Studs's father, Patrick Lonigan, is sitting on the porch of his home in the 5700 block of Wabash Avenue on an evening in June 1916. He owns his own building in this respectable, middle-class neighborhood, and has been here since before his son's birth in 1901. Moreover, he has pleasant associations with this area that go back even further: one of his cherished memories is a Sunday afternoon while courting his wife, when he had rented a buggy at no small expense and "they had driven way out south," to find that "Fifty-eighth Street was nothing but a wilderness," and "it was nearly all trees and woods out here." He also looks back with self-satisfaction to his childhood in poverty "around Blue Island and Archer Avenue," which suggests that, like Tom and Mary O'Flaherty, Patrick Lonigan's father settled near the Chicago River, in or near Mr. Dooley's Bridgeport, one of the first Irish working-class neighborhoods in the city.

Lonigan remembers his parents as "pauperized greenhorns" from Ireland, who raised a large family and never escaped the nets of poverty. His father was a laborer, driven to drink by family and money pressures. Of the Lonigan children, only Patrick has become successful; the others ran away, died young, turned to prostitution, or managed to hold only menial futureless jobs. Lonigan recalls "those days when he was a young buck in Canaryville," the neighborhood around St. Gabriel's Church at Forty-fifth and Lowe. This suggests that, like the O'Neills and O'Flahertys,

his life has also been marked by a series of moves to the south, the
climax of which has been his arrival as a homeowner in Washington
Park. This evening's occasion—his son Studs's graduation from eighth
grade at St. Patrick's School—completes Lonigan's happiness, and the
picture of his situation: he is a Catholic family man and a supporter of
his parish institutions, a typical middle-class Chicagoan whose success
and identity are embodied in his position and property in St. Patrick's
parish, Washington Park.

But Patrick Lonigan is far from secure here. Even on this happy
evening, his complacent revery is interrupted by the thought that "the
family would have to be moving soon. When he'd bought this building,
Wabash Avenue had been a nice, decent, respectable street for a self-
respecting man to live with his family. But now, well, the niggers and
kikes were getting in, and they were dirty, . . . And when they got into a
neighborhood property values went blooey. He'd sell and get out." As
the novel continues, there are more signs of unrest related to the shifting
ethnic and racial makeup of Washington Park. Old man O'Brien, the
father of one of Studs's chums, predicts as early as the summer of 1916
that "one of these days we're gonna have a race riot." When the riots
come in July 1919, Studs and the Fifty-eighth Street gang contribute to
the chaos by roaming the border streets between their turf and the
newest black areas near Garfield Boulevard. In search of black victims
to avenge the cutthroat death of a white boy from Sixty-first Street, they
find only a single ten-year-old, whom they strip and terrorize. Another
sign of the times is the repeated bombing of the home of "the leading
colored banker of Chicago," the first black in the 5900 block of South
Park Avenue, and, ironically, an earnest, contributing Catholic parishioner.

Partly because he has worked so hard to get there, Patrick Lonigan is
unwilling to leave Washington Park, despite the steady movement of
blacks into the area from the north and west and the equally steady
desertion of the neighborhood by his friends. In 1922 the Lonigans move
to a new building on Michigan Avenue, one block east of their old home
on Wabash. But after this concession, Patrick Lonigan becomes the
epitome of the neighborhood die-hard, rejecting a $90,000 offer for his
building, despite his daughter Fran's declarations that "the best people . . .
are moving over to Hyde Park or out in South Shore," and "soon I'll be
ashamed to admit I live around here." In a turn of events based on
Farrell's recollections of St. Anselm's and Father Gilmartin, Lonigan has
put his faith in "Father Gilhooley's" plan to build "St. Patrick's" Church
on the corner of Sixty-first and Michigan. The pastor has assured his
parishioners that Michigan will become "a boulevard straight through,"
and Lonigan believes that the new church will keep the neighborhood

white and double the value of his building at the same time. Two years later, in 1924, Studs attends a fund-raising meeting for the new church, which is still being seen as the potential salvation of the neighborhood. Now that the present buildings are free of debt, the parishioners of St. Patrick's are urged to contribute to a church that will be "one of the most beautiful . . . in this city," and "the fondest dream of your pastor." Of course, the church does get built, but on Father Gilhooley's happiest day, at the first mass in the new building, "standing in the rear of the church were four new and totally edified parishioners. Their skin was black."

Around this time, Studs and some of his friends hear a lecture at the Bug Club (Washington Park's answer to London's Hyde Park Speaker's Corner) on the inevitability of the black migration to the South Side as an "outgrowth of social and economic forces, . . . a pressure stronger than individual wills." But they absorb nothing here, and are merely puzzled at "an Irishman being a nigger-lover." (The speaker is John Connolly, a well-known local radical.) In a few months it becomes clear to all that the new church has not stopped or even slowed the influx of blacks to the area, and many disillusioned parishioners, including the Lonigans, begin blaming Father Gilhooley. A stronger pastor, they contend, would not have "built a beautiful new church, and then let his parish go to the dogs. . . . He'd have organized things like vigilance committees to prevent it."

Ultimately, Patrick Lonigan also gives up on his neighborhood. After reluctantly selling his building to a black man, he moves his family to South Shore (around Seventy-first Street and Jeffery Boulevard) in 1928. The scene at the old house on moving day reveals the emotional cost of such moves to people like the Lonigans, and is important to the overall design of the trilogy. What becomes clear here is that from this point on, both Patrick Lonigan and his son are permanently displaced persons.

Patrick knows immediately that he has lost his last real home; he is simply too old to make another. "You know, Bill," he confides to Studs in the empty parlor on Michigan Avenue, "your mother and I are gettin' old now, and, well, we sort of got used to this neighborhood . . . they were all nearby, and they all sort of knew us, and we knew them, and you see, well, this neighborhood was kind of like home. We sort of felt about it the same way I feel about Ireland, where I was born." (He also says later that it had been his hope to "die in this parish, respected.") The thought of moving to South Shore brings no comfort, for, "out there there'll only be about ten buildings in our block, the rest's all prairie," and "we're not what we used to be, and it'll be lonesome there sometimes." Mrs. Lonigan reports that Father Gilhooley is similarly saddened because "here he built his beautiful church, and two years after it's built, all his parishioners are gone. He's getting old, Patrick, poor man, and he's heartbroken." (Later, Studs learns that, like his real-life counterpart Father Gilmartin, "Father Gilhooley has been changed to a parish back of the yards, and St. Patrick's has been turned over to some order of priests.") Both priest and parishioner thus feel that their lives have been frustrated by forces beyond their control. In his pathetic search for an explanation, Patrick Lonigan comes under the influence of the anti-Semitic radio priest "Father Moylan" (based it seems on Father Charles Coughlin), and at the end of the trilogy, he is blaming most of his troubles on "Jew real estate men" and a conspiracy of "Jew international bankers."

Moving to South Shore also contributes to the failure of Studs Lonigan to find his way in the world. Denied the possibly sustaining context of home in a familiar neighborhood, Studs becomes even more of an aimless drifter. The move, which takes place almost exactly in the middle of the *Lonigan* trilogy, is thus a watershed event in his downward drift to death. No more at home in South Shore than his father, Studs complains that there is "no place to hang out" there. Five months after having moved away, he returns to Washington Park and finds his gang's "old corner" of Fifty-eighth and Prairie looking "like Thirty-fifth and State"—that is, like the center of the Black Belt. The playground, school, and church are all strange to him already, and even Washington Park itself seems alien territory: "It had used to be his park. He almost felt as if his memories were in it, walking like ghosts." Later that night, a drunken Studs goes back to the park looking for the tree he had sat in with Lucy Scanlan twelve years before. He can't find it and gets lost trying.

A stronger indication of Studs's displacement comes on the climactic New Year's Eve that ends *The Young Manhood of Studs Lonigan.* The Fifty-eighth Street Gang have a wild reunion/party—not in one of the neighborhoods where they now live, but "at a disreputable hotel on Grand Boulevard in the black belt." The night of debauched drinking results in the permanent ruin of Studs's health, and he ends up in "the dirty gray dawn" of January 1, 1929, passed out beside a fireplug back at Fifty-eighth and Prairie. It looks as though, in his semiconscious stupor, he has been trying to go home again.

In *Judgment Day,* two years later, Studs is still sick; he is pallid, weak-lunged, subject to coughing and fainting spells and premonitions of death. Desperate for a job to support his pregnant fiancée Catherine Banahan, he foolishly sets out with the want ads under his arm on a cold, rainy day. The job search takes him downtown, where he spends a disheartening ten hours getting doors slammed in his face and wading through puddles of water. He contracts a virulent pneumonia and a few days later he is dead. It is significant that this final illness overtakes him in the alien Loop—the center of business-Chicago but nobody's home.

At the end of *Judgment Day,* Patrick Lonigan also demonstrates how displaced he is for a telling final time. It is the Depression year of 1931, and, along with worrying about his son's failing health, Lonigan is in serious financial trouble. In fact, he is about to lose his business and his house in South Shore. After closing his office, perhaps for the last time, Lonigan embarks on a sad odyssey, in which he literally retraces the steps of his personal history. Driving north through the now-black neighborhood of Washington Park, he stops to look at his old building there and to pay a visit to St. Patrick's Church, on which he had mistakenly placed his trust that the area would stay white. The memory of this dispossession from the home he had built here is sheer agony, especially in the context of his present troubles, and so he leaves the area, and drives blindly, unconsciously northward again. Only when he is detained by a stoplight at Thirty-fifth and Halsted streets, on the outskirts of Bridgeport, does Lonigan realize, with "deep nostalgia," that he is "going back to an old neighborhood, to look at places where he had lived and played as a shaver." As his world spins out of control, he seeks meaning in the steadying power of this most familiar place. Again, though, Lonigan is disappointed, for this visit to his childhood home brings only bitter ironies.

First, the "stockyard smell" reminds him of the poverty of his youth and "the distance he had travelled since those days." But this leads to a despairing question: "What did it mean now," when he is about to have nothing again? Immediately he comes upon a reminder of the Depression that resonates back to his own Irish heritage—he sees the eviction from their apartment of a family of six, who stand huddled by their furniture on the sidewalk. Naturally, he is again reminded of his own lost building and business, "into which he had put all the money earned by the sweat of his own brow." Finally, Lonigan witnesses the sweep of a Communist parade down Halsted Street, and his angry response is the last irony of his visit to Bridgeport. To a policeman-acquaintance that he spots in the crowd, Lonigan simplistically defends "God and America and the home," the very ideals that his own failure seems to have refuted, and condemns the marching "anarchistic Reds, communists, niggers, hunkies, foreigners, left-handed turkeys" (who include a brother and sister of Danny O'Neill). At the same time, he is puzzled that "even these people . . . seemed happier than he." Having found no solace in his attempted return home, Lonigan turns wearily south again—toward the house in South Shore where his son lies dying. On the way he stops at a speakeasy near White City Amusement Park at Sixty-third and South Park, near the old neighborhood of his happiest years. There, he gets so drunk that he has to be driven home, after sinking so low as to scrabble for the pity of strangers by announcing to the bar that Studs is already dead. Patrick Lonigan's disillusionment is complete. All that he believed to be stable has crumbled: the economy of America and Chicago, neighborhood life in Washington Park, and his family. His is a story that can stand for that of thousands of American city dwellers of his unlucky generation.

The power of the Studs Lonigan trilogy has long been acknowledged, but the O'Neill-O'Flaherty novels constitute an even greater achievement, largely because of Farrell's pioneering juxtaposition and structuring of major Irish-American themes. He has made of this five-novel, 2500-page series a single, coherent work of art by means of his brilliant organization of the material around two powerful themes, and he has done so without impeding its realistic narrative flow. Two streams of experience mingle in these pages: the outer stream of social life, a chronicle of the works and days of three generations of Chicagoans, and the inner stream of consciousness, the perceptions of that chronicle by individual members of the O'Neill and O'Flaherty families. Throughout the series, the same two watershed experiences recur, always embodying major themes. These are death and illuminating revery. Deaths in the family constitute the central events of the outer stream and emphasize the most important social theme of the series, what Farrell has called "the tragedy of the worker, the central social tragedy of our times." Solitary reveries are the central events of the individual inner streams of consciousness in the series. They emphasize the most important internal or psychological theme, the inability of these people to articulate to one another their real perceptions, insights, and feelings. Clarifications of life and honest self-assessment come only in dreams and daydreams, and they are never shared. I believe that Farrell's juxtaposition of these two themes conveys a central fact of life for the Irish-American generations in his chronicle. The grim experience of unremitting physical labor beat something out of the American Irish—the gift and luxury of sincere verbal self-expression. Farrell was the first to recognize and to measure this appalling loss. Danny O'Neill is the exception here, for he comes to understand the social tragedy of his family's thwarted lives and the psychological tragedy of their failure to communicate. Furthermore, his development suggests a third important theme of the series: with understanding comes the resolution to act—in Danny's case, to use art as a weapon against both tragedies. The remainder of this essay will concentrate on the last three novels of the series, in which these themes gather force, as three major characters die without having spoken their minds to anyone.

In *Father and Son,* Jim and Danny O'Neill are living only a block apart: Jim with Lizz and their other children in their best apartment ever, at Fifty-eighth and Calumet, and Danny with his grandmother at 5816½ South Park Avenue. Here Danny gropes toward maturity. He goes through St. Stanislaus High School, graduating in 1923, and begins to take prelegal courses at the night school of St. Vincent's College in the Loop. Finally, he enrolls at the University of Chicago, just across Washington Park but an intellectual world away from South Park Avenue, where he is encouraged to write in an advanced composition course. These steps parallel Farrell's own attendance at St. Cyril's (later renamed Mt. Carmel High School) at Sixty-fourth and Dante Avenue, the night school at De Paul University, and the University of Chicago. During these years, Danny also holds down his first full-time jobs—at the Express Company where his father worked and as a gas station attendant. And most important for his growth, he experiences the deaths of his father in 1923 and his grandmother Mary O'Flaherty in 1927.

Although the O'Neills seem finally to be out of the woods, thanks to Jim's promotion and their new apartment, their luck does not hold. In a matter of months, three crippling strokes, the legacy of his years of bone-wearying labor, render Jim O'Neill unemployed and helpless. As presented in this, the central novel of the pentalogy, Jim's life and death embody both the social "tragedy of the worker" and the psychological tragedy of failed communication. Farrell's epigraphs succinctly gloss what will be the major concerns of *Father and Son.* Jim O'Neill's tragedy is set beside that of Tolstoy's hapless burgher: "Ivan Ilych's life had been most simple and most ordinary and therefore most terrible." Danny's growth toward an artist's understanding is compared to Baudelaire's: "—Ah! Seigneur! donnez moi la force et le courage/De contempler mon coeur et mon corps sans dégoût!" ("Ah, Lord! Give me the strength and the courage to contemplate my heart and my body without disgust!")

In the middle of *Father and Son,* Jim attends Anna McCormack's wake and is deeply frustrated by his inability to communicate with her grieving husband: "Aware of how deeply he sympathized with Old Mike, he couldn't think of anything worth saying that would express his feelings. When you most wanted to tell another man something, you were least able to do so. Jim felt a sudden and profound loneliness. He felt himself all alone in a world of men. The words he could say to another man, they did not get him closer to that man. Even with Lizz, he was still alone with himself, alone in the world."[12] All through the series, and especially as he feels death approaching, Jim struggles to express himself to his family. His great frustration is Danny, whom he sees turning into a "dude," and forgetting that he comes "from poor people." One of Jim's greatest sorrows comes from sensing that, after the strokes have rendered him helpless and shambling, Danny is ashamed to walk down the street with him. Jim blames the O'Flahertys in part, but also himself, for having lost his son to his wife's family. Father and son try unsuccessfully to talk throughout this novel, but their only close moment comes when Jim asks Danny to recite Polonius's speech to Laertes. Shakespeare's words briefly bridge the gap between them, as Jim declares, "I'm your father, and I couldn't give you any better advice."

Shakespeare, in fact, is Jim's companion and consolation. After his first stroke, he often sits up late alone, reading *Julius Caesar* and *Hamlet,* and struggling to understand his life and approaching death. The dignity and courage of his solitary questioning make him one of the most memorable characters in Farrell's fiction. Jim's thoughts range widely. He meditates on the mystery of having children, and on the teachings of his Church: "He liked to think that Christ was born in a poor man's home, and never in His life was he rich. . . . A lot of people ought never to forget that." Feeling that "there wasn't a great deal of justice in the world," he tries anyway to tell his children to live right, all the time asking, "would doing right get them anywhere?" Regretting "with such pain the confident days of his youth," he sees that young men "like that kid Studs Lonigan" still have the same careless attitude, and watching children at play in the street "gave you the feeling that it was all so sad because they, too, were going to lose that innocence of theirs. They were going to have to learn the hard lessons of life and they were one day going to lose their health."

More and more, Jim feels "a lonely prisoner in life . . . and the captive of death." Frightened by a new sense of the passage of time, he is "tempted many times these days to get drunk," but realizes that "he couldn't gamble with his health and his blood pressure now, because there was too much dependent on him, his kids, his wife. If he collapsed, they would be sunk in poverty and have no one. No, he had to fight this out with himself." When the last stroke sends him permanently home from work, he knows he will never get better, and feels "that others didn't understand life and that he did. *Vanity, all is vanity.* . . . Yes, men tried and fought and raised hell and wanted all kinds of things, and yes, yes, *vanity, all is vanity.*" When his doctor dies suddenly of heart failure, Jim is terrified at first, but shock gives way to compassion and courageous self-assessment. This was the same man who had failed to minister to his son Artie, but Jim forgives him that: "he would harbor nothing against the dead."

Jim's last weeks are filled with petty indignities. Another of his children, the third, is sent away to the O'Flahertys. Lizz suggests that he put himself in a public hospital. His son Bill takes over as head of the house, and contradicts him on a point of discipline regarding the younger children. He is shamed by a Christmas basket from a Protestant charity which the family is unable to refuse. He has to make an X to get money at the bank, and he loses a five-dollar bill in the street. People on the El think he's drunk, kids mock and mimic his limp, and an apartment-house janitor chases him away as a loiterer. But worse than any of these is the fact that he has no one to talk to. All of his thinking is done in silent revery by the parlor window. He is unable to share his struggle for meaning with another living soul.

Jim's last day, like Ivan Ilych's, is "most simple and most ordinary and therefore most terrible." At lunch, Lizz is full of Mrs. Muldoon's wake, where she stayed all night "because my heart bled with pity for her." When two of his children start arguing over the last bran muffin, Jim lashes out at the whole family: "You don't care about anyone else. You don't care about anything but gorging yourselves. All of you. What if your father is sick? What if your brothers work and put the bread in your mouths, none of you care." Pointing an accusing finger at Lizz ("It's your doing"), Jim leaves the room to lie down, "too tired even to be angry at what had happened." These bitter words are his last. He lapses into coma and dies the next afternoon without regaining consciousness.

Father and Son also records Danny O'Neill's frustrated first attempts to articulate his thoughts. He fails with his father, of course, but also with his peers, most of whom continue to regard him as an oddball, a "goof." Danny is unable to tell a girl who is going to a different high school that he will miss her: "He couldn't say the words." Nor is he able to talk honestly to himself, failing three times in junior high and high school to start a diary of his "real feelings." There are, however, signs of improvement. With an O'Flaherty family fight raging around him, Danny is able to finish a story that he knows is good enough for the high school literary magazine. Also, Danny's reaction to his father's death is a climactic encouraging sign. At first, he is troubled because "he felt empty more than he felt anything." And yet he does recognize immediately two facts that restate the novel's main themes of social and psychological tragedy. First, he sees that "there was something tragic about his father. He told himself that his father was a man who'd never had a chance. His father had been a strong man, and a proud man, and he had seen that pride broken." Second, he sees that "he had never really known his father, and his father had never really known him."

These ending revelations mark the beginning of Danny's coming of

age, which is completed in the fourth novel, *My Days of Anger.* Having
crossed Washington Park to attend the University of Chicago, he is at
once stimulated by new friends and the world of ideas. He writes his first
honest diary entries and goes on to produce a torrent of fiction in an
advanced composition course. He loses his faith, at first in a dream, and
wakes up a nonbeliever, "free of lies." Other liberating rejections follow:
of a pseudo-Nietzschean friend, Ed Lanson, of the university, and of
Chicago itself. At the same time, and gradually through the novel,
Danny's "days of anger" (again the phrase is from Baudelaire) and
confusion slowly evolve toward understanding of his family. In this
process, his grandmother's death in the spring of 1927 is the crucial
event.

Mary O'Flaherty's death, like that of Jim O'Neill, also embodies a
statement of the tragedy of failed communication. Throughout the
series, Mary has been a classic immigrant matriarch, holding her family
together by sheer force of will. She often describes herself as "a hard
woman from a hard country." But the other side of the coin is that the
hard years have left her unable to express love and sympathy to those in
the family who are most in need: Margaret in her emotional crises, Lizz
swamped by the demands of her own large family, and Old Tom O'Flaherty
on his death bed. Nor has she shared her own fears and sorrows with
anyone. As she approaches death in *My Days of Anger*—she is just back
from the hospital with a broken hip, thinner than ever, and eighty-six
years old—a last extended daydream (all of Chapter 26) provides a
summation of her character and concerns. As memories of Ireland and
her parents' generation flood back, she admits the pain of emigration
that she has kept to herself for sixty years. "And sure," she says to
herself, "wouldn't I be giving me right arm to be seeing the steeple of
Athlone in the sunshine, ah, but it was beautiful and wasn't it tall?
Indeed it was."

Of course, she was afraid, "all alone, and the boat going out of
Queenstown harbor, and sure didn't I get down on me knees and pray to
me God." Of course, she was hurt by American mockery of her accent
and her innocence: "So they think I'm a greenhorn, do they? I'll greenhorn them. Greenhorn them, I will." Of course, she was saddened and
frustrated by the news of her mother's death, "and there I was in Green
Bay, Wisconsin, not knowing if me father had the money to give her a
decent burial," and by the death of her own first child: "we christened
him, the little angel, and he died, and what Christian name did we give
him? And here I am forgetting the name of me own son, John. . . . and
his headstone is sinking into the ground."

Mary is still cranky and full of fight though. She claims to remember the day she was born, "and there I was coming out, with the candle on the table." She gloats over having hid the eggs and butter for Danny's breakfast in the top drawer of her dresser, and having offered Tommy Doyle twenty-five cents to beat up a friend of Danny's whom she has judged a bad influence. And she even threatens to chase "Satan himself, the Black Demon," out of Hell, "if I ever get me hands on him."

Not that she is deceived about her condition. There is a refrain running through her mind in this lovely, lyrical chapter—the one word, "Soon." She knows her death is near: "I do see the old men with death in their eyes. Nobody fools me. I won't be long here." She can see the circle of her life closing: "The strength is gone out of me bones. Here I am, and they take care of me just like I took care of them, and they carry me around like a baby." In a typical paradox, Mary now reveals that she has been kept going all these years by both love and love of a fight. "Last Sunday at dinner," she happily recalls, "I put me two cents in to keep them fighting away. And then I told me grandson, I told him, Son, I'm only fooling, and sure it's the fun of it I like. So I kept them at it for all they were worth." At the same time, she acknowledges her love and compassion for her family: for her husband—"Me poor Tom, your Mary that could run swift as the wind and sang you the songs that day of the Mullingar Fair is coming to you," for "me beautiful virgin daughter Louise . . . out with Tom in Calvary Cemetery," for "me poor son Al, carrying those heavy grips to pay all the bills," for "Lizz, me darling Lizz, the poor woman with all of those children, and one coming after the other," and even for Margaret, "wearing her hands to the bone caring for me and bathing and washing me, and cooking and caring for me and emptying me pots, the poor girl." And she also declares what Danny O'Neill has meant to her: "Me grandson, he's me son. Doesn't he call me Mother? Sure, if I didn't have him, wouldn't I lay down in the night and wouldn't I not wake up in the morning? What's kept me alive, with me family raised all these years, but me grandson?" "I'm no scholar but I met the scholars," says Mary, and she is proud of her grandson's chosen vocation: "and sure it's the poet and scholar he'll be, and don't I know that they'll be saying what a fine man he is, and it's poems he'll write."

In the middle of this chapter, Mary is carried to the bathroom by Danny, who then returns to his typewriter and the book, his first novel, on which he is working. Here the point of view shifts for the only time in the chapter, and the focus on Mary's consciousness is interrupted briefly by the thoughts of her grandson: "He wanted to finish this book before she died. If he did and it were published, he'd dedicate it to her. But she couldn't read. . . . What was she thinking of by the window? What went on in her mind?"[13] Imagining answers to these questions is going to be Danny O'Neill's lifework.

Danny learns several important lessons from his grandmother's death a few days later. He is struck immediately by the incalculable value of time: "This life which he had been so spendthrift of, how precious it was." His youthful rebellion, especially against the Church, is tempered by understanding that "The sorrows of death remained, remained in the hearts of the living. . . . He understood now why people did what he could not do, what he could never do—pray." Even his belief that "it was unmanly to cry" gives way to the release of real emotion, and he sobs and calls out his grandmother's name.

Danny's part in the O'Neill-O'Flaherty series leads ultimately to the summer day in 1927, a month after his grandmother's death, on which he prepares to leave Chicago for New York and a new life as a writer. Walking home down Fifty-eighth Street from the El, perhaps for the last time, he feels the weight of Washington Park as "a world in itself . . . a world in which another Danny O'Neill had lived." Feeling that he has "finally taken off a way of life, . . . as if it were a worn-out suit of clothes," Danny now has confidence in the "weapons" of his writer's trade: "now he was leaving and he was fully armed." (In this, he echoes Stephen Dedalus, leaving Dublin for Paris in 1902 with his own "weapons" of "silence, exile, and cunning.") Danny now also has a mature understanding of his position as an artist in relation to his family: "His people had not been fulfilled. He had not understood them all these years. He would do no penance now for these; he would do something surpassing penance. There was a loyalty to the dead, a loyalty beyond penance and regret. He would do battle so that others did not remain unfulfilled as he and his family had been."[14]

The last pages of *My Days of Anger* are a kind of litany to this place and this family, for the weight of both is embedded in Danny's consciousness, even as he leaves them behind. From the street, he turns to "the stones, the buildings" of the old neighborhood. He enters "the alley that he had known since he was a boy," pushes open "the broken backyard gate," and climbs the stairs into the O'Flaherty kitchen. Looking into his grandmother's room, he sees, along with her clothes still hanging in the closet, pictures of Christ and the Sacred Heart, a crucifix, a holy-water fount, and rosary beads—the symbols of her lifelong Catholicism, which he has also left behind but which he no longer scorns. Then Danny walks to the parlor in the front of the apartment to sit "brooding over his plans," and his mind here at the end of the novel comes to rest where his dreams have always been centered: "He listened to the summer wind in the trees across the street in Washington Park."

The first of the novels chronologically and the last to be written, *The*

Face of Time is a perfect coda for the O'Neill-O'Flaherty series. Opening in the summer of 1909, it brings the series full circle to the deaths of
Old Tom O'Flaherty and his daughter Louise, the memory of which
hangs over *A World I Never Made*. Also, in its rendering of Tom and
Mary O'Flaherty's memories of Ireland and their early years in America,
the novel returns to the very beginning of this family's story. The result is
the finest American novel dealing with the felt experience of emigration
from Ireland. In addition, the theme of failed communication gets its
fullest statement here, in the characterization of Old Tom, who lives out
a restless retirement, alternately bored and harassed, and dies of a
painful stomach cancer. Feeling useless and used up, Tom submits
quietly to his wife's nagging, admitting only to himself that "he loved his
Mary but he didn't love her tongue." It is clear here that coming out to
America has affected the O'Flahertys differently. Tom seems not to have
recovered from the early humiliations, while Mary has emerged stronger,
though not always in attractive ways. In fact, her dominance has turned
Tom into the forgotten man of the family. When a shared can of beer
makes both of them melancholy, she stares across the kitchen table at
him and asks, "What have I got but me grandson and me son Al?" And
after Tom has been taken to the hospital, Mary remarks to Al that "Ah,
Pa was no trouble. You'd hardly know he was in the house."

At the end of the novel, the inability to communicate becomes pervasive.
On the day of his hospitalization, Tom's voice fails and he is unable to
say goodbye to Danny. Her voice "breaking," Mary tells her family to
"let me be," and that night they eat dinner "in silence." The old man
doesn't live on for long in the hospital, and in a last daydream-soliloquy,
he reveals all the sad secrets that he has never articulated: he has never
felt at home in America, he is puzzled and embittered at having worked
so hard and ended up with so little, and he wishes he could die in
Ireland. Here is some of his moving revery:

> He'd wanted to tell Mary that he was afraid of America, afraid of it here
> in America, and, sure, if he told her that, what kind of a man would she be
> thinking him to be? Ah, she was a woman with nary a fear in her, not Mary.
> It was a source of wonderment to him that she had nary a fear in her heart,
> and the two of them, greenhorns if you like it, greenhorns in America in
> Brooklyn, New York, and Green Bay, Wisconsin, and Chicago. The strange
> people he'd seen and they were Americans and not his own people. Sure,
> wasn't he afraid to ask them how to find a street in Brooklyn? . . . Lying here
> in his hospital bed, when the pains weren't on him, he would think of all
> this, and think of what he came out here for. Sure, wasn't it to make money
> and marry Mary? Devil a lot of money he made, and until the children grew
> up it had been all they could do to keep body and soul together and put

food in their mouths. And how would the children know what was in him and the work he had done, the saving of money for his own horse and wagon and for the plot of burial ground in Calvary Cemetery?

. . . .

He furrowed his brows as he heard footsteps in the hall. Sure, when he first came to America, he would look at the people in New York and Brooklyn, New York with wonder in his eyes because they were Americans and he was in America. And not a soul on this earth knew how he was always wanting to go back and wishing he had never come out, and himself driving the horse and wagon and not knowing the names of the streets and wanting to ask this man and that for directions and not always asking because of his brogue and his not wanting it thought he was a greenhorn, and getting lost and not knowing where he was and wanting to go home to Ireland.[15]

The Face of Time closes with three final echoes of its major theme of failed communication. During his family's last visit to his bedside, Tom can hear Mary and Margaret discussing his imminent death, but he is unable to speak. When the hospital calls with the news of Tom's death, Mary leaves the family and shuts herself away in her bedroom, to grieve and pray alone. Standing before his grandfather's casket in the parlor, six-year-old Danny thinks, "There was Father. He couldn't talk. He was Father all right, and he wasn't Father." Then the novel (and the series as well) ends with a dying fall of incoherent sound, as Danny hears "whispering voices in the dining room, the low agonized sobs of his Aunt Margaret, and then the noise of a streetcar going by on Indiana Avenue."

Through these five novels, a few large themes build to powerful cumulative statement. Of central importance in that process are the clarifying but unshared reveries and unprotesting deaths of Jim O'Neill and Mary and Tom O'Flaherty. Danny O'Neill's opposing movement in the direction of art provides effective counterpoint, but does not mitigate the force of the presentation of his family's tragedies. In fact, Danny's isolated battling toward significant speech underscores the problems—some internal, some imposed from without—of the culture in which he grows up. In *The Face of Time,* Louise O'Flaherty asks the largest question. Her imminent death from tuberculosis prompts her to reflect: "was this the end of love, one going, dying. . . . Must you, in the end, always be alone?"

Throughout his prolific writing life, Farrell spoke eloquently of the purposes of his art. In his last novel published in his lifetime, *The Death of Nora Ryan* (1978), middle-aged writer Eddie Ryan realizes, while awaiting his mother's death in 1946, that someday he will turn the experience into art. "What was happening now, this present, would be the past and would be in his memory. The experience would have crystallized in his unconscious mind. . . . One morning he would wake up, sit at his desk, and start writing about it." He also thinks of the "simple purposes that his mother and others lived for," and wonders if her dying thoughts are of any consequence. His answer is a central tenet of Farrell's artistic faith: "Yes, it mattered. Nora Ryan's life was a world. For Nora Ryan. These thoughts brought back his most familiar and important ideas. He must one day dignify his mother's suffering in the consciousness."[16] From Old Tom O'Flaherty to Nora Ryan, the line of lives that have been so dignified in Farrell's work runs straight and clear. Toward this end, Farrell perfected an urban American plain style as the fitting mode for registering the self-consciousness of ordinary people living relatively uneventful lives. The forging of this style was a heroic effort of the will for Farrell. Indeed, his plain prose style gave no hint that Farrell was a prodigiously gifted intellectual, fiercely committed to the life of the mind, and encyclopedically well read. In his best work, a hard-won, minimal eloquence emerges naturally from the convincingly registered thoughts of characters such as Studs Lonigan in Washington Park, Jim O'Neill at his window on Calumet Avenue, and Old Tom O'Flaherty in Mercy Hospital.

Farrell was first and always an American realist: scrupulously honest, immune to sentimentality, and committed to giving serious literary consideration to the common life. His sympathetic portrayal of Chicago Irish working- and middle-class families established him as a pioneer in the field of urban ethnic literature. Indeed, Farrell's Washington Park is one of the most detailed settings of any American novel. On a scale far more extensive than Finley Peter Dunne's, Farrell described the inner life of a Chicago neighborhood during the turbulent period from 1900 to 1930. In addition to their undisputed value as literature, his Washington Park novels are first-rate social history, corroborating and clarifying more traditional sources about Chicago neighborhood life in the early twentieth century.

The themes of Farrell's fiction grow from the context of a fully realized narrative world, as complete as Joyce's Dublin and William Faulkner's Mississippi, and consistent with what he saw as "my constant and major aim as a writer—to write so that life may speak for itself."[17] Because these themes are so important and so thoroughly grounded in American, urban, and ethnic realities, it will become clear to more and more readers that James T. Farrell has done for twentieth-century Irish-America what William Carleton did for nineteenth-century Ireland.

Thomas Flanagan's placement of Carleton applies also to Farrell: "From the broken land of gunmen and gallows, of bent men upon bitter soil and lovers 'scattered like nosegays' across the meadows, came a writer so gifted that he could show us everything at once."[18]

NOTES

1. The full texts of the Dooley pieces quoted in this essay appear in *Mr. Dooley and the Chicago Irish: An Anthology,* ed. Charles Fanning (New York: Arno Press, 1976). For a more detailed exploration of Dunne's Chicago accomplishment, see Charles Fanning, *Finley Peter Dunne and Mr. Dooley: The Chicago Years* (Lexington: University Press of Kentucky, 1978). The Dooley pieces appeared in the *Chicago Evening Post* between Oct. 7, 1893, and Jan. 22, 1898.

2. *Observations by Mr. Dooley* (New York: R. H. Russell, 1902), p. 271.

3. *Mr. Dooley in the Hearts of His Countrymen* (Boston: Small, Maynard and Co., 1899). Autograph letter, Dunne to Herbert Small, Apr. 25, 1899, Dunne Letters, Chicago Historical Society.

4. The fiction about Nebraska cited below is collected in *The Nebraska of Kate McPhelim Cleary,* ed. James Mansfield Cleary (Lake Bluff, Ill.: United Educators, Inc., 1958). The biographical information was obtained from James Mansfield Cleary's introduction to the Nebraska book, and from *Poems by Margaret Kelly McPhelim and Her Children Kate McPhelim Cleary, Edward Joseph McPhelim,* "published by her Grandchildren, Vera Valentine Cleary, Gerald Vernon Cleary, James Mansfield Cleary, May, 1922."

5. "The Mission of Kitty Malone," *McClure's Magazine* 18 (Nov. 1901), 88–96.

6. *Like a Gallant Lady* (Chicago: Way and Williams, 1897), p. 231.

7. See Clara E. Laughlin, *"Just Folks"* (New York: Macmillan Co., 1910), and Laughlin's autobiography, *Traveling through Life* (Boston: Houghton, Mifflin Co., 1934).

8. *Studs Lonigan: A Trilogy* (New York: Vanguard Press, 1978), pp. 16–17.

9. Recently, the critical tide has begun to turn. Excellent essays published in the past few years include the following: Ann Douglas, "*Studs Lonigan* and the Failure of History in Mass Society: A Study in Claustrophobia," *American Quarterly* 26 (Winter 1977), 487–505; Ann Douglas, "James T. Farrell, the Artist Militant," *Dissent* (Spring 1980), 214–16; Robert James Butler, "Christian and Pragmatic Visions of Time in the Lonigan Trilogy," *Thought* 55 (Dec. 1980), 461–75; Robert James Butler, "The Christian Roots of Farrell's O'Neill and Carr Novels," *Renascence* 34 (1982), 81–97; Robert James Butler, "Parks, Parties, and Pragmatism: Time and Setting in James T. Farrell's Major Novels," *Essays in Literature* 10 (Fall 1983), 241–54. Farrell's thinking about Irish history and literature has been collected in James T. Farrell, *On Irish Themes* (Philadelphia: University of Pennsylvania Press, 1982), edited with a brilliant introduction by Dennis Flynn. Other relevant criticism of Farrell's "Washington Park" novels

includes the following: Nelson M. Blake, *Novelists' America, Fiction as History, 1910-1940* (Syracuse: Syracuse University Press, 1969), pp. 195-225; Edgar M. Branch, *James T. Farrell,* University of Minnesota Pamphlets on American Writers, no. 29 (Minneapolis: University of Minnesota Press, 1963); Edgar M. Branch, *James T. Farrell,* Twayne's U.S. Authors Series, no. 185 (New York: Twayne Publishers, 1971); Blanche Gelfant, *The American City Novel* (Norman: University of Oklahoma Press, 1954), pp. 175-227; Horace Gregory, "James T. Farrell: Beyond the Provinces of Art," *New World Writing: Fifth Mentor Selection* (New York: New American Library, 1954), pp. 52-64; Alan M. Wald, *James T. Farrell: The Revolutionary Socialist Years* (New York: New York University Press, 1978).

10. All were published originally in New York by the Vanguard Press. It is nothing less than a publishing scandal that of these novels, only *Studs Lonigan* is currently in print.

11. See Charles Fanning and Ellen Skerrett, "James T. Farrell and Washington Park," *Chicago History* 7 (Summer 1979), 80-91. All of the above factual information about these parishes and neighborhoods comes from the research of Ellen Skerrett.

12. *Father and Son* (New York: Vanguard Press, 1940), p. 308.

13. *My Days of Anger* (New York: Vanguard Press, 1943), pp. 362-71.

14. Ibid., p. 401.

15. *The Face of Time* (New York: Vanguard Press, 1953), pp. 334-35.

16. *The Death of Nora Ryan* (New York: Doubleday, 1978), pp. 280, 321.

17. "How *The Face of Time* Was Written," *Reflections at Fifty* (New York: Vanguard Press, 1954), p. 41.

18. Thomas Flanagan, *The Irish Novelists, 1800-1850* (New York: Columbia University Press, 1959), p. 299.

Conclusion

Lawrence J. McCaffrey

Irish-America is an urban ethnic success story. Descendants of Irish Catholics entering early nineteenth-century Protestant America as unskilled, unlettered, unwanted refugees from poverty and hopelessness achieved middle-class respectability. John F. Kennedy's presidency symbolized their progress. But the national profile of Irish-America does have regional distinctions. In many respects Chicago combines the experience of the two main varieties of Irish-Americans: those who first arrived in the United States and settled in eastern cities and those who came later and migrated to the urban frontier.

Like those in the East, the Chicago Irish pioneered non-Anglo-Protestant ethnicity in their city. As unskilled workers they assisted Chicago's emergence as a major industrial and commercial center and the transportation capital of the United States. In Chicago as in the East the Irish were damaged by the transition from rural Ireland to urban America. Psychological dislocation was manifest in antisocial, even criminal, behavior. The impoverished, physically and mentally disabled Irish became America's first group urban social problem. As social pariahs, and more important, as cultural and religious aliens, the Irish became victims of no-popery, anti-urban American nativism. They responded by reaffirming historical associations between Irish and Catholic, seeking and acquiring political power, and championing Ireland's struggle to escape the clutches of Anglo-Saxon Protestant colonialism.

While targeting the Irish for nativist hatred and discrimination, Catholicism also helped in the adjustment between Ireland and America. Its sacramental system, liturgy, devotions, and teachings reduced the differences between rural Ireland and cities in the United States by providing the familiar in a new setting. Catholicism also offered spiritual comfort, community, and a sense of ethnic identity within the pluralistic chaos of a cold, competitive, capitalist America.

As members of the only educated class in early Irish-America, priests played the same role that they did in Ireland, guiding and counseling in secular as well as religious matters. As in Ireland, the Irish in the United States gave their best talent, their loyalty, and their hard-earned money to the Church. After 1830 they took command of and stamped their personality on American Catholicism. Both in Ireland and the United States the Irish entered the priesthood for more than spiritual reasons. In situations short of opportunity for and prejudice against them, part of the attraction was access to power and material comfort. Members of a priest's family shared his community importance. Not until after Vatican II did clerical prestige slip in Irish-America.

Irish Catholicism has been pietistic, puritanical, and authoritarian, but, compared to the Continental version, relatively pragmatic and liberal politically. A long alliance with liberal and democratic Irish nationalism politically civilized Irish Catholicism, enabling its communicants to function within constitutional environments shaped by the British tradition. Because there was no political disparity between their nationalism and their Catholicism and because they had participated in well-organized mass agitations in Ireland for Catholic civil rights, tenant causes, and national liberation, Irish immigrants had the appropriate values and techniques to achieve political power in the United States.

For both practical and ideological reasons most Irish-Americans gave allegiance to the Democratic party. Its leaders were hospitable to Catholic immigrants, speeded their naturalization, and gave them patronage jobs. And as manorial serfs in Ireland and urban proletarians in the United States, the Irish naturally preferred Jeffersonian and Jacksonian egalitarianism to Federalist, Whig, and Republican elitism.

Democratic party Irish shock troops voted often, sometimes in the same election, and battled opponents with fists as well as ballots. But unwilling to remain permanently in the ranks, they began to control their own neighborhoods. By the end of the nineteenth century, Irish political influence extended beyond neighborhoods to dominate a large number of American cities. Irish power had negative as well as positive results.

Perhaps Irish contempt for and evasion of British rule in Ireland encouraged a light regard for law in general, shaping the lax political morality associated with Irish-America. More likely, Irish-American political values drew inspiration from Anglo-America's spoils system and business ethic. Sometimes Irish-American politics featured revenge.

Representing their constituents' response to Anglo-American nativism, some Irish-American politicians looted conquered enemy urban citadels, distributing the spoils among their own people after taking their share. They acquired a reputation as masters of corruption.

Until recently, in all parts of the country, Irish-Americans had little association with political idealism. They entered politics for the same reasons that many of them became priests, to become powerful and comfortable, prospects denied them in business and the professions. Religion and politics were Irish vocations, not avocations. In the case of politics, the calling often became hereditary.

Despite the trinity of power, revenge, and corruption, Irish politics did benefit those it served. Unlike so many Anglo-Americans who considered politics as inferior to business and the professions, at best a necessary evil, the Irish considered it a calling. They rejoiced in power struggles and in dealing with people. Although not as empathetic as they should have been to the problems of other ethnics and races, the Irish still were more tolerant of cultural diversity than Anglo-Americans. They forged coalitions, particularly with other Catholics. While keeping most of the instruments of power in their own grip, they distributed some of its symbols and opportunities among others.

Until well into the twentieth century, Anglo-American reformism was more interested in institutional and moral improvement than in lightening the burdens of poverty. Its attitude toward the poor often reflected the laissez-faire capitalism and the racism of Social Darwinism. In contrast, Irish victims of manorial capitalism in Ireland and industrial capitalism in the United States were not rugged individualists. Their Catholicism was communal. Their politics connected concern for constituents' material needs with votes. Combined, the two meant that the gradual emergence of the American welfare state owed more to Irish machine politics than to liberal ideology.

As in other places, the Irish in Chicago were mostly Democrats. They always have been more prominent as party leaders than their numbers would dictate. Well into the twentieth century Chicago exemplified Irish political corruption. Aldermen and other city officials sold franchises to businessmen ("boodling") and awarded construction contracts for payoffs. Many Irish politicians and policemen took vice lords' bribes not to enact or enforce laws against gambling, prostitution, or the liquor trade.

Despite their nefarious practices, Chicago's Irish politicians provided constituents with jobs and services. As other Catholics and Jews entered the city the Irish incorporated them into the Democratic machine, harvesting their votes, maintaining their own top pyramid power positions but providing their allies with enough clout and patronage to keep them from straying from the party. Like other whites, the Irish were deficient in sympathy for the difficulties of an increasing black population. However, in the 1930s Mayor Edward J. Kelly was a significant exception to this general attitude. His support for public housing and integrated schooling, along with the New Deal, persuaded blacks to switch from the Republican to the Democratic party.

The Chicago Irish joined other Irish-Americans in movements to free Ireland from Britain. With Catholicism, Irish nationalism preserved Irish ethnicity. For some, nationalism was more bitterness toward England than a love of Ireland. Anglophobia released the frustrations of people who never really made it in the United States. They romanticized Ireland while blaming British oppression for their exile in another land where again they had to confront Anglo-Protestant bigotry.

A desire for acceptance also motivated much Irish-American nationalism. Those moving toward or already reaching the middle class were more involved in nationalist movements than working-class people, who were far more interested in bread-and-butter issues of American life than in the troubles of Ireland. A quest for respectability inspired the nationalism of mobile Irish-America. It assumed that Anglo-America's refusal to accept the Irish as equal resulted from their homeland's subservience to Britain and that its independence would confer dignity on them.

There were differences as well as similarities between Irish nationalism in Chicago and in the rest of the country. During the 1880s and 1890s, when the city was at the center of Clan na Gael activities, Chicago's Irish nationalists were more inclined toward terrorism than other Irish-Americans. Leading Irish-American nationalists in the East were contemptuous of politics. They complained of blind Irish loyalty to the Democrats and wanted Irish voters to bargain between parties for their votes, the price to be a commitment to Ireland's freedom. In Chicago, however, particularly during the Clan na Gael phase, nationalism and politics were hand in glove. While most nationalist politicians were Democrats functioning as a machine within a machine, A. M. Sullivan, head of the Clan executive, the Triangle, and a few others were Republican. Chicago's Irish politicians knew that nationalist slogans and celebrations pleased Irish voters.

Irish ghettos in Chicago and eastern cities reinforced fatalism and defeatism derived from dismal historical experiences on two sides of the Atlantic. Pessimism limited perspectives, discouraged a drive for excellence, and encouraged the sacrifice of ambition for security. It also fostered a destructive Irish tendency to escape reality in drink. Insecurity also led the Irish to cling desperately to Catholicism for comfort and identity and to trust in politics for power and economic opportunity.

While Irish parishes were less isolated from the main currents of American life than their German, Italian, or Polish counterparts, Catholic suspicion of American values tended to narrow the Irish mental focus to religious, ethnic, and neighborhood concerns. Chicago Irish provincialism has been reflected in its politics. Irish politicians from the city have not exercised much state or national influence. Viewing downstate Illinois as hostile nativist territory, which it often has been, they have confined their energies to Cook County.

While sharing many of the experiences and attitudes of the eastern Irish, Chicago's Irish were on the urban frontier. They were never as physically ghettoized as those in Boston, New York, or Philadelphia. Initially not as successful as the Irish in some other Midwest cities, they did emerge from the unskilled working-class more rapidly than most of the eastern variety.

In places such as Boston, the Irish settled in cities with rigid social structures, fading economies, and strong anti–Irish Catholic prejudices. But the Midwest and West had dynamic, expanding economies and fluid social structures. Economic necessity had priority over nativism. Immigrants and their children who wanted to work could find jobs and experience social mobility.

Physical and psychological distance from the northeastern literary establishment freed Chicago Irish writers, permitting Finley Peter Dunne in the 1890s to create the first fully realized ethnic neighborhood in American literature. In the 1930s and 1940s James T. Farrell's socially and geographically mobile Lonigans and O'Neills became models for American urban ethnic literary realism.

Midwest Irish achievements distinguished its Catholicism from the eastern expression. Along the Atlantic coast Irish bishops interpreted American life and culture as threats to the faith of their people. They encouraged a ghetto mentality as a means of preserving Catholic values. Bishops resisted social reform and the labor movement as secularism, radicalism, and socialism, advising the laity to postpone justice until the next life. Midwest Irish bishops had a different view of the Church in the United States. They urged its Americanization, praising liberal democracy as an opportunity for, not a threat to, Catholicism. They were involved with social and economic reform, actively defending the right of workers to organize and bargain collectively.[1]

In harmony with its Midwest location, the Irish-dominated Catholicism in Chicago tended to be progressive on social and political issues, and, as far as the Irish were concerned, not culturally ethnic. Priests in the parishes, along with nuns and brothers in the schools, assumed that Irish was Catholic and Catholic was Irish and that was all the cultural and historical identity their parishioners and students needed. Instead of cultivating Irish uniqueness, Irish Catholic educators, particularly on the college level, emphasized a medieval heritage they believed common to all Catholics. Medievalism was intended as more than cohesiveness. It also gave Catholics a historical tradition older than the one claimed by Anglo-Protestants. On the elementary and secondary school levels, Catholics borrowed from and then improved on public education, achieving respectability for their graduates. Women products of Catholic education flocked to the teaching and nursing professions, leading the Irish march toward the middle class.

As in most other parts of the country, after World War II Irish men in Chicago caught up with the women educationally. Taking advantage of the GI Bill they completed the Irish trek in America from unskilled working-class to essentially middle-class status. Since the late nineteenth century residential change has accompanied Irish social mobility. After the Great Fire of 1871, Irish families continually moved farther south, west, and north from the city center. By the late 1950s occupational progress plus pressures from an expanding black population had propelled many of them into the suburbs. Presently, most of the Irish in the Chicago metropolitan area live outside the city.

Suburbanization was a material symbol of Irish-America's social and economic success but challenged the religious core of its ethnicity. Unlike Ireland, where connections between Irish and Catholic have held each in bondage, thus delaying the implementation of Vatican II, the well-educated, assimilated Irish-American middle class welcomed the leadership of John XXIII. Expecting significant changes in the Church, they reacted negatively to the anticontraception message of Paul VI's *Humanae Vitae* (1968). Their initial defiance began a questioning of Church authority which expanded to include such issues as clerical celibacy, an exclusively male priesthood, and divorce. While most still accept the official Catholic prohibition of abortion, a large number would exclude physically or psychologically ill pregnant women or those who were victims of rape and incest.[2]

Currently about 17 percent of American Catholics and 50 percent of their bishops are Irish.[3] But Irish-America no longer contributes its best talent to the Church. So many prospects for the well educated, a decline in the status of organized religion, and less deference to the clergy and their families have discouraged parents from promoting religious vocations among their children. Young people think more about reaching the top in business and the professions than they do about futures in rectories and convents. Conceivably the Poles will replace the Irish as leaders of whatever is left of Catholic America.

In addition to the pursuit of comfort, contemporary middle-class Irish-American Catholicity expresses the questioning, individualistic values of Anglo-American political culture. The result is impatience with stubborn, often unenlightened Church authority. Tensions that have always divided Irish-America in its contradictory allegiances to the religious absolutism of Rome and the political liberalism of the British and American traditions have been resolved in favor of the latter.

The condition of present-day Irish-American Catholicism also indicates fading ethnicity. Thoroughly integrated into a youth-obsessed nation without much respect for the past, most Irish-Americans are unconscious of their cultural and historical roots. Since they were struggling for respectability before ethnicity was fashionable, Irish-American parents hesitated to preserve nationality in their children. And, as just mentioned, the Irish-controlled Catholic Church, through its education system, insisted on Catholic solidarity and an irrelevant medievalism rather than ethnic uniqueness.

Removed from urban parishes, refugees from the city have lost much of their Irishness in suburban melting pots. Association with non-Catholics, the impact of private-conscience theology, the increasingly boring hallelujah liturgies and vapid homilies of post-Vatican religious services which have robbed Catholicism of its history and mystery, and quarrels with the Church, particularly on sexual subjects, have combined to make Catholicism less significant for Irish-America. Since Catholicism was the basic ingredient in Irish cultural identity, ethnicity has receded with fading religious commitment.

Success has altered Irish politics as well as Catholicism. After John F. Kennedy's assassination, such former and current Irish-American senators as his two brothers, the late Robert F. (New York) and Edward M. (Massachusetts), Eugene McCarthy (Minnesota), Mike Mansfield (Montana), and the late Philip A. Hart (Michigan), and the former Speaker of the House of Representatives, Thomas P. O'Neill (Massachusetts) have served as liberal political voices in Congress. But ethnic vagueness added to middle-class economic self-interest have meant that a large number of Irish suburbanites have forsaken hereditary allegiance to the Democratic party. They voted for Richard M. Nixon in 1972 and Ronald Reagan in 1980 and 1984.

There are exceptions to the profile of the general upwardly mobile, well-educated, suburban Irish-American. Many, including most recent immigrants, still live in cities. However, since World War I, American immigration laws, economic depression, World War II, and the availability of work in the nearby United Kingdom directed the mainstream of Irish emigration from the United States to Britain. Now only a few thousand Irish arrive yearly in urban America. In 1970 there were only 14,709 Irish born in Chicago, placing them eighth among those with foreign origins.

Of all American cities, still-ghettoized Boston best represents early Irish-American economic and social situations. But pockets of retarded Irish mobility and insecurity exist in other cities, including Chicago. Efforts to preserve the psychological securities of cohesive neighborhoods and ethnic values have joined Irish and other inner-city Catholics in resistance to open housing and busing to achieve integrated education.[4] Defensiveness has also made them more consciously Catholic than suburbanites. Many believe that the Church's positions on sex and marriage are essential to family stability and social order. While suburban Irish parents send children to parochial schools out of some loyalty to the past and to protect them from drugs and sexual dangers, those in the city are more concerned with preserving the faith, which means white ethnicity, and with a quality education seldom available in public schools.

Among the Irish and other ethnic blue-collar workers and marginal middle-class people in cities and collar suburbs there is an angry conviction that since 1972 elitist, sanctimonious ideologists who view them with contempt and cater to blacks, feminists, and homosexuals have captured the Democratic party. In retaliation, they spurned presidential candidates George McGovern (1972), Jimmy Carter (1980), and Walter Mondale (1984) for their Republican opponents.

Differing responses to the situation in Northern Ireland since 1969 measure the complexities of Irish-America. Although the Irish, British, and American governments have accused Irish-Americans of sustaining terrorism with their dollars, only a minority of them aid the Irish Republican Army. In 1969, when Northern Irish officials and policemen responded to the Catholic civil rights effort with oppression, violence spread through the streets of Derry and Belfast. Irish-America reacted in anger to the results of centuries of British stupidity and insensitivity in Ireland. They saw their own kind, Irish Catholics, brutalized on television screens. In time, however, when tempers cooled, most middle-class Irish-Americans flinched at collaborating with an indiscriminate terrorism that often killed and maimed women and children, and they rejected the macabre masochism of hunger strikers. They also heeded the advice of such prominent politicians as Tip O'Neill and Teddy Kennedy, who told them not to assist death and destruction in Northern Ireland. And gradually, in the good old American tradition, they became bored with what appears to be an insoluble problem.

Among the minority of Irish-Americans involved in Northern Ireland some are nationalist idealists convinced of the justice of the United Ireland cause. Most, however, are post–World War II immigrants. They left Ireland bitter about the failure of its government to provide jobs and found it difficult to meld into the new, middle-class Irish-America. They continue to hate Britain and to search for respectability—themes of nineteenth-century Irish-American nationalism. They fit Isaiah Berlin's definition of nationalism "as the inflamed desire of the insufficiently regarded to count for something among the cultures of the world."

Despite class and value differences between old and new diasporas, recent additions contribute to rather than contradict the Irish-American success story. Like their predecessors, recent Irish immigrants are socially mobile and their American commitment is loving and permanent. On sentimental occasions they may shed a tear for "Old Ireland" but unlike many other ethnics, the Irish always have come to the United States without reservations and quickly become citizens. For the Irish the United States remains the land of opportunity.

Chicago is a good example of recent Irish immigrant progress. Political power has provided them with more jobs than come to other Catholic white ethnics, blacks, Puerto Ricans, or Chicanos. They invest much of their incomes in higher education for children who attend such universities and colleges as Loyola, DePaul, University of Illinois at Chicago, Mundelein, Rosary, and St. Xavier. Following graduation, sons and daughters of immigrants join the suburban or urban-condominium middle-class, with the result that differences between old and new Irish-America tend to adjust within a generation.

Despite few new immigrant arrivals and large departures from the city, Irish political power in Chicago has continued to exceed their share of the population. Except for Croatian Michael Bilandic (1976–79), Irish mayors presided over the city from 1933 to 1983. The Irish also maintained their hold on key positions in city government, on the judicial bench, and in the police and fire departments. While higher education has polished and improved the quality of Irish politicians, occasionally they still get caught with hands in the public till.

Irish political power in Chicago reached its zenith during the administration of Richard J. Daley (1955–76). As mayor and chairman of the Cook County Democratic Central Committee he perfected Irish machine politics. Differing from his "boss" predecessors in Chicago and other cities, Daley attached more importance to the city's future and the common good than to the interests of the patronage parasites attached to the organization. He could have been more sensitive to the plight of blacks and Spanish-speaking people and more tolerant of political dissenters within the party, but the mayor truly loved Chicago. During his administration it became physically one of the most beautiful of American metropolises and one of the most efficient in services.

Though they lost the 1983 Democratic mayoralty primary to Harold Washington, a black, two Irish candidates, the incumbent Jane M. Byrne, and the State's Attorney son of the former mayor, Richard M. Daley, garnered approximately two-thirds of the vote. Still, considering relative Irish and other white ethnic population decline and Hispanic and black increase, plus the developing organizational skills of the latter, and the breakdown of the machine into self-interest fiefs, Chicago is not likely to have another Irish mayor. Gradually Irish numbers in the city council, in the police and fire departments, in the judiciary, and in the patronage structure will all decrease.

Few non-Irish Chicago tears will fall over the passing of Irish political power in Chicago, but on the whole it served the needs of the people. Certainly the Irish should receive as much credit for the beauty, charm, hospitality, and dynamic quality of the city as they have blame for its graft and corruption. They have helped make Chicago's politics the most interesting in the country.

Not even all of Chicago's Irish lament the decline of their political influence. Some realize that overconcentration on politics has limited achievement in other directions, particularly the creative arts. Chicago has an abundance of Irish politicians, lawyers, doctors, dentists, teachers, social workers, civil servants, and businessmen, but the city that inspired an Irish-American literary tradition has not produced worthy successors to Finley Peter Dunne and James T. Farrell.[5]

Catholic education's emphasis on respectability steered the Irish away from the creative arts into more secure occupations. Politics also has played a role in the Chicago Irish failure to make a significant cultural impact on city, state, or nation. Politics was a step toward Irish-American power and opportunity. Unfortunately, in Chicago it became an end in itself. And while Chicago's Irish politicians have been skilled in acquiring power, they have had little influence over events beyond the borders of Cook County. Chicago Irish political provincialism and tribalism reasserted themselves after Daley's death, particularly after Washington became mayor. Instead of helping him solve the city's many problems, particularly in the areas of economics and education, Irish and other white ethnic aldermen face the mayor in racial confrontation.

In Chicago and elsewhere, Irish-America's pulse falters. Despite the popularity of soda bread, the Irish have abandoned the unimaginative cooking of their ethnic heritage for the excitement of French and Italian cuisine. But thanks to such groups as the Clancy Brothers and Tommy

Makem and the Chieftains many Irish-Americans have come to appreciate the merits of traditional Irish music. And throughout the United States college students have an interest in the genius of Irish literature and the diversity and relevance of the Irish historical experience. Perhaps these enthusiasms are of the moment, or alternatives to a fading Catholicism in the search for Irishness, and will diminish or vanish in the post-college suburban melting pots or marriages with non-Irish partners. On the other hand, perhaps many young Irish-Americans have found a permanent pride in and consciousness of nationality abandoned by their progenitors. Irishness might survive in a reduced but more refined and vital context.

Traveling to extinction or a new creativity, Irish-America has marked the history of the United States. Irish pioneers of the American urban ghetto have previewed the adventures of other non-Anglo-Protestants. While confusing and contradictory allegiances to Roman Catholic authoritarianism and Anglo-Saxon and Anglo-American liberal democracy have tormented the Irish mind, they have enabled it to accommodate American Catholicism to the political culture of the United States. Irish leadership saved Catholic America from developing an impregnable siege mentality and enabled it to participate in the diversity and freedom of the American experience.

NOTES

1. John Cogley, *Catholic America* (New York: Dial Press, 1963); James Edmund Roohan, *American Catholics and the Social Question, 1865-1900* (New York: Arno Press, 1976); Robert D. Cross, *The Emergence of Liberal Catholicism in America* (Chicago: Quadrangle Books, Inc., 1967); Andrew M. Greeley, "The Chicago Experience," *The Catholic Experience* (New York: Doubleday Image Books, 1969).

2. According to Marjorie R. Fallows, a sociologist, evidence indicates "a majority of Irish Catholics in metropolitan areas of the North support the legal availability of abortion for those who wish to use it—especially in cases of rape, a threat to the mother's life, or the likelihood of birth defects." (*Irish-Americans: Identity and Assimilation* [Englewood Cliffs, N.J.: Prentice-Hall, Inc., 1979], pp. 109-10.)

3. Michael Novak, *The Rise of the Unmeltable Ethnics* (New York: Macmillan Publishing Company, 1973), p. 55.

4. In "Race and Housing: Violence and Communal Protest in Chicago, 1940-1960," in *Ethnic Chicago,* ed. Peter d'A. Jones and Melvin G. Holli (Grand Rapids: William B. Eerdmans Publishing Co., 1977), Arnold Hirsch's description of Chicago Irish resistance to black expansion into white neighborhoods indicates that they could be as insecure as the Boston Irish discussed in J. Anthony Lucas,

Common Ground: A Turbulent Decade in the Lives of Three American Families (New York: Alfred A. Knopf, 1985).

5. James Carroll is an exception. He was born and raised in Chicago but his novels are set in eastern cities.

Chicago's Irish settlements, 1880

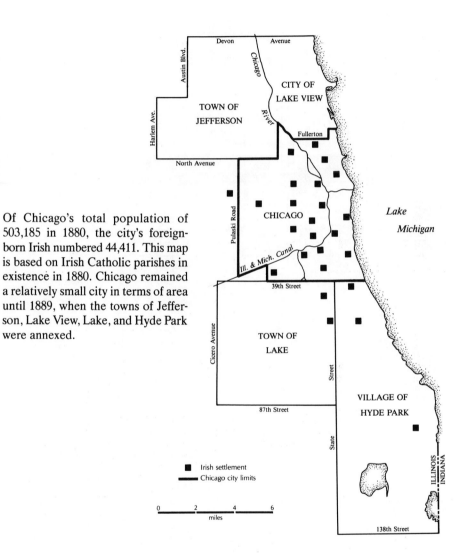

Of Chicago's total population of 503,185 in 1880, the city's foreign-born Irish numbered 44,411. This map is based on Irish Catholic parishes in existence in 1880. Chicago remained a relatively small city in terms of area until 1889, when the towns of Jefferson, Lake View, Lake, and Hyde Park were annexed.

Chicago's Irish stock population, 1930, by community area

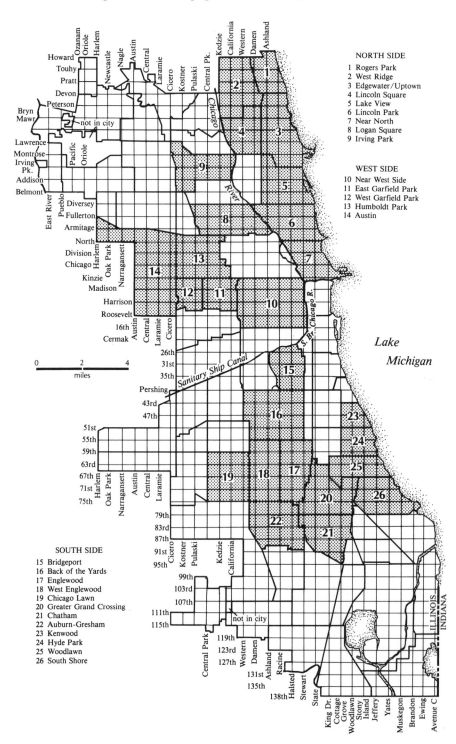

NORTH SIDE

1 Rogers Park
2 West Ridge
3 Edgewater/Uptown
4 Lincoln Square
5 Lake View
6 Lincoln Park
7 Near North
8 Logan Square
9 Irving Park

WEST SIDE

10 Near West Side
11 East Garfield Park
12 West Garfield Park
13 Humboldt Park
14 Austin

SOUTH SIDE

15 Bridgeport
16 Back of the Yards
17 Englewood
18 West Englewood
19 Chicago Lawn
20 Greater Grand Crossing
21 Chatham
22 Auburn-Gresham
23 Kenwood
24 Hyde Park
25 Woodlawn
26 South Shore

Lake Michigan

Chicago's Irish stock population, 1930, by community area

This map is based on the 1930 U.S. Census and the community areas
defined by the Social Science Research Committee, University of
Chicago. Shaded areas indicate communities with Irish stock populations in excess of 2,000 persons. "Irish stock" includes persons born
in the Irish Free State and Northern Ireland as well as native-white
persons whose parents were born in the Irish Free State or Northern
Ireland. Of the city's total population of 3,376,438 in 1930, Chicago's
Irish stock numbered 193,555.

Community area	Irish stock, 1930	Total community population
1 Rogers Park	3,733	57,094
2 West Ridge	2,201	39,759
3 Edgewater/Uptown	7,447	121,637
4 Lincoln Square	2,131	46,419
5 Lake View	5,695	114,872
6 Lincoln Park	5,587	97,873
7 Near North	5,044	79,554
8 Logan Square	2,362	114,174
9 Irving Park	2,207	66,783
10 Near West Side	6,235	152,457
11 East Garfield Park	6,413	63,353
12 West Garfield Park	8,570	50,014
13 Humboldt Park	3,657	80,835
14 Austin	15,738	131,114
15 Bridgeport	3,452	53,553
16 Back of the Yards	9,687	87,103
17 Englewood	12,001	89,063
18 West Englewood	9,532	63,845
19 Chicago Lawn	4,485	47,462
20 Greater Grand Crossing	7,439	60,007
21 Chatham	3,863	36,228
22 Auburn-Gresham	11,716	57,381
23 Kenwood	2,116	26,942
24 Hyde Park	2,951	48,017
25 Woodlawn	5,913	66,052
26 South Shore	7,603	78,755

Col. James A. Mulligan served as leader of the Chicago Irish Brigade from 1861 to 1864. His dying words, "Lay me down and save the flag," inspired a popular Civil War song. (Courtesy Chicago Historical Society)

The Great Chicago Fire began Oct. 8, 1871, in a barn behind Patrick and Catherine O'Leary's wooden cottage at DeKoven and Jefferson streets. Although the fire destroyed nearly four square miles, including downtown Chicago, it spared the O'Leary cottage. (Courtesy Chicago Historical Society)

The Irish Industrial Village at the 1893 World's Columbian Exposition in Chicago featured a replica of Blarney Castle. (Courtesy Chicago Historical Society)

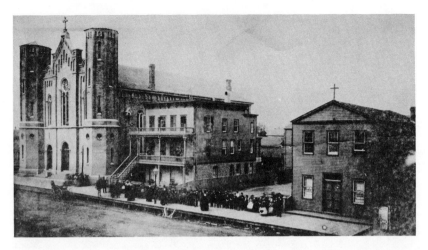

St. Patrick's parish, Adams and Desplaines streets, c. 1875. The frame building at the right is the original church, constructed in 1846 for the burgeoning Irish community on Chicago's West Side. Rev. Dennis Dunne, uncle of Finley Peter Dunne, was pastor when the building was completed in 1856. (Courtesy *The Chicago Catholic*)

St. Bernard's Church at 66th and Stewart Avenue in the Englewood neighborhood was a powerful symbol of middle-class Irish respectability. Established in the midst of a Protestant community, the marble church was completed in 1898. (Courtesy *The Chicago Catholic*)

Graduates of Holy Family's parochial schools parade through the Near West Side neighborhood. (Holy Family Church, courtesy Jane Addams Hull-House)

May crowning at Visitation parish, Garfield Boulevard and Peoria Street, 1950s. (Gibson Studios, courtesy *The Chicago Catholic*)

Corpus Christi parish, 49th and South Parkway, was founded in 1901 by "steam-heat" Irish. James T. Farrell attended Corpus Christi grammar school from 1911 to 1915. He later used the parish as a setting for his Danny O'Neill novels. (South Parkway is now Dr. Martin Luther King, Jr., Drive.) (Courtesy *The Chicago Catholic*)

In 1933 Corpus Christi became the third black Catholic parish in Chicago, serving families in the "Black Belt." (Courtesy *The Chicago Catholic*)

The Michael J. McCaughey family, 1939, was a model of Irish social mobility. They lived in the fashionable South Shore neighborhood, and all six McCaughey children attended Catholic institutions, from St. Philip Neri grammar school to St. Mary College and Notre Dame University. (Courtesy *The Chicago Catholic*)

In the early 1920s, James T. Farrell lived in this graystone building at 5816 South Park Avenue. It was in the second-floor apartment overlooking Washington Park that he "dreamed . . . and resolved to write." Farrell's Washington Park novels and *Studs Lonigan* detail the lives of Chicago's "steam-heat" Irish between 1900 and the Great Depression. (Courtesy John C. O'Malley)

Finley Peter Dunne (1867–1936), creator of "Mr. Dooley" and the first voice of genius in Irish-American literature. His depiction of Bridgeport in the 1890s is the first fully realized ethnic neighborhood in American literature. (Courtesy Chicago Historical Society)

The Shannon Rovers Pipe Band, organized in 1926, performs at every significant Irish event in Chicago. This photo was taken in 1966 to celebrate their fortieth anniversary. (Courtesy St. Patrick's Day Parade Committee)

Archbishop George W. Mundelein and Eamon de Valera, president of the Irish Dail (Parliament), 1919. De Valera was in the United States attempting to achieve American recognition of the Irish Republic during the Anglo-Irish War. (Courtesy *The Chicago Catholic*)

Mayor Richard J. Daley and Admiral Daniel V. Gallery lead the 1956 St. Patrick's Day Parade, the first in downtown Chicago since the nineteenth century. Admiral Gallery, the grandson of William J. Onahan, directed the capture of the U-505 German submarine in 1944. (Courtesy St. Patrick's Day Parade Committee)

The Nov. 4, 1960, torchlight parade in Chicago was John F. Kennedy's last public appearance before his election as president. Mayor Richard J. Daley (center) and Kennedy represent the transition in Irish politics from power to power with purpose. (Courtesy St. Patrick's Day Parade Committee)

Police Commissioner James Rochford and Mayor Richard J. Daley install the Haymarket statue in the new Police Training Academy, 1976. This statue, modeled after a Chicago Irish policeman and unveiled in 1889, commemorates the seven police officers killed as a result of a bomb explosion at a workers' rally May 4, 1886. To the Irish, policemen and firemen are heroes who make life possible in the urban jungle. (Courtesy St. Patrick's Day Parade Committee)

This picture of Jane Byrne, the first woman mayor of a large city, with Bishop Nevin Hayes and Daniel P. Lydon of the plumbers union, demonstrates the connection between the Irish in politics, religion, and the labor movement. The occasion was the Irish Fellowship Club's St. Patrick's Day banquet, 1981. (Courtesy St. Patrick's Day Parade Committee)

Selected Readings

History, Sociology of the Chicago Irish

Clark, Dennis. *Hibernia America: The Irish and Regional Cultures.* Westport, Conn.: Greenwood Press, 1986.

Doyle, David N. "The Regional Bibliography of Irish America, 1800–1930: Selected Readings, A Review and Addendum." *Irish Historical Studies* 23 (1983), 254–83.

Fallows, Marjorie. *Irish Americans: Identity and Assimilation.* Englewood Cliffs, N.J.: Prentice-Hall, 1977.

Fanning, Charles; Skerrett, Ellen; and Corrigan, John. *Nineteenth Century Chicago Irish: A Social and Political Portrait.* Urban Insight Series, No. 7. Chicago: Center for Urban Policy, Loyola University of Chicago, 1980.

Ffrench, Charles, ed. *Biographical History of the American-Irish in Chicago.* Chicago: American Biographical Publishing Co., 1897.

Fleming, George. "Canal at Chicago." Ph.D. dissertation, Catholic University of America, 1950.

Flinn, John J. *History of the Chicago Police from the Settlement of the Community to the Present Time.* Chicago: Police Book Fund, 1887.

Funchion, Michael F. "Irish Chicago: Church, Homeland, Politics, and Class— The Shaping of an Ethnic Group, 1870–1900." In *Ethnic Chicago.* Edited by Peter d'A. Jones and Melvin G. Holli, pp. 9–39. Grand Rapids, Mich.: William B. Eerdmans Publishing Company, 1981.

Greeley, Andrew M. *The Irish Americans: The Rise to Money and Power.* New York: Harper and Row, 1981.

——. *That Most Distressful Nation: The Taming of the American Irish.* Chicago: Quadrangle Books, 1972.

——. *Why Can't They Be Like Us?* New York: Dutton, 1971.

McCready, William C. "The Irish Neighborhood: A Contribution to American Urban Life." In *America and Ireland, 1776–1976: The American Identity and the Irish Connection.* Edited by David Noel Doyle and Owen Dudley Edwards, pp. 248–56. Westport, Conn.: Greenwood Press, 1980.

Pierce, Bessie Louise. *A History of Chicago.* 3 vols. New York: Alfred A. Knopf, 1937–57.

Piper, Ruth M. "The Irish in Chicago, 1848–1871." M.A. thesis, University of Chicago, 1936.

Skerrett, Ellen. "The Development of Catholic Identity among Irish Americans in Chicago, 1880 to 1920." In *From Paddy to Studs: Irish-American Communities in the Turn of the Century Era, 1880 to 1920.* Edited by Timothy J. Meagher, pp. 117–38. Westport, Conn.: Greenwood Press, 1986.

Literature

Cleary, Kate. *Like a Gallant Lady.* Chicago: Way and Williams, 1897.

Collected works of Finley Peter Dunne:
  Mr. Dooley in Peace and in War (1898). Boston: Small, Maynard
  Mr. Dooley in the Hearts of His Countrymen (1899). Boston: Small, Maynard
  Mr. Dooley's Philosophy (1900). New York: R. H. Russell
  Mr. Dooley's Opinions (1901). New York: R. H. Russell
  Observations by Mr. Dooley (1902). New York: R. H. Russell
  Dissertations by Mr. Dooley (1906). New York: Harper
  Mr. Dooley Says (1910). New York: Scribners
  Mr. Dooley on Making a Will and Other Necessary Evils (1919). New York: Scribners
  Mr. Dooley and the Chicago Irish: An Anthology. Edited by Charles Fanning. New York: Arno, 1976.

Fanning, Charles. *Finley Peter Dunne and Mr. Dooley: The Chicago Years.* Lexington: University Press of Kentucky, 1978.

James T. Farrell's Chicago Novels and Collected Short Stories:
  Gas-House McGinty (1933). New York: Vanguard
  Studs Lonigan: A Trilogy (1935). New York: Vanguard
  A World I Never Made (1936). New York: Vanguard
  The Short Stories of James T. Farrell (1937). New York: Vanguard
  No Star Is Lost (1938). New York: Vanguard
  Father and Son (1940). Reprinted, 1976. New York: Arno
  Ellen Rogers (1941). New York: Vanguard
  $1,000 a Week and Other Stories (1942). New York: Vanguard
  My Days of Anger (1943). New York: Vanguard
  The Face of Time (1953). New York: Vanguard
  The Dunne Family (1976). Garden City, N.Y.: Doubleday
  The Death of Nora Ryan (1978). Garden City, N.Y.: Doubleday

Laughlin, Clara E. *"Just Folks."* New York: Macmillan Co., 1910.

———. *Traveling through Life.* Boston: Houghton, Mifflin, 1934.

Politics

Allswang, John M. *A House for All Peoples: Ethnic Politics in Chicago, 1890–1936.* Lexington: University Press of Kentucky, 1971.

Becker, Richard E. "Edward Dunne, Reform Mayor of Chicago, 1905–1907." Ph.D. dissertation, University of Chicago, 1971.

Biles, Roger. *Big City Boss in Depression and War: Mayor Edward J. Kelly of Chicago.* DeKalb: Northern Illinois University Press, 1984.

Buenker, John D. *Urban Liberalism and Progressive Reform.* New York: Charles Scribner's Sons, 1973.

Duis, Perry R. *The Saloon: Public Drinking in Chicago and Boston, 1880–1920.* Urbana: University of Illinois Press, 1983.

Funchion, Michael F. *Chicago's Irish Nationalists, 1881–1890.* New York: Arno Press, 1976.

Gleason, William F. *Daley of Chicago.* New York: Simon and Schuster, 1970.

Green, Paul Michael. "Irish Chicago: The Multiethnic Road to Machine Success." In *Ethnic Chicago.* Edited by Peter d'A. Jones and Melvin G. Holli, pp. 212–69. Grand Rapids, Mich.: William B. Eerdmans Publishing Co., 1981.

Keefe, Thomas M. "Chicago's Flirtation with Political Nativism, 1854–1856." *Records of the American Catholic Historical Society of Philadelphia* 82 (1971), 131–58.

Levine, Edward M. *The Irish and Irish Politicians.* Notre Dame, Ind.: University of Notre Dame Press, 1966.

O'Malley, Peter J. "Mayor Martin Kennelly of Chicago: A Political Biography." Ph.D. dissertation, University of Illinois at Chicago, 1980.

Walsh, James B., ed. *The Irish: America's Political Class.* New York: Arno Press, 1976.

Religion

Brewer, Eileen M. "Beyond Utility: The Role of the Nun in the Education of American Catholic Girls, 1860–1920." Ph.D. dissertation, University of Chicago, 1984.

Dahm, Charles W. *Power and Authority in the Catholic Church: Cardinal Cody in Chicago.* Notre Dame, Ind.: University of Notre Dame Press, 1982.

Gaffey, James P. "Patterns of Ecclesiastical Authority: The Problem of Chicago Succession, 1865–1881." *Church History* 42 (1973), 257–70.

Garraghan, Gilbert J. *The Catholic Church in Chicago, 1673–1871.* Chicago: Loyola University Press, 1921.

Kantowicz, Edward. *Corporation Sole: Cardinal Mundelein & Chicago Catholicism.* Notre Dame, Ind.: University of Notre Dame Press, 1983.

Keefe, Thomas M. "The Catholic Issue in the Chicago Tribune before the Civil War." *Mid-America* 57 (1975), 227–45.

Kirkfleet, Cornelius. *The Life of Patrick Augustine Feehan, Bishop of Nashville, First Archbishop of Chicago, 1829–1902.* Chicago: Matre and Co., 1922.

Koenig, Rev. Msgr. Harry C., ed. *A History of the Parishes of the Archdiocese of Chicago.* 2 vols. Chicago: Archdiocese of Chicago, 1980.

McGirr, John E. *Life of Rt. Rev. Wm. Quarter, D.D., First Bishop of Chicago.* Des Plaines, Ill.: St. Mary's Training School Press, 1920.

McGovern, James J. *The Life and Writings of the Right Reverend John McMullen, D.D.* Chicago: Hoffman Brothers, 1888.

McGovern, James J. *Souvenir of the Silver Jubilee in the Episcopacy of His Grace the Most Rev. Patrick Augustine Feehan, Archbishop of Chicago.* Chicago: privately printed, 1891.

Sanders, James W. *The Education of an Urban Minority: Catholics in Chicago, 1833-1965.* New York: Oxford University Press, 1977.

Schaefer, Marvin R. "The Catholic Church in Chicago: Its Growth and Administration." Ph.D. dissertation, University of Chicago, 1929.

Shanabruch, Charles. *Chicago's Catholics: The Evolution of an American Identity.* Notre Dame, Ind.: University of Notre Dame Press, 1981.

Thompson, Joseph J., ed. *The Archdiocese of Chicago, Antecedents and Development.* Des Plaines, Ill.: St. Mary's Training School Press, 1920.

Walch, Timothy G. "Catholic Education in Chicago and Milwaukee, 1840-1890." Ph.D. dissertation, Northwestern University, 1975.

Walsh, John Patrick. "The Catholic Church in Chicago and the Problems of an Urban Society, 1893-1915." Ph.D. dissertation, University of Chicago, 1948.

Notes on Contributors

Lawrence J. McCaffrey received his B.A. from St. Ambrose College, Davenport, Iowa, his M.A. from Indiana University, and his Ph.D. from the University of Iowa. Since 1970 McCaffrey has been professor of Irish and Irish-American history at Loyola University of Chicago. He has written five books and a number of articles on Irish and Irish-American topics, and edited the *Irish-Americans* series. McCaffrey's two latest books are *The Irish Diaspora in America* (1984) and *Ireland from Colony to Nation State* (1979).

Ellen Skerrett, a Chicago writer, received her B.A. from Rockford College, Rockford, Illinois, and her M.A. from the University of Chicago. She has written *Chicago: City of Neighborhoods* with Dominic A. Pacyga (1986) and is a contributing author to *From Paddy to Studs: Irish-American Communities in the Turn of the Century Era, 1880 to 1920,* edited by Timothy J. Meagher (1986). Skerrett has written several articles about the Chicago Irish based on research from a National Endowment for the Humanities Youthgrant and she researched and coordinated the two-volume *History of the Parishes of the Archdiocese of Chicago,* edited by Rev. Msgr. Harry C. Koenig (1980).

Michael F. Funchion, professor of history at South Dakota State University, received his B.A. from Iona College in New Rochelle, New York, and his M.A. and Ph.D. from Loyola University of Chicago. He is the author of *Chicago's Irish Nationalists, 1881-1890* (1976) and "Irish Chicago: Church, Homeland, Politics, and Class—The Shaping of an Ethnic Group, 1870-1900," in *Ethnic Chicago,* ed. Peter d'A. Jones and Melvin G. Holli (1981). Funchion edited *Irish American Voluntary Organizations* (1983) and is now at work on a study of the Irish in the rural Midwest.

Charles Fanning has written widely about the immigrant and ethnic experience of the Irish in America. His work includes a number of essays on such writers as

Finley Peter Dunne, James T. Farrell, Elizabeth Cullinan, Brendan Gill, and William Kennedy. He has also produced two annotated anthologies, *Mr. Dooley and the Chicago Irish* and *The Exiles of Erin,* and his critical study *Finley Peter Dunne and Mr. Dooley: The Chicago Years* won the 1979 Frederick Jackson Turner Award of the Organization of American Historians. His work has been supported by fellowships from the National Endowment for the Humanities, the Rockefeller Foundation, the Newberry Library, the American Antiquarian Society, the Ancient Order of Hibernians, and the American Irish Foundation. He was a Fulbright Senior Lecturer in American Studies in New Zealand. Now professor of English at Bridgewater State College in Massachusetts, he lives in Bridgewater with his wife Fran and their two children, Stephen and Ellen.

Index